IN
WHITEST
AFRICA
THE
DYNAMICS
OF
APARTHEID

IN WHITEST AFRICA

THE DYNAMICS OF APARTHEID

By William R. Frye

PRENTICE-HALL, INC., ENGLEWOOD CLIFFS, N.J.

". . . of a truth I perceive
that God is no respecter of persons:
But in every nation he that feareth Him,
and worketh righteousness,
is accepted with Him."

—Acts 10:34–35

PREFACE

Prominent among the landmarks in Port Elizabeth, South Africa, an attractive city near the southeast corner of the African continent, is a monument dedicated in genuine sentiment to horses that fell in the Boer War (1899–1902). It shows a soldier kneeling before his horse, holding a bucket of water for it to drink. The inscription reads: "The greatness of a nation consists not so much in the number of its people or the extent of its territory as in the extent and justice of its compassion."

I paused a long time before this memorial. "The extent and justice of its compassion." How many South Africans, I wondered, can read that inscription today without a twinge of conscience?

The answer, I fear, is a great many—indeed, probably most. A few miles from the monument there was a sandy beach, a portion of the great sweep of beautiful waterfront with which Port Elizabeth is blessed. This was the "African beach," the mile or so set aside under laws of apartheid, or "separate development," for use by the city's 134,000 Africans. (The words "African," "Bantu," and "Native" are used in South Africa to mean Negro.)

It was empty. It was so close to a sewage drain that when tide and current were right, it was contaminated with filth—so much so that the beach had been condemned as a hazard to health for everyone of lighter-tinted skin. Moreover, access to the beach area was difficult, around an industrial complex with no public transportation available.

So all during the hot summer, there was rarely anyone to be seen in swimming. There was enough other waterfront in the city for everyone within miles to have swum in perfect comfort; but the Africans could not legally use any of it. To get a dip in clean water, they would have had to trek some fourteen miles.

South Africa is a majestic country, a country of breathtaking

vii

scenic beauty with a climate fit for the gods. It is a land of great superhighways, towering skyscrapers, and rich farmlands on a rolling green countryside. It is a rich country, whose industrious and imaginative people have spurred the economy to an extraordinary 5½ percent growth rate.

But South Africa has yet to demonstrate the extent and justice of its compassion.

Because of its treatment of the nonwhite majority, the very phrase "South Africa" has become a curse in a large part of the world, a profanity used with some of the worst expletives in the language. An editor of the Afrikaner newspaper *Die Burger* referred to his country as "the skunk of the world."

Most Afrikaners are deeply religious men. One wonders if they have pondered in this context that searching question of the Master's: "For what shall it profit a man, if he shall gain the whole world, and lose his own soul?"

Many nations have built prosperity in part on the ill-paid labor of an uneducated class. This is not South Africa's principal offense.

Nor is it her principal offense to have crushed an indigenous people and occupied their land. Other nations have done this; Americans won their country from Indian tribes. Indeed, in some parts of South Africa, there is an active debate as to who arrived first.

South Africa's principal offense is an unwillingness to give the African hope—hope for a better future, hope of sharing in the good things of life, hope of joining in the government of the country even when he is fully able, hope of being judged by his capacities and character rather than his color.

The law of the land deliberately and ruthlessly crushes this hope. It classifies the African as an inferior being and sets out to guarantee that he is forever kept inferior.

Such a policy is an anomaly in the twentieth century. There is under way in our time a worldwide social revolution, a revulsion against the idea that the worth of a man can be measured by his color. Race riots, civil rights marches, and massive ghetto demonstrations are manifestations of this upheaval in the United States. Sharpeville was a result of the same phenomenon abroad. So, in a different way, are outraged protests by Africans at the use of white mercenaries in the Congo, and the inordinate fury Afri-

cans displayed in 1964 when Belgian paratroopers, aided by the
United States and Britain, swooped down on Stanleyville (now
Kisangani) to rescue white hostages from a primitive band of rebel
African tribesmen.

Some of the manifestations of this social revolution are ugly,
but its wellspring is a call for justice. Nonwhites are determined
that men shall be judged and treated according to merit, with
color utterly irrelevant to any significant action or opportunity.
They are determined, in a word, that the biblical concept of man
as the image of his Maker, possessing "glory and honor" and
"dominion over the works of Thy hands," shall be universally
accepted. Nowhere does the Psalmist say this birthright is reserved for men of white skin.

In Asia, men with yellow and brown skins won recognition in
the tumultuous years before and immediately after World War
II. There were bloody colonial wars, and a Pearl Harbor, before
the concept was accepted. Now it is Africa—held in darkness for
decades, indeed for centuries, to facilitate external rule—which is
demanding, and widely getting, recognition.

One corner of the African continent is attempting to hold out
against this wave of history. The southern tip, consisting of the
Republic of South Africa, South-West Africa, Rhodesia and Portuguese Africa (Angola and Mozambique), has made of itself a
kind of white redoubt, a fortress in which white supremacy is still
the law and the practice. Here, white men have set out consciously, with much determination, to keep black men inferior.
(In Portuguese Africa, the discrimination is not racial; at least,
there is no legal segregation. The white supremacy is political and
economic. Sophisticates quip that the Portuguese have just begun
their second 500-year plan for African development.)

Having achieved one of the manifestations of equality—self-
rule—in the rest of the African continent (with minor exceptions),
black men now have come face to face with the white redoubt
and are storming it. They are calling on the rest of the world for
help in their siege and are noting with care the response.

Calls for help have gone out with particular urgency to the
United States and Britain, which hold in their hands economic
weapons which could, if used to maximum effect, shatter the de-
fenses of the redoubt. But economic weapons injure the man who
uses them as well as the one on target. Hesitancy to accept such

injury has earned for Washington and London the enmity, or at least the furious impatience, of much of Black Africa, a fact which has led, in turn, to backlash against American and British interests north of the Zambesi River, that is, north of the redoubt.

What to do? Aid in the African siege? Resist it? Try to stay neutral, working both sides of the street (and antagonizing both)? Few problems have posed more difficult choices for policy-makers.

And the time in which to avoid decisions may not be unlimited. A fearsome storm is brewing. One day, perhaps not long hence, if there is no hope of peaceful change in southern Africa, that part of the continent may explode in a bloody race war, with the Africans turning to communism for help because they cannot get it elsewhere. Indeed, some underground leaders have already despaired of the free world and sought out communist arms, money, and training.

What, if anything, can be done to prevent the tragedy of race war and communism in this part of the world? What are the real interests of America and Britain? Can we of the West afford to get involved? Can we afford not to? Are we, indeed, already inextricably involved? What kind of outside action, if any, would be effective in heading off disaster? It was in an effort to answer such questions that this book was written.

I owe much to African specialists who have read the manuscript and made suggestions as to its content. They include Professor Vernon McKay of the School of Advanced International Studies, Johns Hopkins University; Lord Caradon, Permanent Representative of the United Kingdom to the United Nations; J. Wayne Fredericks, former Deputy Assistant United States Secretary of State; Robert C. Good, United States Ambassador to Zambia; William R. Duggan, formerly of the State Department Policy Planning Council and now consul-general in Durban; Waldemar B. Campbell and Horace Byrne, State Department specialists on South Africa; Professor Gwendolen M. Carter of Northwestern University; Professor Cornelis W. deKiewiet of the American Council on Education; William E. Lang, Deputy Assistant Secretary of Defense; Senator Frank Church of Idaho; Elmore Jackson, of the United Nations Association of the U.S.A.; Mrs. Helen Suzman of Johannesburg; E. S. Reddy of the United Nations Secretariat; Bishop C. Edward Crowther, formerly of Kimberley; Mrs. Ted Cott of New York; and Arthur M. Cox of Washington.

Miss Lucy Young of New York and Larry Fabian of Washington did valuable supplementary research, notably, in Mr. Fabian's case, on the historical chronology which is appended to the book.

In addition, I had the privilege of interviewing scores of highly knowledgeable people, including other State and Defense Department officials; other United Nations delegates; Dr. Hilgard Müller, Foreign Minister of South Africa; F. W. Waring, then South African Minister of Information; the late Chief Albert Luthuli, winner of the 1960 Nobel Peace Prize; Alan Paton, the distinguished author; the Rev. Kenneth N. Carstens of New York; and a wide range of diplomats, businessmen, journalists, politicians, educators, and African underground leaders in South Africa and neighboring countries. None of these people would, I am sure, wish to take responsibility for my conclusions, and all officials acted in a private capacity. My wife and children went through the ordeal of silence and sacrifice familiar to families of authors everywhere, and came through with remarkably good grace.

In the hope that I may be able to contribute to avoidance of anguish and bloodshed, and to the advancement of racial harmony, these pages are dedicated to men of compassion and conscience everywhere.

WRF

CONTENTS

CONTENTS

IN
WHITEST
AFRICA
THE
DYNAMICS
OF
APARTHEID

CHAPTER ONE

What God Hath Joined Together

Matsokolo Mapheele was married at the age of nineteen in an Anglican church in Herschel, South Africa—a tiny village of the Transkei, where green mountains and rolling valleys are, as Alan Paton would say, lovely beyond any singing of it. Jackson, her husband, who had left Herschel in his youth for Paarl in the Western Cape, returned some six hundred miles to win her, probably traveling that spectacular coastal route along the south ern tip of Africa where, for mile after breathtaking mile, mountains plunge directly into the sea, and from time to time, tidal lagoons form a diamond necklace at their feet. It was a romantic beginning. Especially for lovers, South Africa is a Riviera in eternal spring, a California of sunshine and beauty.

"What, therefore, God hath joined together, let not man put asunder." Matsokolo was to recall the words of the priest many times during the five-year ordeal that began in 1958.

Jackson Mapheele could not stay in Herschel more than a few days without losing his right to return to Paarl as a resident. No African in South Africa may freely choose where he is to live or work. His movements are strictly controlled under the laws of apartheid (pronounced "apart-hate"), the South African Govern- ment's unique contribution to the social mores of the twentieth century.

For a nonwhite, Jackson Mapheele had a reasonably good job in a textile plant in Paarl. He had won the respect of his employ- ers, had been able to save a little money, and most important of all, had been in one place long enough to earn, under the laws then in effect, residence rights to which a great many Africans were not entitled.

Matsokolo, his bride, could not legally go with him to Paarl until he had found a place for them to live. But this can be dif-

1

ficult for an African in South Africa. Even if he can afford it, he is forbidden to go into the real estate market to buy or rent a home. He must live in specified "locations" or "townships." These are housing developments which, though the houses, or barracks, are often of relatively good quality, have much of the appearance and atmosphere of concentration camps. Guard towers are not used, but the development is usually surrounded by a fence, "to protect the Africans." The township is removed at least five hundred yards from white areas, thus providing both physical segregation and space for the army or police to use tear gas or heavy weapons in case of need. Water and electricity can readily be shut off at central control points in the white areas.

When available, dwellings in the townships are rented by the government to Africans considered qualified. An African ceases to be qualified when, for example, he loses his job and does not promptly get another. He can then be "endorsed out"—forcibly removed—to the *kraal,* or mud hut, in the countryside where he or his ancestors lived. The right to live in "white areas" and work for the white man is regarded by the government as a privilege. It is extended to limited numbers of black men who make themselves "useful." Anyone who is not useful—a widow unable to work, a child deserted by his parents, an agitator for higher wages—can be endorsed out. Sometimes the cruelty of the law is softened by compassionate exemptions, but there are thousands of heartbreaking cases every year in which an exemption is refused. In 1965,* for example, at least 86,186 persons were endorsed out of Bloemfontein, Cape Town, Durban, East London, Kimberley, Pietermaritzburg, Port Elizabeth, Pretoria, and the Witwatersrand. The consequences of no longer being regarded as useful make Africans markedly polite to white men.

Jackson Mapheele had a bed in a single men's barracks in Mbekweni township, Paarl. No family dwellings were available there. Since the law did not permit Matsokolo to come to Paarl and live separately from her husband, and since she could not join him in bachelor quarters, she could not legally come to the city

---

* Asked in Parliament for more up-to-date figures, the Minister of Bantu Administration and Development said he regretted they could not be furnished. It would be too much work to compile them, he said.

at all. Suddenly the word apartheid, which means apart-ness, took on special significance for them.

The first two years of the Mapheeles' married life consisted of separation forced by the law of the land. Finally defying this cruel and unnatural law, Matsokolo surreptitiously moved in with an uncle in Langabuya location, a squalid shantytown near Mbekweni. As if coming to some sordid assignation, Jackson visited her at night and slipped out the following morning, praying the authorities would not find out.

The Mapheeles lived this way for another two years, until their first child, Alfred, was born. Then the authorities either found out what was happening or decided they could no longer look the other way. Matsokolo was endorsed out.

She got help and took her case to court. Lower-ranking magistrates in South Africa are appointed and may be dismissed by the Minister of Justice, and hence are vulnerable to political pressure. But many of the higher courts are fiercely independent, the judges being appointed, in effect, to life terms. Mrs. Mapheele found both lawyers and judges sympathetic. The Judge President of the Cape Supreme Court, commenting bitterly on "the absurdities of this country," said openly that he would "try to find" in her favor. But the government prosecutor was technically right.

The case turned on whether, in the legal sense of the phrase, Mrs. Mapheele "ordinarily resided with her husband." African wives who do so reside may sometimes share their husband's residence rights. Mrs. Mapheele's lawyers contended that in a very real sense she did reside with him; and that in the more literal sense, she had wanted desperately to do so, but it was impossible. There was sworn testimony from a government official that "even if Mrs. Mapheele had asked permission to live with her husband, it would have been refused." Must she be punished, her lawyers asked, for not doing what she would not have been allowed to do?

"It would be most unfortunate," the court said in reluctantly finding for the government, "if, as a consequence of this judgment, husband and wife were forced to live apart. It appears that Parliament intended to ensure that, as far as possible, natives who are in lawful employment in a proclaimed [i.e., white] area should be permitted to have their wives in the area; indeed, it would be unthinkable that Parliament intended otherwise."

This comment touched off an explosion of public sympathy for the Mapheeles, first in Paarl and then in the rest of the country. The sympathy was not limited to nonwhites. Many white South Africans saw the case in a religious context, and were disturbed. Here was a couple, married according to Christian rites in an Anglican church, being ordered to live apart, in direct defiance of what the church taught as God's law. Moreover, there was a newborn baby to be cared for.

Much of white South Africa has both a heart and a conscience, though these attributes sometimes seem engulfed by fear and other emotions. A small but significant group detests the government's policy. Many realize, too, what the eventual consequences must be for a white minority, outnumbered more than 4–1, which allows explosive hatred to build up in the majority. Just what proportion of the white community was involved in the Mapheele protest is not clear. No doubt a large body of government supporters kept discreetly silent; but protest there was, and it was vocal.

Some 250 residents of Paarl petitioned the government on Mrs. Mapheele's behalf. The principal political opposition, the United Party, which supports segregation and white domination but proposes that they be less rigidly practiced, demanded remedial action. The English-language press, which often is sharply critical of the government, played up the story. Sermons, letters to the editor, editorials, and columnists expressed outrage.

"This arbitrary law, inflexibly applied, has imperiled just about every Christian, western value that South Africa exists to uphold," one editorial writer stated.

Another wrote: "We have no doubt that the world will take note that a government which claims to uphold the Christian and western way of life has had no compunction in separating a man and wife, the parents of a child. It is this sort of action, taken in the name of apartheid, that gives support to allegations made in international forums that four-fifths of the population of South Africa are rigidly controlled by inhuman laws. . . .

"We have no doubt what would have happened if an administrative regulation had separated a white man from his wife. But in this case the married couple are black, and when Mrs. Mapheele comes to say good-bye to her husband, only they will shed a tear.

"After all, a technicality of apartheid has been upheld; and does

South Africa really worry about the moral cost involved?"

J. Hamilton Russell, a United Party MP (now a member of the Progressive Party) did. He also saw practical objections. He wrote for a Cape newspaper:

"A man like Jackson Mapheele, with a wife and child to care for, has a sense of responsibility. He makes no trouble. Give him a good job and home for his wife and family and you have a happy, contented, productive worker. Take these things from him, and you create unnatural conditions in which communism thrives and violence is provoked.

"These are the conditions our government creates. This is the cause of trouble. If our government cannot see the inhumanity of getting rid of Mrs. Mapheele, can they not see the insanity of it?"

Apparently they could not. Mrs. Mapheele was given two extensions, but the order remained in force. In the court's eyes it might be "unthinkable" for the law to be applied in such a way as to separate an African woman from her husband. But it was by no means unthinkable to the cabinet of the late Prime Minister Hendrik F. Verwoerd, the former psychology professor and newspaper editor who presided over South Africa from 1958 until 1966, when he was stabbed to death on the front bench of Parliament. Nor was it objectionable to many of his supporters.

Hundreds of thousands of Africans from the countryside and from territories neighboring South Africa were imported each year to work in South African mines and farms. Their wives were barred from following them. Was an "urban African," a South African native who had grown up in the city, to be necessarily more privileged? He could not be if the government was to achieve its overall purpose—to control, and if possible reduce, the ratio of nonwhites to whites in areas designated "white."

Breaking up families and forcing African men to live as bachelors in barracks areas served to keep down the nonwhite population and/or to render a large part of it illegitimate, and hence rootless. It also helped prevent Africans from thinking of themselves as a permanent part of the community, with rights of citizenship—including that most dangerous right of all, the right to vote. Less than half of the African workers in white areas had their wives with them. Why should Jackson Mapheele be specially privileged? Moreover, Mrs. Mapheele had taken "provocative action," M. D. C. de Wet Nel, then Minister of Bantu Administration and Development, complained: she had "challenged the law of the country." It was clear she had embarrassed the ruling Nationalist Party. She must go.

During the court action, Mrs. Mapheele had again become pregnant. Now, in all the upheaval, she had a miscarriage and was confined to bed. This won her another temporary stay.

Her husband faced an anguished decision. If he went back to Herschel with her, he would lose his job in Paarl and all the rights that derived from it, as well as the associates he had known for years. He would also have to undertake an entirely new life in the country. He might not be able to support his family on jobs available in Herschel, where the total population was approximately 100. If he stayed in Paarl, population 38,000, he could at least send money for Matsokolo and Alfred to live on. A forced return to primitive rural surroundings is no light matter for the urbanized African, already one step up the economic ladder. But the alternative for Mapheele was to bid his wife and son good-bye, perhaps for good. This he could not do.

The time between the Mapheeles' initial expulsion order and the day it took effect was eighteen months. That final day was anticlimactic for everyone but them. Newsmen converged on Paarl. They watched Mapheele's bachelor quarters, his wife's residence, and the railway station. No one appeared. The Mapheeles had dropped completely out of sight. Apparently they had left or been taken from Paarl ahead of the deadline.

Where they had gone, no one seemed to know. Perhaps an embarrassed government did not want the world to know.

CHAPTER TWO

A Nation Torn Asunder

The experience of Jackson and Matsokolo Mapheele is in many ways characteristic of South Africa today: the cruelty of the law, the rigidity of its application, the compassionate reaction of some whites, and the speed with which the case was forgotten—for it was soon forgotten.

South Africa is a land of bewildering contradictions. Its whites, both Afrikaners * and English-speaking, are among the most enterprising and talented people in the world. They have a frontier spirit, a zeal for economic conquest, a sense of boundless opportunity for the imaginative and talented (provided they are white). There is a kind of early-American flavor to the zest and sweep of South Africa. Rags-to-riches stories among the whites are not uncommon. One of the world's great tragedies is that such admirable qualities should be overhung by a cloud of fear, prejudice, and extremism.

Few of these people are intentionally cruel; most are devout, hospitable, and even tenderhearted. Yet they do cruel things, and a majority of them vote for a government that enshrines their prejudices and practices into law. ("If an Afrikaner wants to break a chap's heart, he makes a law.") Then they turn around and deplore what has happened, finding a rationalization for it: "We must maintain civilized standards"; or, "We would be overwhelmed." And they desperately want the world to understand why they have acted as they have.

There is just enough logic in the law that crushed the Mapheeles to make the government's policy comprehensible. Without

---

* Afrikaners (roughly 60 percent of the white population) are descendants of the original white settlers, primarily Dutch. Afrikaans, a simplified form of Dutch influenced by English, French, Malay and local African tribal dialects, is their home language.

"influx control," South Africa's cities would be swamped by migrants from the countryside, as scores of cities, like Bombay and Mexico City, have been swamped. All the pressures that have produced a worldwide movement from farm to city are present in South Africa: population pressure, poverty on the farms, opportunity at the centers of industrial growth.

Such migration became significant in South Africa in the 1920's and reached extremes during World War II. The cities were then especially prosperous, and the government was either deliberately indulgent, with new industries requiring new workers, or preoccupied with winning the war. Local city councils neglected the resulting housing problems, so the influx created a rash of ugly slums and, with them, crime, misery, hazards to health, and other familiar blights of slum life. When mass migration continued after the war, the Smuts government, despairing of successful slum clearance in these conditions, sought to regulate the flow of migrants with a system of legislative sluice gates. This system barred people who would be a burden on the white economy but permitted a convenient influx of cheap labor to industrial areas. (After all, the objective of a "white South Africa" could not be taken too literally.)

Under the circumstances of Paarl at the time Mrs. Mapheele was married, she was a burden on the city's economy. Despite a considerable building program—fifty houses a day in the country as a whole—there was no place in the "nonwhite area" for the family to live. The inexorable logic of the law, therefore, sought to bar her from coming to Paarl. The fact that she was married to a man who lived in Paarl was irrelevant in the eyes of the authorities: she had simply shown bad judgment by marrying him.

Any massive interference with the law of supply and demand sets up its own complications. The intricacies are greatly multiplied when it is human beings who are manipulated, especially if bureaucratic bungling, rigidity, and corruption are involved in application of the controls, as is the case in South Africa. Had the government undertaken, soon enough, to create a significant magnet in the opposite direction—back to the farm—by introducing into nonwhite rural areas the modernization that was transforming the cities, influx control might have worked. But little of this nature was attempted until very late in the game, and in point of historical fact, influx control has had very limited success.

In 1950, two years after the Nationalist Party came to power, 28 percent of the nonwhite population lived in cities. In 1967, despite progressive tightening of the regulations, between 33 and 40 percent was there, and by 1990, best estimates are that it will be 70 percent.*

Thus, influx control may well have slowed, but it has not stopped African migration from country to city—and the government holds out little or no hope of its doing so before 1978, if then. Nevertheless, there is no prospect of relaxation in the incredibly complex and virtually unmanageable system of regulations which influx control has required.

For Africans, the heart of the control system was and is what they call the *dom pas* (stupid passbook), now officially known as a "reference book." (All South Africans over 16 years of age are required to carry at least an identification card, but only Black Africans must have the elaborate "reference book.") A document of 90-odd pages, resembling in some respects a passport, it contains a miniature life history of the owner. He must have it on his person at all times. Without it, he (or she) cannot travel, take up residence, obtain employment, or even legally exist. No fewer than 479,114 persons—an average of 1,313 a day—were prosecuted for passbook irregularities and related offenses in the year ended June 30, 1966. The demonstrations at Sharpeville and elsewhere in 1960, resulting in bloodshed which shocked the world, arose out of protests against the pass laws.

These laws produce all kinds of anomalies. A gardener in Port Elizabeth named Welcome M—— lost his passbook. Not having 2 rand ($2.80) to buy another, and being unable to get a job without a passbook, he attempted to steal the money. This landed him in jail, and while he was there, his wife left him. His sentence up, but still caught in a vicious circle of no passbook and no job,

---

* Figures for the six principal "white" cities (Johannesburg, Cape Town, Durban, Pretoria, Port Elizabeth, and Bloemfontein) show the ratio between whites and blacks to have been 10–9 in 1951; in 1963, 14.1 to 14.8. Taking the population as a whole (that is, including Asians and mulattoes as well as blacks and whites), the blacks in these cities grew from 36 percent in 1951 to 39 percent in 1963.

METROPOLITAN AREAS		South African Census—1951	South African Census—1960	Estimated 1961	Estimated 1962	Estimated 1963
JOHANNESBURG	Asians	21,720	28,993	29,772	30,551	31,330
	Coloreds	37,544	59,467	61,816	64,165	66,514
	Africans	465,266	650,912	670,803	690,694	710,585
	Whites	359,477	413,153	418,904	424,655	430,406
	TOTAL	884,007	1,152,525	1,181,295	1,210,065	1,238,835
CAPE TOWN	Asians	8,099	8,975	9,069	9,163	9,257
	Coloreds	272,314	417,881	433,477	449,073	464,669
	Africans	49,793	75,200	77,922	80,644	83,366
	Whites	247,442	305,155	311,339	317,523	323,707
	TOTAL	557,648	807,211	831,807	856,403	880,999
DURBAN	Asians	160,674	236,477	244,599	252,721	260,843
	Coloreds	17,457	27,082	28,113	29,144	30,175
	Africans	150,732	221,535	229,121	236,707	244,293
	Whites	151,111	196,398	201,250	206,102	210,954
	TOTAL	479,974	681,492	703,083	724,674	746,265

PRETORIA

Asians	6,024	8,046	8,262	8,478	8,694
Coloreds	5,848	7,452	7,588	7,724	7,860
Africans	122,407	199,390	210,691	221,492	232,293
Whites	151,100	207,202	213,213	219,224	225,235
TOTAL	285,379	422,590	438,754	456,918	474,082

PORT ELIZABETH

Asians	4,157	4,247	4,336	4,409	4,490
Coloreds	41,050	68,532	69,892	71,482	74,152
Africans	65,110	123,183	127,042	130,996	134,128
Whites	78,670	94,931	96,559	98,112	99,807
TOTAL	188,987	290,693	297,829	304,999	312,577

BLOEMFONTEIN

Asians	2	2	2	2	2
Coloreds	3,719	6,281	6,556	6,831	7,106
Africans	56,574	75,944	78,019	80,094	82,169
Whites	49,074	63,046	64,543	66,040	67,537
TOTAL	109,369	145,273	149,120	152,967	156,814

he fell in with a gang of *tsotsis* (a *tsotsi* is a cross between a juvenile delinquent and a gangster), and spent the proceeds of petty larceny on liquor and prostitutes. The spiral might have carried him all the way to alcoholism and felony had a white family not taken an interest in him, lent him the money for a passbook, and given him a job.

Only a small percentage are this fortunate. Few who get caught in the incredible maze of passbook regulations are helped to escape. Even getting caught momentarily without the book can bring punishment.

"I was arrested near my house while on my way to buy a paper," Cameron B—— of Johannesburg related. "My family brought my pass to the police station, and it was in order; but I was not released, and the next day I was fined 8 rand [$11.20]." This is six days' pay for the average urban African.

Other pass violation cases are handled more quickly—much more quickly. A Bantu Affairs Court in Johannesburg sometimes disposes of pass violators at an average rate of about a minute and a half per case. Africans are brought before the magistrate, questioned, and sentenced to terms ranging from a week to two months, all in little more than the time it takes to describe it.

The New York Times' Joseph Lelyveld, whom the government later expelled, tells of visiting the Bantu Court in September, 1965.* He saw 71 cases handled before lunch, 57 of them in 80 minutes.

"Why were you in Johannesburg?" the magistrate asks an accused.

"I was looking for my child."

"Where's your child?"

"Lost."

"Fourteen days," says the magistrate, and bangs his gavel.

In Cape Town, a man named Reuben S—— came into an Advice Office operated by the Black Sash in conjunction with the South African Institute of Race Relations. The Black Sash was formed in the 1950's. It is an organization of earnest, dedicated, and courageous white women, who protest against injustices to nonwhites and do what they can within the law to correct them. ("Kaffirboeties"—nigger-lovers—some white Afrikaners contemp-

---

* *The New York Times,* September 9, 1965.

tuously call them.) The scene was described as follows in a Cape Town newspaper:

You can look in there [at the Advice Office] any morning be-tween 9 and 12 o'clock and see the dark folk sitting on hard shiny benches waiting their turn for interviews and advice.

The interviewers—two, three or more—sit at little tables scribbling notes as they patiently unravel involved stories and study grubby passbooks and precious scraps of paper faithfully preserved by their owners down the years.

These people know the value of bits of paper. References, baptismal certificates, doctor's certificates, marriage lines, any one of these may help to save them from the dreaded fate of endorsement out.

Take a long breath of fresh air before you enter that room. It smells of squalor and the intangible miasma of despair. . . .

The first case I listened to was that of Reuben, the cowman. Young, nice-looking, expressionless till his slow smile broke to display fine gleaming teeth. His family was in the Transkei.

His problem was simple. He had worked at the Cape since 1950 [it was then 1963], first as night watchman in a factory. The factory had gone into liquidation, throwing Reuben into the labour pool [government employment office] which had found him employment in a dairy, where, after seven years, he received 13 rand [$18.20] a month with quarters.

The dairy was reducing staff and Reuben was once more in the labour pool. But he had his own solution—if the authori-ties could be persuaded to allow him to take his golden op-portunity. He produced a note addressed to the registration authorities. It was signed by the manager of a well-known fac-tory.

"I wish to report a vacancy for a Bantu employee in our factory. Reuben S—— has applied to us for employment and it would be appreciated if you would grant him the necessary permit to enable him to start work for this firm."

Across this note had been written "Regret. Not in this cate-gory."

A factory cleaner and sweeper is more highly paid than an agricultural labourer, and it was Reuben's modest ambition to better his circumstances and break into industry.

The interviewer frowned. Only after fifteen years [from 1950,

when he first began work] could he hope to change his category; but there was a small loophole here. She did her best.

She telephoned the registration official in question, explaining that originally Reuben had been in the industrial category.
The labour pool had switched him years ago.

The official couldn't help that. He made an offer. She returned to Reuben.

"I'm sorry. I am told it's impossible for you to change your
category. There is a dairy job for you at 4 rand [$5.60] a week
and quarters. Now. At once."

Reuben fingered the note with the factory heading. After
an endless pause he said, "This is the job I want."

Her indignation at the injustice of the system manifested
itself in the sharpness of her voice.

"My advice is to take the dairy job while you can. Soon
you'll qualify to change your category if you want to."

Soon? Two more years! He knew he had no option. If he
refused the job and remained "idle" for even three days, he
would be endorsed out to watch his family starve in the Reserve.

His face darkened visibly and seemed to close as he put the
tantalizing note back with his passbook. He went out reluctantly with all his bitter disappointment apparent in the slump
of his shoulders.

The interviewer watched him with lips compressed.

"After thirteen years with a clean record," she said to me,
"he hasn't the right to create or use an opportunity to better
his wretched standard of living!"

"So it's back to the cowshed."

She nodded and veiled the flash of her eyes as she turned
to examine the next problem.

A revolutionary could be born in a cowshed, I thought.

Many South Africans would agree that "a revolutionary could
be born in a cowshed." Mrs. Helen Suzman, for example, has
repeatedly warned the government that influx control, pass laws,
and other inequities are making revolutionaries out of Africans.
Mrs. Suzman is the only Member of Parliament elected from the
Progressive Party, which favors voting rights for all men and
women, regardless of race, who meet certain qualifications. Leaders of the much larger United Party have said somewhat the same

thing, though they would ease, not repeal, pass laws. The government dismisses such warnings as "lying propaganda," and many
South Africans consider them politics.

The problem was further highlighted by this story:

Gertrude —— had been married in 1949 and had lived in
Cape Town ever since. Of her seven children, only two had
survived.

The authorities had found that her husband owned a "home"
in Butterworth [a rural area] to which she could return. This
"home" was an unproductive patch of ground which they admitted had long since "gone to rack and ruin."

Solomon, her husband, had worked in Cape Town since
1946, but, when "the ladies" went into the case, they found
that the proofs of his continuous employment were inadequate
to satisfy the authorities.

Gertrude and her children must go.

The pondok [the hut in which the family lived] was gaily
painted with a pretty design on the door and the inside parti-
tions were covered with coloured pictures cut out of old maga-
zines. The family had some fowls, a dog and a mealie [corn]
patch.

The edict of exile made an end of these things. The pondok
toppled like a house of cards, and with it, all hope.

The children said good-bye to their more fortunate school
friends, and Solomon, heavy-hearted, took his family to the
evening train. He must stay and earn money to support them.

As the train drew out of Salt River station in the dusk and
the sombre silhouette of Devil's Peak dwindled, Gertrude cried.
She knew that her life with Solomon was finished. She was
going into the wilderness and she feared for her children.

How would she feed, clothe and educate them, or shelter
them on that derelict patch of earth? How soon would it be
before Solomon took a "town wife" who would spend his
meagre wages? How long would it be before he stopped sending money to his family in this place the authorities insisted
on calling "home"?

Now her little ones cried out of naughtiness. Soon they would
cry out in hunger.

Solomon returned to the grim single quarters, his heart like
lead, his mood black, What to do? Get drunk . . . find company to cheer him up . . . join these others who talked of

Poqo [a violent underground organization]? What was Poqo?
Poqo was revenge. Destroy those who destroy your life and
liberty. Interesting. . . ."

There are tens of thousands of similar stories. Virtually every
aspect of influx control produces its own special inequities and
cruelties. Without government permission, children may no longer live with their parents after they reach the age of eighteen.
They are thus forced onto the labor market to become useful.
The Johannesburg authorities in 1966 ruled that an African
mother residing on her white employer's property may not keep
an infant child with her even until she has finished nursing it.
Presumably it would reduce her usefulness to the employer.

In Johannesburg, the parents of two young boys were both
working to make ends meet. Because the parents could not adequately care for the youngsters during the long working-day, they
sent them to live with their grandparents in the country.

When the children finished school, they sought work. Unable
to find it in the country, they returned to Johannesburg. But
they were not allowed to stay. They were endorsed out. The authorities maintained that because they had not lived continuously
in the city, they had forfeited their right of residence there. And
when they returned to the country, they suddenly were endorsed
out of there, too, because they had been born in Johannesburg.
They were legally prohibited from living in either place.

They sneaked back to the city, lived illegally with their parents,
and kept out of sight. They could not take jobs because their
passbooks were not in order. At night they roamed the streets,
impoverished, hungry, resentful, fearful of being picked up, with
no prospect of ever living a normal life. The moment they applied for a job, their passbooks would be examined, and they
would be back on the official shuttlecock.

Excellent material for the underground.

And the regulations are steadily getting tougher. On January
1, 1965, it became impossible for Africans to win unchallengeable
residence rights anywhere in white South Africa. Even though a
man had lived and worked in an area fifteen years or worked for
the same employer for ten (the previous qualifications), he was
no longer entitled to remain as a matter of right, if the authorities
wished to evict him. No length of stay would give him such a

right. Regardless of how deep his roots—even if he had been born there—no African was exempt from being endorsed out of his home if he was considered a burden or a peril.

This law, embodied in the so-called Bantu Laws Amendment Act of 1964, has been widely denounced, both in and out of South Africa, as one of the most extreme apartheid laws ever enacted. It made every Jackson Mapheele, every Reuben S., every urban African, a migrant laborer, or as Mrs. Suzman put it, a "disembodied pair of hands." He was completely at the mercy of the authorities, however responsible a citizen he might be. "Temporary sojourner" in a white area, the government called him.

The Bantu Laws Amendment Act made influx control—in legal theory—absolute. It enabled the government to isolate potential revolutionaries, idlers, delinquents, and criminals. But it also served to create furious grievances. For every revolutionary the government might segregate under this law, four—or perhaps forty—would be created in his place.

Nor is influx control the only aspect of apartheid which stirs revolutionary feeling. "All thinking people," J. Hamilton Russell has said, "know of hundreds of other apartheid laws and regulations which cause despair, distrust, humiliation and resentment that is always ready to boil into violence."

One such law is the Group Areas Act of 1950 (called by its critics the "Ghetto Act"), a massive zoning ordinance which seeks to rearrange South African society into a predetermined pattern with all the whites housed in certain areas, all the "Coloreds" in others, all the Asians in still others, and finally all the Africans in what is left.*

Gathering all members of a group into its designated area has meant uprooting and resettling hundreds of thousands of people in what surely must have been, and still is, one of the largest involuntary movements of peoples in modern times.

For many Africans, the change from slums to government townships or locations, even with their concentration-camp appearance,

---

* "Asians" or "Asiatics" in South Africa are almost entirely Indians and Pakistanis. "Colored" is used to describe not Africans but mulattoes, persons of mixed racial origin. South Africa's Coloreds originated in miscegenation between the original white settlers and Malay or Hottentot women. Today they form a distinct cultural group, the great majority of whom use Afrikaans as their home language.

has been a dramatic physical improvement. The government dwellings are simple, but they have small yards and are equipped in most cases with electricity and plumbing. Africans like them well enough to consider it a tragedy when they are endorsed out, though there are many elements in the tragedy other than loss of a dwelling.

On the other hand, the change from slum to township or location involves certain hardships: loss of familiar surroundings; an increase in rent, which is sometimes severe; the inconvenience and expense of living in an isolated district, many locations being some miles out of town; severe restraints on one's movements (Africans may not, for example, be outside the fence after 11 P.M.); and perhaps most galling of all, acquiescence in apartheid. From the moment an African settles in a government township or location, the ceiling on his advancement becomes clear and visible. Even if he is moderately successful—some are, despite the enormous obstacles—he cannot move up to better housing unless it is available inside the fence. He is kept at the level the government considers appropriate for people of his color.

Moreover, he is dependent on the sometimes-capricious government, not just for his residence, but for everything else of importance he possesses. As Jackson Mapheele found out, he may not even marry freely under all circumstances and expect to live a normal life. If he is married to a mulatto or an Asian, he and his wife may never be able to make a home together. One or both may be restricted to a location or township for people of that racial group. Africans lack the essential ingredient—freedom— without which life is an empty routine.

A group of some 1,000 African squatters in a shantytown called Holpan, forty miles north of Kimberley, the diamond center, was ordered to transfer to a nearby location in late 1965. Many had lived in Holpan all their lives and did not want to shift. The rent to be charged for the government houses ($5.60 a month) was, for them, very high; it would be one third of all they could earn at nearby farms and diamond diggings, even in the best months. They refused to go.

One day, about a week before Christmas, government trucks pulled up abruptly. The Africans were taken with their possessions, not to the designated location but to the Mamuthla Reserve, twenty-five miles away. There was nothing there but barren veld—no shelter, no food, no opportunities to earn a living, no schools for the children, nothing. The trucks dumped them, and left them to fend for themselves.

The Anglican Bishop of Kimberley, the Right Reverend C. Edward Crowther, a naturalized American, heard of their plight and went to the Reserve. He found the Africans huddling, impoverished, in lean-tos, many not having eaten, they said, for five days. The bishop went to a general store and bought them some mealie meal (corn meal). Indignant, he issued a statement saying: "I feel ashamed to be associated by the accident of race with those responsible for this disregard for humanity and ordinary human wants of food and shelter."

What happened then is related by Lelyveld (*The New York Times,* January 1, 1966): *

The Bishop's statement raised a furor. Officials in the Bantu Affairs Department in Pretoria, pressed for comment, were reported to have declared that the squatters had forfeited their right for sympathy by refusing to be relocated.

"Can you tell me," the Bishop asks, "how old people and children can forfeit their right for sympathy—especially at the Christmas season?"

When the keeper of the general store brought the maize to Mamuthla the next day, he was unable to distribute it because, he said, an official told him "he had no right to feed the Natives." The Bishop immediately announced that he would return to Mamuthla to distribute the maize himself.

Two carloads of officials were waiting for him when he arrived. The local Bantu Commissioner told him that he had no right to enter the Reserve, and that, anyway, no one there needed or wanted food. He offered to let the Bishop come along and satisfy himself that this was so.

The two men approached a crowd of about 100. The Bishop spoke. "I told them I came as their Bishop and they need not be afraid of telling the truth," he recounted. "I asked all those who were without food for themselves or their children to stand. The whole crowd stood."

The officials nevertheless forbade him to distribute the food. But he returned the following day, Christmas Eve, in a "convoy" of three trucks, bearing not just corn but hundreds of pounds of dried milk, dried soup, and canned goods. Clothing had been contributed by sympathetic whites in the Kimberley area, and money had come from all over South Africa. Most striking of all were hundreds of Christmas toys, which white children from Kimberley had taken from under their own trees and given to the children at Mamuthla. By this time, the case was spread over the front pages of every English-language newspaper in the country, and the authorities did not dare bar the convoy. It went through. (Bishop Crowther was accused of "deliberately embarrassing" the government, and later was expelled from the country.)

This is the kind of incident that can accompany proposed transfers to locations, even when the Africans involved are being offered a physical improvement. For Asians, as distinct from Africans, there is not even that much compensation; in their case, on top of everything else, the move often represents a physical downgrading. It can also be accompanied by severe financial injury, despite government efforts to mitigate it. Property often cannot be disposed of advantageously when its occupants have been ordered to vacate, and when the neighborhood has been closed to those who would normally seek to buy into it. Some Asians are small entrepreneurs, and for them, enforcement of the Group Areas Act may mean damage to their livelihood as well, since their place of business may also be uprooted. One elderly Indian in Pretoria, Nana Sita, a disciple of Mahatma Gandhi, has served three prison terms rather than move from a home he has occupied for thirty-seven years.

The impact of the law has been, and is being, felt with especially cruel force in Cape Province. "Cape Coloreds" (mulattoes living in that Province) are being uprooted from homes their families had occupied for as long as one hundred years. In the port city of Durban, a semitropical resort and commercial center on the east coast, where a large percentage of South Africa's Indian population lives, more Indians are being moved to nearby townships than there are whites in the city. Some of these Indian families had also lived in the same neighborhood for nearly a century.

The rationale for this policy is that different races, or "nations,"

as they are now being called, must be compartmentalized "for
their own good." While much of the world is striving to become
color-blind, South Africa persists in seeing men not only in terms
of their color, but of their shades of color. "Our task in South
Africa," Foreign Minister Hilgard Müller told the United Nations
General Assembly in December 1964, "is not primarily that of
solving a problem of races, it is a problem of nations, a problem
of bringing about a situation where peaceful coexistence of the
various nations living in our country will be possible. We believe
that this can only be achieved by the independent development
of each people toward the full realization of its separate nation-
hood. . . ." A "fully integrated multiracial society" such as
critics urge, he said, would amount to "completely ignoring the
rights of the various distinctive nations."

Carried to its logical conclusion, this would produce a kind of
forced Balkanization of the country. But the government does
not wish to go quite that far. It cannot, or does not wish to,
separate people entirely. Within limits, they are allowed to use
the same cities, work in the same buildings, shop in the same
department stores, serve the same employers—that is, they are
"economically integrated." It would be totally impractical to try
to prevent it. Moreover, the availability of nonwhite labor serves
well the interests of the white "nation."

However, no contact which remotely implies equality between
races is permitted. Not only must the various "nations" live in
separate areas at night (the government would even like to eliminate sleep-in servants), but they travel, with rare exceptions, in
separate trains and buses, eat in separate restaurants, sit on separate park benches, walk through separate doorways, and are buried
in separate graveyards. There are separate hospitals, separate am-
bulances, separate telephone booths, and separate taxi stands. The
main Afrikaner churches are strictly segregated. (Some smaller
denominations are integrated, but the authorities can forbid it.)
There are separate clubs, schools, and movies. Factories even make
workers punch separate time clocks, and comic books deal almost
exclusively with characters of a single color.

Until recently, legitimate theatres occasionally permitted multiracial audiences, but now, except on special permit, it is prohibited even if seating is to be segregated. There are separate
hours for nonwhites at zoos, art galleries, museums, and public

gardens. Stiff penalties are meted out for sexual intercourse between white and nonwhite. Spectators at a track meet often used
to stand in line for more than an hour at a ticket window for
"whites only"; they would not be served if they sought a general
admission ticket at an empty window designated "Asiatics." Now,
unless the sponsors get a special permit—not easily obtained—
they cannot attend the same meet at all (a restriction which may
have been prompted in part by the fact that at international
events, nonwhites had taken to cheering against the South African
team). In 1967–68, Vorster bowed to demands by the International
Olympics Committee that as a condition for readmittance to the
games, South Africa field an integrated team. Vorster's consent
to do so was, from his point of view, a considerable departure.
But he did not agree to make try-outs for positions on the team
multiracial, or otherwise ease customary and legal barriers to
interracial sports at home. As a result, the Olympics Committee's
decision in February 1968 to accept South Africa for the summer
games in Mexico City was explosively unpopular in Africa and
caused a major upheaval in the sports world. It finally was reversed.

Curiously enough, there is one set of facilities in Cape Peninsula
that is still nonsegregated: public lavatories. How they have es-
caped, no one is quite sure. They are widely regarded, the Port
Elizabeth *Evening Post* wrote in November 1967 (tongue well in
cheek), as "the last line of defense against total apartheid in South
Africa" and "multiracialism's last stand." One was in the process
of being reserved for nonwhites last fall, but the rest were holding
out against the times.

The paper wrote:

They are still the only places in the Republic where men of
all colors can stand shoulder to shoulder without so much as
a word or look that could lead to racial friction. They are free
conveniences, and the only authoritarian notices that appear
in them are "spitting prohibited—penalty £5", and "stand close
in".

Lawyers believe, however, that the chalets, as they are officially called, will remain multiracial because in terms of the
Group Areas Act a person using the toilets would only be
breaking the law if he "occupied" them. Although the word
occupation means more than mere presence, it does not mean
presence for an ephemeral purpose.

However, under Section 1 (4) of the Act, the words occupation of premises are directed at people of different races sitting down together as in restaurants. If they were prohibited from standing, most restaurants would go out of business.

Lawyers say that if the same criterion were applied to the lavatories, standing in them would be legal for people of all races, but sitting in them would be a crime. According to the Greenmarket Square lavatory attendants, the standing trade is by far the highest.

"Petty apartheid," as segregation practices of a minor character are called, may be designed to protect the "separate rights" of "nations." But nonwhites may perhaps be forgiven for wondering if the government's prime concern is not the rights of the white "nation."

Petty apartheid sometimes gives rise to curiously strained logic. The 150-odd Japanese businessmen in Johannesburg are treated as "honorary whites," a concept that would certainly have startled the authors of the "yellow peril" legend in the 1920's. This special concession can perhaps be explained by the fact that so few people are involved. A more likely explanation, however, is that Japan now is one of South Africa's most important trading partners, along with Britain, the United States, and West Germany.

Some 6,500 Chinese, on the other hand, are not considered white, though they are accorded special treatment. They could perhaps be described as "white by government permit." Chinese born in South Africa are usually issued permits to live and work in white areas; foreign-born Chinese, still whiter, have additional privileges.

Even among native-born South Africans, classification is not always an easy task. A white man may have a dark complexion, and a mulatto a light one. Many Coloreds quietly crossed the color line and were accepted as whites until, in August 1966, the government sought to halt the practice. It required everyone over 16 to obtain an identification card stating, among other things, his racial classification.

The process of identification has led to much anguish, heartbreak, and even broken families—for sometimes, until the law was amended, natural brothers and sisters, with different appearances, were differently classified. People on the border line who appeal their classification are brought before government appeal boards which scrutinize their complexion, take testimony from witnesses about their habits and associates, and sometimes even question barbers about the texture of their hair. The appeals process can, and often does, take more than a year, during which time the appellant's whole life is, in effect, held in suspension. He does not know where he will be allowed to live, whom he will be allowed to marry, what jobs he will be able to take, where his children may go to school, what property he may buy, or even what beach he will be able to use to take a swim.

The ordeal of Sandra Laing, an 11-year-old girl in Pretoria, has been widely publicized. Her parents are white, knowing of no Colored ancestors on either side; her two brothers are obviously white, and are treated as such. The family's associates are all white. But Sandra had a darker face and crinkled hair. After she spent four years at a boarding school for whites at Piet Retief, in the Transvaal, her father was told there had been complaints from the school board and that he must take her out. He refused. School officials, accompanied by a policeman, then escorted her home.

This not only meant that Sandra could not go to a white school —any white school—but that, if the classification stood, she could not even live in a white area. The other Laings could not live in a Colored area; so it seemed they would have to be separated. Mr. Laing told the *Rand Daily Mail* in Johannesburg that his wife was near suicide, and had threatened to kill Sandra as well. "What do I have to do to keep our daughter?" he asked. "Will we have to register her as a servant to keep her with us?" *The New York Times* commented editorially, "Here . . . is the crowning commentary on the attempts of cowardly men everywhere—the United States as well as in South Africa—to enforce separation of human beings on the basis of color or race. Humanity one day will sit in awful judgment on such men."

Mr. Laing went to court, but the school's decision was reluctantly upheld.

However, the world-wide publicity which the case had received helped to push through an amendment to the law which provided that, if both parents are white, natural-born children are automatically given that classification. Sandra thus became officially white.

By this time (August 1967), she had been out of school for 18 months. The Transvaal Education Department ruled that she could return, but that "in her own interests," apparently because of possible hostility from other children, she could not live at the school. When she sought to transfer to a white public school near home, many of the parents threatened to pull out their children. Finally, Sandra was offered, and accepted, a place in a church boarding school.

There are many other, less well-known, cases. A Colored woman in Durban married an Indian. They adopted a Colored girl, who was then officially classified as Indian. The husband died, and at about the same time, the area in which the family had lived was zoned for whites only. The mother was told she must move to a Colored area, but could not take her daughter with her because the daughter was "Indian." This was too cruel an absurdity even for South Africa. She appealed, and got the child reclassified.

According to the Institute of Race Relations, there has been at least one case where a white man was classified nonwhite because he had worked in the sun for a long time and gotten a deep tan. On appeal, he was restored to white status. Other problems have arisen with "Mediterranean" complexions. In such cases, the Institute's 1967 Survey of Race Relations states, if "no clear-cut decision can be reached about a person's appearance, then his associations became the criterion. Appeal boards have frequently insisted that an appellant must satisfy them on every point. A man who looks white, and is readily accepted by the community as being white, for example, could be refused registration as such if many years previously he attended a Colored school, or if a large proportion of his friends were Colored, or if he had not rejected and forsaken all family members who were not classified as white." The courts have refused to uphold the latter test, calling it unwarranted and insupportable; so legislation has been introduced in Parliament to require that they do. In all, according to the Minister of the Interior, investigations into a person's classification have proved necessary, because there was a measure of doubt, in some 308,500 cases: 48,000 whites, almost 179,000 Coloreds, 14,000 Malays, 27 Indians, 14 Chinese and 26,500 Africans.

The form of "coexistence" amongst the various "nations" that apartheid produces is not consistently peaceful, though it often appears tranquil to a casual observer. In January 1949,

Africans and Indians in Durban clashed in one of the bloodiest race riots the country has ever seen. An Indian storekeeper punched an African he believed had stolen some merchandise. Before the ensuing riot could be checked, more than twenty-four hours later, at least 145 Africans and 122 Indians had been killed, 1,807 persons had been injured, and more than 2,000 buildings had been destroyed or damaged.

This kind of hostility, not merely between Africans and Indians but between different tribes of Africans, is one reason the government cites for keeping them apart. But it is at least debatable whether apartheid minimizes or intensifies this hostility. Indian leaders charged that apartheid had directly contributed to the disturbances in Durban.

When the opposite policy is tried, there is harmony. At Isipingo Beach, near Durban, during a period of transition between all-white and all-Indian residence, the two races were temporarily permitted to live side by side. During this period, Isipingo Beach was a model of racial concord. Much the same thing is happening in Umtata, capital of the Transkei, where roughly one third of the community is being changed from all-white to all-African zoning, the existing residents being permitted to remain, if they wish, for their lifetime.

One aspect of apartheid unquestionably intensifies hostility between races. It is "job reservation," the law or custom that certain types of jobs must be filled only by members of the race considered "suited" for it. Regardless of a man's qualifications, he may not legally cross the barrier which artificially defines his occupation. A nonwhite may sacrifice and struggle to gain expertise badly needed by the economy; it is formidably difficult for him to get education and training beyond the elementary level, but a few manage it. Then, after getting his degree, he is expressly forbidden by law to seek a job on the open market commensurate with his skill. Except in his own milieu, such jobs are—with rare exceptions—for whites only. There are ways to get around some of the requirements, and others are not strictly enforced; but for many nonwhites, and especially for the unemployed, the impact of the law is heavy.

A 1967 UNESCO report on the effects of apartheid on education, science, culture, and information in South Africa told of two particularly striking cases. One was of an Indian, Dr. Dorasamy Chetty, a graduate of the University of the Witwatersrand and the London School of Hygiene and Tropical Medicine. Despite many years of experience on malaria eradication programs in the Far East with the World Health Organization, Dr. Chetty was unable to obtain a post in South Africa where he could practice and teach preventive medicine. The other case was of a highly qualified African doctor, not named, who was refused an appointment to the Livingstone Hospital in Port Elizabeth—a hospital exclusively for nonwhite patients—because in his post he would have had several whites working under him. The South African Government recognizes that this kind of thing is unfortunate, but feels the answer is to limit and channelize the education of nonwhites in such a way that they will not gain skills the law will not let them use—or (in Verwoerd's words) will not have "expectations in life which circumstances in South Africa do not allow to be fulfilled immediately." *

Job stratification is intended primarily for the benefit of whites, but it also applies (the government is at pains to point out) among Africans, Coloreds, and Indians. This is at best a very mixed blessing. It sets up strains between categories of nonwhites. Africans resent the fact that Indians and Coloreds take from them some of the few opportunities they might otherwise have. In turn, Indians and Coloreds look down on Africans and discriminate against them socially, fearing their potential competition and hence sharing with whites an economic motive for repressing them. Psychologically, too, prejudice is a contagious disease. Feeling repressed by the whites, the Asians and Coloreds seek, perhaps unconsciously, to enhance their own status by shoving the Africans further down the scale.

---

* This statement was made when Verwoerd was Minister of Native Affairs. He further told Parliament:
"When I have control of Native education, I will reform it so that Natives will be taught from childhood to realize that equality with Europeans is not for them . . . People who believe in equality are not desirable teachers for Natives . . . When my Department controls Native education it will know for what class of higher education a Native is fitted, and whether he will have a chance in life to use his knowledge. . . . What is the use of teaching the Bantu child mathematics when he cannot use it in practice? . . . that is quite absurd. . . . The Bantu must be guided to serve his community; there is no place for him in the European community above certain forms of labor."

Fear of job competition from nonwhites ("cheap black labor") is strongest among ill-educated and unskilled or semi-skilled whites—"poor whites," some of them would be called in the American South, although the parallel is not precise, their position on the socioeconomic ladder being a rung or two higher. Unable or unwilling to compete with nonwhites on even terms, they are given specially protected status. For them, job reservation is a kind of social subsidy—a convenient cushion, but one that removes what could otherwise be a useful stimulus to self-improvement.

In the 1920's, one out of every five whites in South Africa was below the subsistence level, with a powerful motive to seek such a subsidy. Since then, because of job reservation, white unionization, and the economic boom which accompanied and followed World War II, the poorest of the poor whites have virtually disappeared. Those below the subsistence level today are estimated to number between one and six percent of the white population. But the artificial protections continue.

Job reservation produces some of the most extraordinary anomalies of all. South Africa's boom has brought a major shortage of housing-construction workers; yet in many places African plasterers may not legally be hired, no matter how desperate a contractor may be for labor. So unemployment and a labor shortage exist side by side in the same field.

The government attempts to ease the pressure by importing white Italians, sometimes bringing them all the way from Europe by air. This unusual step is justified on the ground that it also contributes to white immigration, one of the government's major objectives; but this is not a very persuasive explanation. The total number of Italians of whatever occupation who entered the country in 1965—1,403—did not make much of a dent on a country of 18,000,000 people. Nor, indeed, did it make much of a dent on the shortage of labor in the housing industry. The fact is that the government and the white workers (though not the employers) would rather see jobs unfilled than officially ease the color bar. This is true generally—so much so that if the policy continues into 1969, the London *Economist* has estimated that in the country at large there will be 230,000 unemployed nonwhites and 47,000 vacant jobs reserved for whites only.

Efforts to adjust ideology to suit economic necessity are strongly resisted. In mid-1964, eleven of the fifty-five operating gold mines in South Africa tried an experiment in which certain low-ranking African supervisors ("boss boys") were given a little added authority which previously had been reserved for whites. There was a severe shortage of supervisory personnel, with some 2,000 unfilled jobs—so no white supervisors were in danger of injury. The mining industry, caught between rising costs and the fixed price of its principal product, gold, was eager to fill some of the vacancies with Africans, since Africans earned only $15 to $50 a month (whites get $319 to $420). The white labor union endorsed the experiment, confident it would increase mine efficiency and make higher white salaries possible. Everyone stood to benefit—the upgraded Africans, the white employees, and the companies.

A "rebel" group of white supervisors, however, protested, arguing that it was "the thin edge of the wedge" and that the "principle of job reservation" was in danger. They threatened to stage a wildcat strike if the practice were continued. A government commission of inquiry looked into the matter in 1965 and, after a three-month study, reported that the experiment had "dangerous implications" and must be halted. Other industries might also try it, the commission warned. "The color bar in the mining industry should be maintained," the Minister of Mines declared. And he so ordered. Ideology was more important to the government than economics.

This particular decision was unpopular, and efforts were made to overthrow it. A subsequent case affecting the state-owned railroads went the other way, with Africans being upgraded to fill empty posts, the white union retaining a veto over specific decisions. A similar problem in the coal mines in 1967 was also solved by upgrading Africans. But each such step toward logic and common sense has had to be taken against formidable resistance. Anyone who counts on economic pressures to erode apartheid must be thinking in very long-range terms indeed.

The assumption that whites are better suited to certain jobs than nonwhites has been disproved time after time without undermining devotion to job reservation. Anglo-American Corporation, Harry Oppenheimer's giant empire of diamonds and other minerals, originally hired Africans as elevator operators. The government later reserved this job for whites. The company then had to fire its efficient African operators and search the scarce labor market for white replacements. In some cases the people it had to settle for were slow, clumsy, and discourteous. They did not use the company shower room each morning as the Africans had been instructed to do; white men cannot be subjected to such indignities. With South Africa's relatively warm climate, the result was a severe annoyance and a handicap to business—so much so that Anglo-American spent the equivalent of thousands of dollars converting the elevators to an automatic system. Both white and African operators were then out of jobs.

Job reservation is subject to many unofficial exceptions. Walk through an automobile assembly plant near Port Elizabeth, the "Detroit" of South Africa, and the guide may point to Africans performing the same function as whites. It is illegal, but it is overlooked. Stop at a gasoline station. Behind a screen there may be an African mechanic, repairing a car. He was hired as a menial laborer, is listed as a menial laborer, and may be paid as one; but he is in fact doing a much more skilled job. As a general rule, white men are paid up to six times as much as non-whites for the same work. The African has no recourse. He cannot go to the authorities or to a white union and demand proper pay for it, for then he would be announcing that he has been breaking the law. Most white unions are determined to maintain the differential.

Underlying all this inhumanity to man is *baasskap* (boss-ship). *Baasskap* is the doctrine—the utter conviction—of white superiority, with a determination to keep things that way. "We want to make South Africa white," Verwoerd told Parliament in 1963, a time when euphemisms and circumlocutions were less in style than they are today. "Keeping it white can only mean one thing, namely white domination—not leadership, not guidance, but control, supremacy." This kind of statement has a greater ring of sincerity than Dr. Müller's elaborate concern in the United Nations for "peaceful coexistence of the various nations living in our country."

Apartheid, however, cannot safely be presented to the world in the form of bald white supremacy. The outside world's hostility is an economic disadvantage to South Africa, as well as an inconvenience and an embarrassment, and the government wishes to minimize it. To do so, and to help silence domestic opposition as well, the government has devised an elaborate structure of theory and logic with which to rationalize its policy. It has even ceased to use the word "apartheid," preferring to call the policy "separate development" of whites and nonwhites in their "respective areas."

The centerpiece of this structure of rationalization is a plan to establish eight "Bantustans," or black-ruled states, one of which has already been set up. In these states Africans will theoretically possess the rights of which they have been deprived in white areas: the right to elect their own rulers, to run their own economy, to own property, to choose where they will live and work.

The Bantustans are to comprise roughly the 264 present tribal areas or Reserves, plus a little additional land, a total of about 13 percent of the country. Each Bantustan will embrace the "homeland" of a tribe or group of tribes (a "nation"); Africans of that tribal origin who are not presently living in the Bantustan, or homeland, but instead are "temporarily sojourning" in white areas, will be allowed to exercise civil and political rights in absentia. Ultimately, government literature promises, the Bantustans will take their place within a "Commonwealth of South Africa," in which "the white state and the black states can cooperate together, without being joined in a federation, and therefore without being under a central government, but cooperating as separate and independent states."

On paper this ingenious plan accounts for much. Africans living in "white" areas can be said to be away from their home "state." Like aliens in a strange country, they cannot expect to take part in the government of the state of residence. They can reasonably be required to carry passports; they can be deported at will by the local authorities; the terms of their employment can be arbitrarily determined. They can even be forbidden to own land, though few countries treat aliens this severely. Being legally migrant, they are not to be regarded as a regular and permanent part of the community, even if they and their forebears have in fact lived there for generations. Having thus conjured away the majority of the population, the minority becomes a majority, the area becomes "white," and white men can exercise "control, supremacy."

The South African Government has invested a great deal of time and money, domestically and abroad, in promoting "under-

standing" of the Bantustan scheme. High-powered public relations firms and lobbyists have helped in the promotion. It is
more than a rationalization of the treatment of the urban African
and a framework for population control. It is clearly intended
to be the capstone of the apartheid edifice, the ultimate realization of "separate development." Though not formal partition,
which Verwoerd used to say is "nonsense," it is obviously something of that general character.

It gives the government a context in which to contend that it
is treating all its people equally and benefiting them all by keeping them separate. Known as "grand apartheid," by contrast with
the "petty apartheid" of separate taxi stands or job reservation,
it clothes government policy in wise and beneficent garb, giving
the government a useful vehicle for both domestic politics and
foreign propaganda.

"It is our objective," Dr. Müller told the United Nations, "to
provide to every individual the fullest chance of development
within his own nation and, where possible, in his own homeland."
An advertisement in American newspapers, one of many published
by the South African Information Services, expands on the theme:

"The peoples of South Africa are distinctly different in language, history and culture. These differences are evident not only
between black and white, but also between black and black. The
Bantu nations are quite as different one from another as are the
nations of Europe—and just as intent on preserving their separate identities.

"South Africa recognizes, and provides for, the divergent aspirations of its multi-national population. Its goal is to assist
these separate nations to develop their human and material resources as they advance to self-government."

This, the government argues, is the kindest thing that can be
done for the Africans. They are happier in their own milieu, can
compete more effectively, will not come into contact with antag-
onistic groups, and can preserve their own ways and customs.
"Emancipation without chaos," the government calls it. Indeed,
in sheer rapture over the possibilities, government spokesmen
sometimes even say the Bantustans will "eliminate discrimination." There will no longer be any necessity for it; everyone will
be the equal of everyone else in his own compartment. The "separate but equal" doctrine once proclaimed by the United States

Supreme Court will have been made a reality, they imply, on a national scale.

In fact, the Bantustan scheme as outlined on paper and as tested in the Transkei, a coastal area below Durban, falls so far short of the theoretical optimum as to raise serious doubts about the government's real motives. There are gaping holes both in the theory and in the practice.

Urban Africans—the roughly four and one half million living in "white" cities—are not in fact being separated from the white men for whom they work, at least not in the daytime. They can scarcely be said to have been "emancipated" by the right to cast absentee ballots for a Parliament which has no jurisdiction over their daily lives. They are not benefited by the opportunity to "develop" economically in a primitive area which may be hundreds of miles from where they live and which offers fewer economic advantages. The cruel realities of daily life will not have been changed for them by legal fictions. Urban Africans will in fact be neither separate nor equal.

Rural Africans in the Reserves, numbering perhaps another four million, will be separate, but they will certainly not be equal. They will face these handicaps:

1. The allocation of land between "black" and "white" areas is not equitable. Africans constitute 68 percent of the population of the country; those now in the Reserves, roughly 27 percent of it.* This many people clearly cannot be accommodated properly on 13 percent of the land (even if that area represents a greater percentage of South Africa's arable land). The "black" area includes none of the country's rich gold or diamond mines, none of its principal ports, none of the manufacturing centers— in short, little except underdeveloped agriculture and forestry on which to build an economy. And much of the agricultural area is suited primarily to grazing.

2. No adequate effort is being made or proposed to render the African areas viable. Africans, most of whom are at or below the subsistence level, have virtually no savings to invest in de-

---

* As of mid-1967, the Bureau of Census and Statistics estimated South Africa's total population at 18,733,000, of whom 12,750,000 were black, 3,-563,000 white, 1,895,000 Colored, and 561,000 Asian. A rough rule of thumb is that one third of the Africans live in Reserves, something over one third in white cities, and something under one third in white farm areas.

velopment projects. White capital, without which there can be no real development on a significant scale, has been authorized only under strictly controlled conditions (on the curious theory that otherwise it would preempt black opportunities). White men are being permitted and, indeed, encouraged and assisted to build industries outside the borders of the Reserves, the workers commuting across the frontier to their jobs. However, fewer than 250 factories, employing only 44,600 Africans in all, were built or expanded between 1960, when the program began, and mid-1966. Moreover, these totals are arrived at, in government reports, by an extraordinarily broad definition of the word "border." Some factories are included which are located scores of miles from the African Reserve which they presumably adjoin. And the program is running out of steam. Except where the government has made special concessions, such as tax rebates and authorization to pay unusually low wages, these industries rarely have been striking financial successes, and the government is having a hard time persuading investors to establish more of them.

The government publicizes the statement that 114,000,000 rand ($159,000,000) was devoted over the five-year period 1961–66 to development of Bantu areas, including (until 1964) the Transkei. A new five-year plan for 1966–71 has 490,000,000 rand ($686,-000,000) as its target. In addition, Pretoria has been subsidizing the budget of "independent" Transkei since 1964, the 1966–67 subsidy being 10,466,000 rand ($14,652,400). Some of this goes for development projects—such as irrigation, forestry, soil conservation, and animal husbandry—and some for current obligations, such as education.

All this adds up to a praiseworthy program, but it scarcely scratches the surface. Independent experts and, indeed, some government specialists estimate that this development effort would have to be multiplied many times and be continued for twenty years if the "Bantu homelands" were to have any real hope of supporting the people who live there now. But even the limited expenditures currently being made lack enthusiastic support among some white taxpayers, complaints being voiced that "too much" is being done for the "Natives."

There is serious doubt that the government will ever genuinely want the Bantu homelands self-supporting. It is conve-

nient to have them dependent upon white South Africa. It means
they will continue to have to export labor—that is, send out
workers on limited-term contracts—to white mines and farms,
as they have done for decades. Thousands of youths sign up
each year for stints ranging from three to ten months, the white
recruiters portraying the tour as a "badge of manhood." While
away, part of their pay is withheld and sent home to their rela-
tives in the form of "remittances." Some $1.4 to $2.8 million is
believed to be transmitted in this manner each year to the Transkei alone, providing a sizable share of the net income of the
territory, one without which it could not survive. The young
men then return home bringing a few lengths of cloth, some
jewelry, a Coleman lamp or stove, and/or some cash—which they
may use as *lobola* with which to buy a bride.

If it were easier for African men to earn a living at home, they
would be under less pressure to sign up with the recruiting officers. The Reserves (and/or Bantustans) would cease to be so
readily available to white South Africa as labor pools on which
to draw, when necessary, on terms dictated by employers. Wages,
now as low as 3 rand ($4.20) a week,* might have to rise, per-
haps all the way to the $2.80 a day requested by workers in many
parts of the country, and resisted by most employers.

3. The prospect of self-government for the Reserves is largely
on paper, and may well be a fraud. At best, the process of "emancipation" is likely to move at a very slow pace, indeed. In the
Transkei, the one Bantustan thus far established, African self-
rule is largely illusory. The constitution severely limits the field
in which Africans may exercise jurisdiction. Pretoria has reserved
for itself authority over matters having to do with foreign affairs, the armed forces, police, aliens, public utilities, communications (including national roads and railroads), currency,
customs, and constitutional amendments.

Transkei cabinet ministers all have white "advisers" with
whom they rarely disagree. Decisions of Parliament are strongly
influenced by Pretoria, which pays the salaries of a majority of
the members, the hereditary chiefs. Laws may even be vetoed
by Pretoria, if necessary. And the white South African secret

---

* Some mine workers start for as little as 7 cents an hour, plus board,
lodging, and medical treatment.

police is active throughout. The idea that the Transkei will be
approaching genuine self-rule in the near future is sheer fantasy.
In answer to opposition charges, during the 1966 election campaign, that the Africans were gaining dangerous footholds, a
government-party MP assured his constituents that freedom would
not be granted for 200 years. And few observers think the other
Bantustans, if and when established, will be significantly different.

A visit to the Transkei, the "Land Across the Kei River," bears
out this impression. It is 16,500 square miles of rolling piedmont
on the east coast of South Africa, roughly the size of Switzerland
or Denmark. On this land live more than 1,500,000 blanket-wear-
ing, Xhosa-speaking Africans. (Xhosa is the language involving
clicks of the tongue, the language of singer Miriam Makeba.)

Scenically much of the Transkei is superb, with steep green-
brown hills, river valleys, and a seacoast. The very topography
which makes it spectacular to look at, however, renders it hard
to live on. Only 24 percent of the land is arable, and there are
few known mineral resources—factors accounting for the export
of labor to white South Africa.

The capital, Umtata, a one-dimensional frontier town, was until recent years a "white" enclave, in legal theory, with nonwhites
legally alien. (Port St. John's, the only potential harbor, still is.)
When I was in Umtata (1964), the only hotels were strictly segregated, admitting whites only. The white authorities had just
turned down a proposal to build one for the Africans. This made
Umtata just about the only "national" capital in the world where
the prime minister could not hire a hotel room. Since then, about
one third of Umtata has been designated a "black" area, and a
small motel connected with a filling station has been purchased
for African use.

The Transkei has a unicameral legislature in which the 45
elected representatives are outnumbered by 64 traditional chiefs,
whose position is hereditary but who can be dethroned by the
South African Government. The election of November 1963 was
the first and as of this writing the only territory-wide election
to be held. The party of the Paramount Chief of Western Pondoland, Victor Poto, a soft-spoken, barrel-shaped man who opposes
apartheid, won 33 of the 45 elected seats, but Poto failed to
become prime minister. Instead his rival, Chief Kaizer D. Matanzima, a man more responsive to Pretoria, put together a

parliamentary majority, obviously composed primarily of hereditary chiefs. It was taken for granted that Pretoria had twisted
arms and greased palms among the chiefs to make sure the right
man was elevated.

Chief Matanzima's policy is to apply apartheid, or separate development, to the Transkei in reverse: that is, to make the Transkei, except for Umtata and St. John's, all black. Whites have
been, or are being, barred from owning property, voting, taking jobs reserved for blacks, and so on. The principal practical
effect of this policy is to number the days of the "white traders,"
once numbering 600 to 800, who run "trading stations" (general
stores) on the countryside. Each of these traders acts as a combination doctor, lawyer, adviser, and great white father for his
captive clientele of several thousand Africans. Many of the traders are an important stabilizing influence, but they are being
sacrificed to the doctrine of race separation. As of August 1966,
246 stations had been offered for sale.

Chief Poto would prefer a multiracial society. He told me
Chief Matanzima keeps his parliamentary majority in line by
threatening chiefs with withdrawal of their benefits. Poto said
he favors establishment of more Bantustans, but only if they are
made multiracial—that is, opened to whites. In such multiracial
societies he would not want unqualified majority rule, one-man-
one-vote. He would set up qualifications for the franchise, including especially literacy. But African voters would inevitably be
in the majority.

I also talked with some of the white "advisers" designated by
Pretoria to sit at the right hands of the cabinet ministers. Matanzima's alter ego was J. T. H. Mills, a tough and supremely
self-confident man with an extensive, detailed knowledge of the
Transkei.

He seemed very much in charge. He controlled the prime minister's appointments, apparently without the balderdash of con-
sulting the prime minister. He said with a straight face that
there was no way to judge Chief Matanzima's independence:
since the chief had "not clashed" with Pretoria, there had "never
been a difference of policy." * He acknowledged that "ten to

---

* When Verwoerd was assassinated, Matanzima called him South Africa's
"greatest statesman of all time."

fifteen" of the sixty-four chiefs were being given "protection" by white secret police because "people imported from liberal centers" had tried to assassinate them. (Some time thereafter, two members of the opposition party were haled into court on charges of attempting to assassinate Matanzima. One formal charge specified that on a witch doctor's advice, they had used, or caused to be put into operation, a medicine of crushed leaves and roots, which had been buried in the ground and calculated to cause the death of Chief Matanzima.)

Mills gave the impression of full personal mastery of the government, a mastery which his colleagues said he liked to have acknowledged with due deference. In Pretoria, he might have been a low- to medium-grade functionary, but in Umtata he was, in effect, the prime minister.

Chief Matanzima is not quite the puppet that Mr. Mills, perhaps unwittingly, implied. The chief has put public pressure on Pretoria for wider authority. In one daring speech in Johannesburg, for example, he appeared to urge Africans in white areas to insist upon the right to own property and make their own local laws.

There have been other instances in which Transkei politicians, by displaying independence, have prompted speculation that perhaps the lesson of self-rule was being learned faster than Pretoria intended. The Transkei legislature voted in 1965 to educate its children, not (except for the lower primary grades), in the tribal mother tongue, as Pretoria preferred, but in English and Afrikaans, the languages which afford opportunity for progress in contact with white South Africa and (in the case of English) with the world at large. It was as if the legislature, while agreeing to apartheid in most respects because there was no choice, was hoping to prepare the next generation for a better existence.

Considering that the Transkei is totally dependent upon white South Africa for its political identity and its economic survival, the impulsion behind this remarkable demonstration of independence must have been enormous. The outsider is forced to the conclusion that separation of races, or "nations," is unnatural, irrational, and unworkable except in the short run. It flies in the face of instinct, self-interest, and human nature.

Pretoria offers a variety of rejoinders. It claims that outsiders do not understand the unique character of South Africa's problems. It says the government knows what is good for the primitive "Natives" better than they do. It claims that white men pioneered the country, as Americans pioneered the United States; that they conquered and displaced the "Natives," as Americans conquered and displaced the Indians—if anything, less inhumanely; that they developed the land by their own sweat and ingenuity, as did Americans, and are therefore entitled to regard it as their country. South Africans maintain that outside interference is illegal, immoral, and counterproductive. Finally, they say the outside world will one day awaken to the fact that racial integration leads to conflict, not harmony, viz Watts, Detroit, and Chicago. A variant of this argument, not used so frequently of late, is that South Africa is really not so very different from the American South.

There is some truth to the contention that outsiders do not fully understand South Africa's problems, but not much substance to the rest of this case. The paternalism of the argument that "papa knows best" what is good for the "Natives" is often a cloak for determination to remain papa. Efforts of the "child" to develop his talents are rarely encouraged or rewarded. The parallel with treatment of American Indians, while superficially valid, has little or no relevance. The one would not justify the other unless the world had made no moral progress in the past 100–150 years.

White South Africans did indeed contribute ingenuity, hard work, and enterprise to the development of their splendid country. Nonwhites contributed much of the physical labor. There is no apparent reason why both should not reap the harvest, sharing its benefits in proportion to ability and contribution, as in any freely competitive, shared society. It is the determination of the white man to retain a disproportionate share of benefits by the exercise of naked power that offends the outside world. It is the belief of the whites that they must have all or will be left with nothing that is at the root of the trouble.

Outside "interference" to help awaken South Africans to this mistake is certainly neither illegal nor immoral, and if carefully honed, need not be counterproductive. Nor is it true that too much integration has produced racial discord in the United States. During the Newark riots in July 1967, *Die Vaderland*, a progovernment newspaper, recommended that the United States try apartheid as a remedy for its social ills. "America's obsession with integration only causes chaos, strife and destruction," it commented. The truth, as most thoughtful Americans know, is that "chaos, strife and destruction" have sprung from too little, not too much, integration. Despite progress in recent years, Negro ghettos still afford too little opportunity for adequate education, too few job openings, too much slum misery. It would scarcely be a satisfactory answer to round up "troublemakers," unemployeds, and drifters and ship them to a partially Negro-governed state in, say, West Virginia.

Nor is South Africa the American South with an Afrikaans accent. There are important differences of kind, as well as degree, between discrimination in the two areas. Even before Congress passed the Civil Rights bill of 1964 and the Voting Rights bill of 1965, the comparison was invalid. It is not just that the central government in the United States is fighting against, not for, white supremacy; even the policies of the most conservative southern states are not comparable to apartheid. As actor Sidney Poitier, just back from making an American movie on location in South Africa, once commented: "Mississippi is paradise compared to the racial, political and social levels of South Africa."

George Wallace in his worst nightmares never forcibly separated a Negro from his wife and children by government decree, deported him from the city to the countryside, or passed a law requiring his employer to fire him and hire a white replacement. Hard as it is for Negroes to get good jobs in the South—and sometimes in the North—they are not forbidden by law to take them, if employer (and union) are prepared to give them an opportunity. They have had trouble getting registered to vote in the deep South; people have been murdered for attempting it. But they are legally entitled to the franchise, and more are getting on the rolls each year. Some Southerners may find apartheid (especially petty apartheid) congenial as a doctrine, but more are coming, with varying degrees of reluctance, to the same conclusion that is being reached elsewhere in the world: that white supremacy is an impractical and immoral anachronism in the twentieth century, a denial of the most fundamental tenets of the Christian religion, which proclaims that God "is no respecter of persons, but in every nation he that feareth Him and worketh righteousness is accepted with Him." It is because South Africans are making little or no progress toward this recognition—because, in fact, they have embodied racial discrimination in law and enshrined it as an eternal verity, even claiming scriptural authority for it—that they have set themselves apart, not merely from the American South, but from the overwhelming majority of mankind.

CHAPTER THREE

The Rumbling Volcano

On the surface, there is an atmosphere of calm in South Africa. Most cities are relaxed, with little violence in the streets except in certain areas at night. In normal times, a white man feels in no more danger in Cape Town than he does in New York or Los Angeles, and perhaps not as much.

Nonwhites defer elaborately to whites; the latter are called "master" and "boss," and treated correspondingly. These words have come to be regarded as ordinary parts of the language, comparable to "sir." "Master's tea is ready," a nonwhite waiter will say to a white stranger. "Will master have milk and sugar?"

Remarkably enough, there is also a considerable fund of genuine goodwill between the races, despite all that has happened. It is reciprocal. Africans often respect and sometimes even love their employers, showing a capacity for patience and forgiveness which astounds a visitor. In turn, many whites feel a compassion for the Africans which, for all its paternalism, is nonetheless real. Individual acts of kindness are done for "our blacks." Collectively the government provides hospitals, housing, and health services. These latter may sometimes reflect as much a desire to demonstrate one's virtue to oneself, and to the outside world, as an impulse to be compassionate. But they are approved by most white taxpayers for reasons that often reflect genuine concern.

The calm is deceptive. Beneath the surface, a volcano is rumbling. Seeds of hatred planted thousands of times, year after year, are taking root. Few Africans hate easily, but they can learn.

Emotions boiling inside a deferential exterior can burst forth unexpectedly, in curious ways. The fury with which a crime against a white man is committed (some murderers hack their victims to death with *pangas,* or cleavers) . . . the momentary look of triumph when a white man is arrested for a traffic violation . . . the resentment, not quite successfully concealed, at an arbitrary order: like flashes of sheet lightning, these things illuminate inner feelings.

The crime rate—22.8 convictions * a year per 1,000 population in 1966–67—is also eloquent testimony, since much anger and frustration is taken out in this form. Because it is especially risky for nonwhites to assault whites, nonwhites themselves become the principal victims. For each white person robbed by a nonwhite, 14 nonwhites are robbed by nonwhites. For each white murdered by a nonwhite, 138 nonwhites are murdered by nonwhites. "A lot of people die in Soweto," an African remarked, referring to the 21-square-mile township just outside Johannesburg, "and not all of them have been sick." Twenty murders there in a single weekend are a common occurrence, many taking place on Friday night when hundreds of thousands of wage-earners come home with weekly paychecks. In 1962–65 inclusive, 1,192 cases of death by violence were reported to police in Soweto, and estimates are that roughly three times this many go unreported. The *Rand Daily Mail,* in a survey of crime in Soweto, estimated that 1,000 or more people are killed there each year. Moreover, more than half the persons in Soweto convicted for murder, culpable homicide, and assault resulting in death, 1962–65, were under 21 years of age.

The immediate motive for a crime of violence may often be robbery, the pressures of hunger and poverty being what they are. But underlying it all is a current of frustration, fear, and anger. The man who swings the *panga* or jabs with the *ntshumentshu* (a needle-sharp bicycle spoke) may not himself be fully aware of how he has been influenced by this mental atmosphere, but the crime rate is vivid testimony to the fact that he has.

There are indications of where the resentment is really directed. No matter how compassionate he feels, no white man in South Africa dares to stop and help an African he has struck with his automobile if there is a crowd of other Africans in the vicinity. He would be in very real danger of being lynched. He must drive to the nearest telephone and summon help. Twice in 1966 when

---

* For crimes of all kinds, including pass-laws violations. Comparisons are difficult because the pass laws are unique to South Africa. The figure normally cited for crimes of all kinds in the United States is 13.6 per 1,000.

African commuter trains were derailed, keyed-up Africans rioted and attacked the white engineer.

In the Indian marketplace in Durban on market day, Indians and Pakistanis stroll deliberately en masse down the middle of the street, slowing traffic. They do so because it is a long-standing practice to walk there and because there is little room to walk anywhere else. But also, one suspects, it is because this is one occasion when self-assertion is permitted—and is safe. White men in their cars must sit and wait.

Along with resentment there is fear. A white man stops and asks an African for directions on the road. The African may not know the way, but he does not dare say so for fear he will be thought deliberately uncooperative. So he says, "Go down the road three miles, boss, and turn right." Long before boss has discovered the directions are incorrect, the African will have vanished.

Whites fear Africans at least as intensely as Africans fear whites. Indeed, their fear is a major motive for apartheid. A family which had camped thirty miles from Umtata on the banks of a river, where the men were engaged in road construction, woke up one night with their caravan on fire. When they fled to the veld, they were attacked by tribesmen with *assegais*—broad-bladed spears. They were stabbed and hacked to death, their bodies mutilated. It was a relatively isolated case—but it happened.

Parlor raconteurs settle down with their after-dinner coffee and tell the story, presumably apocryphal, of a man who asked a well-loved children's nurse whether, if there were a revolution, she would slit the throats of the family. "Oh, no, boss," she replied. "I would go over to the neighbors'. Neighbors' cook-boy would come over here."

Fear of revolution pervades much of South African life. Among the 3,563,000 whites, there are some 2,000,000 privately owned firearms. An estimated 35,000 women have joined pistol clubs in recent years, giving rise to talk about "pistol-packin' mamas." One gun fancier, François Joubert of Johannesburg, has designed a "brassiere holster," a cloth gun-holder which snaps onto the strap of a bra and enables the wearer to carry a .38-caliber revolver under her arm. To deal with the possible servant peril, white families in municipal areas have recently been required to obtain permits if they have more than one sleep-in servant—a restriction which, however, is unpopular and is said to be widely evaded. Every able-bodied white South African man or woman from 17 to 65 can be called up for military training if he has not already had it.

In its more acute form, this fear of revolution is a relatively recent phenomenon. Until 1961, the policy of African underground leaders was to protest peacefully. The oldest nationalistic movement, the African National Congress (ANC), which dates from 1912 and was legal until 1960, clung to the policy of peaceful resistance until some time in 1961. At a secret meeting that summer in Bechuanaland, now Botswana, it endorsed violence, and Umkonto we Sizwe (Spear of the Nation) was founded by some of its leaders. Spear was to be separate from the ANC and, unlike the ANC, was to include whites. In effect, however, Spear was to be its action arm, engaging in sabotage and other violence against property.

Earlier, in 1959, a group of younger ANC members, impatient with what was then the organization's policy of passive resistance, broke off and founded a second, rival group, the Pan Africanist Congress (PAC) under Robert M. Sobukwe, an impressive lecturer in Bantu languages at the University of the Witwatersrand, in Johannesburg. Parallel to the PAC, and loosely associated with it, were violent activists who, beginning in late 1961, called themselves members of Poqo ("Pure").

The PAC stepped promptly to the forefront. Soon after its formation, it organized massive demonstrations against the pass laws. Its first major demonstrations were held on March 21, 1960, when scores of thousands of Africans in many parts of the country appeared at police stations without their passbooks, inviting arrest.

One of the largest of these demonstrations was at Sharpeville, an African township thirty miles south of Johannesburg, where a crowd of Africans estimated at between 5,000 and 20,000, on strike for the day, gathered outside the fence surrounding a police station. On the other side of the fence were some 300 police armed with rifles, machine guns, and four Saracen tanks. Pictures taken at the time show no visible weapons in the possession of the Africans and much indication of a holiday mood. The crowd was singing songs and shouting. Women were carrying umbrellas and children were playing. A few men held sticks. (The previous month, at Cato Manor, in Durban, a crowd had attacked a group of policemen conducting a liquor raid and beaten nine of them to death with sticks.)

Nothing happened for several hours. No one ordered the crowd to disperse. Police officers walked through the crowd without incident. But suddenly, for no reason that was ever adequately explained, the police started shooting. In some twenty to forty seconds of horror, 705 rounds of ammunition were poured into the crowd: 69 Africans were killed on the spot (three others died later) and 178 wounded. More than 80 percent were shot in the back as they fled. There was no return fire.

Government propaganda sought to justify the police action. Many of the wounded Africans were arrested. Some were jailed with their wounds still incompletely dressed. Seventy-nine were charged, and twenty-three actually tried, for "public violence." None of the police was charged with criminal wrongdoing. At a formal investigation, an effort was made to show that the crowd had been ugly, armed, and menacing, but few independent observers were persuaded. A government witness undoubtedly came closer to candor when he complained that the Africans had been "lacking in respect and humility."

Near the end of the testimony, after the long tragic story had been told and retold, the police officer in command at the time of the shooting, a Lieutenant Colonel Pienaar, was asked if he had learned any useful lesson from the investigation. "Well," he replied, "we may get better equipment."

The government seemed, for a time, to have been more profoundly affected. A shock wave from the "Sharpeville massacre" had echoed around the world, and many South Africans, too, were outraged. There were minor relaxations of some restrictions; there was also some tightening. Leaders of the protest movement were arrested. The government seemed off balance, unsure of its course.

On March 30, the country got another big scare. Thousands of Africans marched from their locations into the nearest white community to protest the arrest of their leaders. The biggest march was in Cape Town. Some 30,000 grim Africans, led in the later stages by one youth, Philip Kgosana, marched in lock step— slowly, rhythmically, inexorably—from Langa township to within a few blocks of the Houses of Parliament. The sight must have been terrifying—as, of course, it was intended to be. On a hillside above the center of town, the marchers were induced to halt while

Kgosana negotiated with officials. He was persuaded, apparently on the promise of an interview with the Minister of Justice, to disperse the men. Kgosana did disperse them, but he never got his interview. He was arrested, and a national crackdown began in earnest. In the course of the next few weeks, under a state of emergency, 11,503 were jailed. Many thousands more were arrested and released. The ANC and PAC were outlawed, thus driving them underground. On April 9, in the midst of the tension, a mentally disturbed white farmer tried to assassinate Verwoerd.

Not until the following year were Poqo and Spear of the Nation founded, and not until 1962 did they begin to make themselves felt. It takes time for violent resistance to organize and gather momentum. Poqo's principal centers of strength proved to be Langa and Nyanga townships in Cape Town and Mbekweni in Paarl. Its growth appeared to be partly spontaneous and partly the result of recruitment and intimidation. Most of all, however, it was a reflection of the conditions of African life.

Because many African workers were forbidden to have their wives with them, men outnumbered women at Langa by perhaps 10–1. Similarly at Mbekweni, where Jackson Mapheele was quartered, many of the 2,000 men in "single" barracks were in fact married, as he was, but were forbidden to live with their wives. In the Cape as a whole, 68 percent of African men in bachelor quarters were married but unable to live as such. Prostitution, venereal disease, illegitimacy, homosexuality, and crimes related to sex were the result, along with great discontent and an ever-present danger of violence.

The night of November 21, 1962, is another of the vivid landmarks in South Africa's racial history. About one hundred men from the "single" men's barracks at Mbekweni strode into downtown Paarl. There had previously been eight murders of African and mulatto men and women in the vicinity. Three of the women had been hacked to death in the "bachelor" barracks, apparently because they were causing men to stay away from Poqo meetings. Seven men had been arrested in connection with the murders. The mob marched to the police station and stormed it, seeking to release the seven. The police replied with gunfire, and some of the Africans fell.

Infuriated, the mob swept through the main street of town,

burning two shops, trying to set fire to a post office and a gas station, and smashing windows. A group broke away from the main demonstration and attacked two private houses, breaking windows and trying to force open doors. A white woman who sought to escape and a man who came to her aid were killed. Three other whites were seriously injured. Neighbors and policemen fired on the Africans, killing five and sending at least four others to the hospital.

A full-scale investigation followed. Among the men's principal grievances was their forced separation from their wives. They also complained of rough handling and assault by the police, harsh penalties for petty infractions, overcrowding (eight to twelve men in a barracks room), and regular midnight police raids in which they were abruptly awakened while the police checked for squatters and rent defaulters.

The judge conducting the investigation said there was impressive and convincing evidence that three men—the municipal Director of African Affairs, a town councilor, and a senior African clerk—had been guilty of corrupt practices. Africans seeking work permits had been required to pay bribes, despite their meagre resources, and others had had to work for a period without pay. Africans resented the fact that prosecutions for similar offenses the previous year had resulted in acquittals. They also resented officials' lack of sympathy for victims of influx-control regulations; their "petty autocracy"; and what was called their "mechanical and impersonal approach." The situation, the investigation said, was "ready-made for Poqo."

Some of the shortcomings uncovered in the investigation were corrected. Not long thereafter, the mayor and municipal councilors who had been reluctant to take action against the corrupt Director of African Affairs were voted out of office by the white electorate. At its first meeting, the new town council suspended the director, asking the central government to fire him.

The government's principal weapon, however, in dealing with unrest—in Paarl as elsewhere—was repression. The white secret police infiltrated agents into the townships and bribed Africans into playing informer. The going rate was said to be 5 rand ($7), which is nearly four days' pay for the average African in Johannesburg. It was and is enough to tempt many Africans. South African officials tell the story of 47 African labor union leaders who met secretly one night in Soweto to discuss strategy. The next day, 23 of the participants separately gave the police detailed accounts of the meeting.

In response to such police methods, Poqo tried to become better organized, setting up a counterintelligence system and dealing brutally with government "stooges." One way of disposing of them was, and is, to drive a bicycle spoke into their abdomen or through their backbone, thus paralyzing the victim. When the police caught Poqo members, they were treated only a few degrees more gently.

Police methods first came dramatically to public notice in 1964 at a trial of four constables and a clerk of court from a community called Bulfontein. The five white men were charged with murdering a suspected thief, an African named Izak Magaise, one of four Africans accused of stealing 13.60 rand ($19). Constable Jacob Barend Maree, one of the police on trial, testified to a shocked court that when Magaise did not confess, he and a second constable lifted the suspect about three feet from the floor (it must have been a long three feet) and dropped him, repeating the process twice thereafter. The third time Magaise did not get up. He was dead.

The other three Africans, according to Maree's testimony, had lived through the "interrogation" but had been struck, given electric shocks, whipped with a *sjambok* (a whip made of rhinoceros hide), and/or suffocated with a plastic bag in an unsuccessful effort to extract confessions. The electric shocks came from wires attached to a hand generator. "While shocking Africans I tell them it is the *tokoloshe* or a cat scratching them," Constable Maree said. (A *tokoloshe* is a mythical dwarflike creature of which many Africans are terrified.) "Some of them seem to believe it." He said the shocks caused reactions similar to convulsions.

Asked by the judge how he could be familiar with these methods and the use of this equipment after only a short time at a new post—for he had recently been transferred—he replied: "It is done at more places. I don't think there is a police station in the country that does not use violence during questioning." He indicated he thought things had gone too far, however, when the suspect died.

The accused policemen were found guilty and sentenced to jail terms varying from three to nine years. White South Africans appeared to consider the sentences severe (and by comparison with glaringly unjust acquittals by some white juries in the American South, they may have been). But Africans can be, and have been, sentenced to similar terms in South Africa for nothing more than distributing "objectionable" pamphlets.

Questions were asked in Parliament about widespread police brutality. It was denied, and the commissioner of police reminded all stations of standing orders to use "only such force as is absolutely necessary to overcome resistance on arrest." Few people, however, took the denials seriously.

The following year, 1965, a courageous and outspoken opposition newspaper, the *Rand Daily Mail,* published a series of three articles by a former political prisoner, Harold (Jock) Strachan (as told to reporter Benjamin Pogrund). Mr. Strachan, a 40-year-old white artist, had been jailed for three years on charges of conspiracy to cause explosions. He gave a vivid description of prison life, saying—among many other things—that he had been forced to brush his teeth in a flush toilet, and that a letter from his wife, the only word from outside that he was allowed in a six-month period, was waved under his eyes and then withheld, as a form of psychological torment.

The treatment he received as a white man, however, was mild indeed by comparison with what he said was meted out to nonwhite prisoners. He told how he had seen nonwhites beaten with fists, whipped with leather straps, forced to stand dripping wet in cold winter winds, and in some cells driven literally insane— to the point of self-mutilation—by months of total, absolute silence.

> The worst assaults I saw anywhere in jail [he wrote] were those on Africans . . . in the hospital at Pretoria Local [prison]. For most of my time there, the hospital yard was straight under my window.
>
> All prisoners when they came into prison went to the hospital to get examined and so forth. Non-European [i.e., nonwhite] prisoners who had to see the doctors were brought out at about 6:15 in the morning, and it could be freezing cold in Pretoria.
>
> They stood naked, 60, 70, 80 of them at a time. Huddled up like birds trying to keep warm. Like poultry. Stark naked.
>
> They had to stand with frost thick on the ground, barefoot, clutching each other to try to keep warm. Shivering.

And they would stand there until the doctor came at nine o'clock, sometimes later. Now and then one of the poyisas [non-white guards] would allow them to pick up a garment to drape over their shoulders. Otherwise they just stood naked until the doctor came.

I have seen prisoners get a blow, as they were inoculated, from a poyisa or from one of the prisoners who worked in the hospital. Sometimes this happened in the presence of a doctor.

I also saw occasional assaults on the patients themselves. I saw one man, who was apparently suspected of smuggling dagga [a narcotic] dragged out of the hospital by a warder [prison guard]—Kruger—whom we called "Florence Nightingale."

This warder was a burly man with a deformed face. He dragged out this prisoner who was wearing the hospital grey robe and forced him to kneel down on all fours [and] strip naked in front of all the other patients. . . .

The African prisoner who acted as hospital orderly stood with an enema can of soap and water. The enema was administered.

The prisoner was stood up; blood was dripping down his legs; he was not allowed to get rid of this soapy water. It was blue soap. I saw them making it. He had to stand with his buttocks clenched together with his hands.

He was then forced to jump around from leg to leg, doing a sort of quick march, a sort of knees up to a horizontal position but still clutching his buttocks so the stuff couldn't come out.

The burly warder kicked him as he jumped in this way, kicked him on his arms, his back, his hips and his belly. Until finally a pot was brought out by one of the African prisoners.

The man then sat on the pot and got rid of all this water in the presence of the warder and everyone else. And while he was doing it he was being beaten over the head.

Where the man had been standing and jumping there was a puddle of blood. When he got up from the pot, Kruger went and poked around in it with a stick [presumably searching for the narcotics]. I did not see him pull anything out.

On another occasion I saw a prisoner carried into the prison yard on a blanket, the corners held by other African prisoners. He might have been shamming, because many prisoners, like soldiers . . . like to get into hospital where the food is slightly better.

Anyway this man was put on the ground and he was lying there immobile. After a while he stirred.

Two of the warders had a consultation and apparently decided the man was shamming.

One of the warders took his wooden truncheon and, sitting down, let it fall on the forehead of this man on the ground— I suppose about 20 or 30 times. Bong, bong, bong—as you might do with a pencil on a table letting it fall with its own weight.

But this was a truncheon falling from six inches. As it turned out, the man was unconscious—fortunately, for he didn't feel this lot going on.

Several times I saw warders kicking or assaulting prisoners lying on the ground, who had been carried into the hospital ward.

I assumed this was to test whether they were shamming or not. Some suddenly jumped up whereas before they had been apparently unable to stand.

But otherwise these were potential patients, and this was no way to treat a man who came in as I saw some of them come in.

At one point, Mr. Strachan and another political prisoner complained to the superintendent. "What about regulations?" they asked. "Don't talk about regulations," Mr. Strachan quoted him as replying. "There is no such thing as regulations."

Conditions at another of the prisons in which Mr. Strachan was held, just before his release—Maritzburg jail—were much better. "I saw no vicious assaults [there]," he wrote. "Only a few odd cuffs on the back of the head. In Maritzburg, imprisonment was no burden to me because of the humanity of Section Warder Kriel. He was a gentleman to all prisoners, speaking to them courteously and intent on their rehabilitation."

On the day the second of the three Strachan articles was published, six detectives from the South African Special Branch (secret police) raided the offices of the *Daily Mail* and seized the reporter's notes and other documents, including the manuscript of the third article. Either Mr. Strachan and Mr. Pogrund rewrote it, however, from memory, or else they had a carbon copy of the original. At any rate, the third article appeared on schedule. The government then "banned" Mr. Strachan for five years, severely restricting his movements and making it illegal in South Africa to publish anything he said or wrote during that period.

Seven weeks later, Mr. Strachan was arrested. Under the Prisons Act of 1959, it is an offense to publish "false information concerning the behavior or experience in prison of any prisoner or ex-prisoner or concerning the administration of any prison. . . ." Conviction carries a fine and/or a year in jail. The key word, of course, is "false," and a normal defense would be to establish the accuracy of what had been stated or the good faith in which verification had been sought. Confiscation of the *Daily Mail*'s supporting documents during the police raid and other, similar raids that followed was, therefore, a severe blow, both to Mr. Strachan and to the paper, which was also liable to prosecution if it could be shown that it had failed to take "reasonable steps to verify" the information. Mr. Pogrund and officials of the paper were in fact later charged.

Shortly before Mr. Strachan's sensational allegations were published, a white prison warder of seventeen years' experience, Johannes A. Theron of the staff of Cinderella Prison, Boksburg, complained officially, in private, of brutality and corruption by his superiors. He said prisoners were subjected to beating and to electric shocks to force false statements in court, and that prison officials accepted bribes from farmers in return for supplying prison labor.

Mr. Theron got results, but not the ones he sought. He himself was brought before a departmental court on a disciplinary charge. He then told his story in a sworn statement to the *Sunday Times* of Johannesburg, a sister paper of the *Mail*, adding that warders who spoke out against "these appalling conditions" had been "victimized." The *Times* published his statement, and he was promptly suspended from the prison force and confined to barracks.

Once Strachan and Theron had spoken out, others came forward. Two of Theron's colleagues at Cinderella Prison, Gysbert Johan van Schalkwyk and Herhardus Prins, both white men, told similar stories.

Van Schalkwyk, a 22-year-old warder, provided detailed corroboration of an important part of Theron's story. He told the *Mail* he had witnessed fifteen to twenty-five electric-shock tortures, describing one as follows:

"Erasmus [the warder] held the one shiny point on Aaron's body—on his stomach, his legs, private parts, chest, neck—and when Aaron screamed, also on his mouth and tongue." In another case, the shock treatment was given to a prisoner, Mr. van Schalkwyk said, to force him to give evidence against Warder Theron in the latter's departmental trial.

Two former prisoners at Cinderella Prison, both Africans, further corroborated the charges. One of the prisoners, Filisberto Nyabetse, said he had been forced to strip and lie down on a table covered with rubber matting. His body and the mat were sprinkled with water, and he then was prodded with live electrodes. "I had this pain all over," he said in a statement to the *Mail*. "My head felt as if it would split into many parts. I screamed aloud and prayed."

The government reacted vigorously, though not by ordering the judicial inquiry the *Mail* demanded. (A departmental investigation was said to be under way.) Typically, it attempted repression and intimidation of its critics. It raided the *Mail* again, questioned the editor, Laurence Gandar, for forty minutes, searched Mr. Pogrund's desk, and began legal proceedings against Mr. Theron, Mr. van Schalkwyk, and the two African prisoners on charges of perjury.

In court van Schalkwyk recanted on some of the statements he had made. He pleaded guilty and waived defense counsel, a fact which made it impossible to cross-examine government witnesses. Mr. Gandar and Mr. Pogrund applied for the right to testify, but their applications were denied. Thus no rebuttal to the government's case could be presented in court.

The accused cooperated fully with the prosecution. The machine he had previously said was used for electric-shock torture was, in fact, he now asserted, a massage machine for the therapeutic treatment of nervous cases. He had manufactured the earlier story, he said, in order to "make a good impression" on the reporter for the *Mail* and on Warder Theron. The head warder of the prison testified he had "not even heard whispers" of torture at his institution.

Since no challenge or contrary testimony was allowed, this extraordinary proceeding succeeded in giving the impression that the *Daily Mail* had engaged in politically motivated libel of a virtuous government, and that Mr. van Schalkwyk was a publicity-seeker who had been paid to assist. The pro-government press and government-controlled radio did their utmost to magnify the impression. A common man-in-the-street reaction was that "it looks as if the *Mail* has gone overboard again."

Despite his "repentance," Mr. van Schalkwyk was given three years in jail, the maximum sentence, and the mother of his fiancée broke off the young people's engagement. The two African prisoners who had spoken out were also convicted; they got six-month sentences. Later, apparently regretting his decision to co-operate with the government, van Schalkwyk decided from a jail cell to appeal the sentence, and it was cut in half. Theron got thirty-two months, which similarly was reduced on appeal to sixteen.

The fight thus continued, but all the advantages were on the government's side. In a fourth raid on the *Mail* in two months, police seized documents and notes having to do with additional planned disclosures, and court action by the *Mail* failed to force their return. Men interviewed by the paper on the subject of prison conditions were visited by the secret police—despite efforts by the paper to keep their identity confidential (suggesting that the newspaper offices may have been "bugged" and/or infiltrated). In an unusual twist, Mr. Pogrund successfully sued the prosecutor of the prison trials for defamation, and won 500 rand ($700) damages plus costs. The prosecutor also filed a cross libel against the *Mail*. It had not come to trial as this book went to press.

Mr. Strachan, the man who had touched off the whole struggle, was prosecuted for perjury and violation of the Prisons Act. The magistrate expressed skepticism about the testimony of guards and prisoners called by the government to refute Strachan's description of prison conditions. "The suspicion is strong," he said in his judgment, "that such witnesses might well be endeavoring to paint too rosy and perfect a picture," not being above "considerations of self-interest." (They were vulnerable to reprisals, and could see what had happened to others who criticized the government.) Nevertheless he convicted Mr. Strachan and sentenced him to two and one-half years in jail, observing that defense witnesses also had been suspect. This sentence, too, was reduced on appeal.

All of the people who had been quoted by the *Mail* having been prosecuted and convicted, it became progressively more difficult for the paper to find witnesses willing to come forward, as the government no doubt intended it to be. The passports of Mr.

Gandar and Mr. Pogrund were seized, and in 1967 they, too, were haled into court, along with Joel Mervis,* editor of the *Sunday Times,* Leycester Walton, managing director of the firm which publishes the two papers, and Kelsey Stuart, its legal adviser. All were charged with violations of the Prisons Act.

As of this writing, although the two papers have not been silenced, they have been badly hurt financially by the necessity to fight a series of court cases. The *Mail* is said to have spent more than $350,000 on them. Meanwhile the government has threatened to ask Parliament for legislation to crack down even more severely on all "untrue" press reporting.

Abroad, the *Mail* has been honored; the American Newspaper Publishers Association Foundation awarded it the World Press Achievement Award for 1966. Mr. Gandar, however, has been "kicked upstairs" to the post of editor in chief, where he still writes one crusading editorial a week but does not supervise the day-to-day operation of the paper. Pressure from advertisers, themselves under pressure from the government, is understood to have forced the paper's corporate directors to shelve him. They did not dare fire him; virtually the whole staff would have walked out.

There have been repercussions in the United Nations. In March 1967, the UN Commission on Human Rights, "deeply disturbed," it said in a formal resolution, "by the evidence . . . of continuing torture and ill-treatment of persons in the Republic of South Africa who have been detained by the police or imprisoned for opposition to, or infringement of, apartheid laws," condemned these practices, requested Secretary-General U Thant to convey to South Africa the commission's "deep distress and serious concern," and established a "working group" of "eminent jurists and prison officials" to investigate further and write a report.

The group began its work in May 1967, but could not make an on-the-spot survey. South Africa scorned the group as "flagrant interference" in her internal affairs, in effect refusing to let it see the prisons. The International Committee of the Red Cross had already visited them in 1963, 1964, and 1967, Pretoria pointed out. This was true; but what South Africa did not say was that the Red Cross visits had been planned in detail in advance, the Red Cross representative rarely if ever seeking to depart from the

---

* Proceedings against Mr. Mervis were withdrawn in January 1968.

itinerary. The fact that his arrival was never a surprise enabled prison officials to prepare carefully for him. Prisoners later said that in one institution a cockroach nest had been cleaned out, and in others, pajamas and shoes were issued temporarily, sick prisoners were put in beds instead of on mats on the cement floor, and the overflowing enamel pots which served as toilets in many cells were emptied. Thus the visits fell considerably short of searching and independent investigations, and did the International Committee of the Red Cross little credit. Even so, there were some constructive repercussions from them.

The UN working group held hearings in New York, London and Dar es Salaam, Tanzania, taking sworn testimony from 20 former political prisoners, white and nonwhite. Among them was a white American woman, Mrs. Mary Louise Hooper of California and New York, a one-time permanent resident of South Africa who worked with the late Chief Albert Luthuli. Others were teachers, lawyers, writers, clergymen, and medical practitioners— even one former member of a provincial council. They had been jailed for offenses ranging from preparing a document for the ANC (in Mrs. Hooper's case) to complicity in an attempted explosion in a post office. Several had been held for interrogation, without charge.

The stories they told were grim descriptions of filth, brutality and perversion. Earlier descriptions of South African prison conditions were fully corroborated and expanded upon. Witnesses said that, as "pogos," or political prisoners, they had been deliberately treated, as a matter of policy, more severely than murderers, thieves and rapists, being allowed fewer privileges and often being subjected to special humiliations, such as being required to clean a latrine with their hands. The juxtaposition of "politicals" and common criminals, some of the latter serving long sentences, led to special hardships, they said. In short-staffed prisons, criminals were sometimes given disciplinary power over other prisoners, including politicals, and it was used with great cruelty, they testified. In other places, witnesses said hardened criminals sought to force young political prisoners into homosexuality. Some charged that this was done with the indulgence and actual connivance of a prison warder. One witness in the inquiry, a 42-year-old writer and former high-school teacher, said a young political prisoner in a cell near his "had been repeatedly assaulted for re-

fusing to consent to homosexual intercourse with criminal prisoners. At the time I saw him, he was receiving treatment for alleged
insanity; he was certainly behaving abnormally and had periods
of ravings. I had no way of knowing what became of him after
he was removed on a stretcher."

Beatings and other assaults against nonwhites were common,
it was testified. Minor assaults were described as "almost part of
the routine." Women who washed clothing of what warders called
the "kaffir pogos" (nigger political prisoners) said it often was
impregnated with blood and ointment. One witness said he protested the assaults to the authorities, pointing to the blood stains
on shirts. "I was told by the chief warder," he said, "that all the
shirts had blood stains in that prison. It was not sufficient proof
to refer to blood stains . . ."

Conditions were so bad in one prison, according to testimony,
that four convicts "confessed" to a 10-year-old murder they had
not committed—risking a possible death sentence—in order to be
brought before a court where they could be sure of a hearing.
(Complaints to the immediate authorities often brought nothing
but reprisals; law suits sometimes were successful, but often a
court denied jurisdiction.) When the "murderers' " complaints
were heard, a prison representative replied by saying he couldn't
understand what the fuss was all about. In the previous year, he
was quoted as telling the court, only one prisoner had committed
suicide and several had cut their tendons; otherwise the prisoners
were very satisfied with their conditions.

There was no one on the United Nations investigating panel
who reflected South Africa's point of view, or who subjected the
witnesses to hostile cross-examination. Some exaggerations and
hearsay evidence may therefore have gone unchallenged. The witnesses had abundant reason to strike back in anger at the South
African Government.

But even if only one fifth of what they said was true—and
testimony, taken on three continents, was consistent in many
respects—it was one of the most damning indictments ever spread
on the international record. Perhaps in part because of embarrassment at earlier disclosures, the South African authorities improved conditions in some of the worst prisons in 1964–65,
witnesses said. They pleaded for more exposures in the hope that
there would be further improvements. Independent observers,

however, believe prison conditions are affected more directly by the government's sense of security, or lack of it. When the police are afraid of sabotage and potential revolution, as they were in the period 1960–64, they crack down hard on political prisoners; when fears ease, as they did (in a relative sense) after the Rivonia Trial,* some of the worst extremes—physical tortures during interrogation, for example—tend to cease.

The behavior of police and of prison officials can be explained in part by the makeup of the two forces. Many white police and warders, especially in rural areas, are young, brutal, ill-educated men of the "poor-white" type. Their superiors do not always insist on strict discipline. In 1959, the year before Sharpeville, more than three hundred white policemen were convicted of serious crimes, but only one in five of them was thereupon discharged from the force. One out of three on the force was under twenty-one years of age.

In the ten years 1955–65, South Africa's prison population doubled; the daily average for the year ended June 30, 1967, was 73,285—more than three times as many, in proportion to the population, as the United States, and more than five times as many as Britain. In January 1967, the Minister of Justice acknowledged there were 1,221 persons in custody who had been "convicted of serious offenses against the public safety and security of the state." (He declined to call them "political prisoners.") The maximum ever held, he said, was 1,825. Observers, however, believe a more realistic breakdown as between "political" offenses and "criminal" ones would produce a much higher figure. In any event, the percentage of "politicals" has sharply increased since 1960.

Sentences are getting more severe. In 1962, sabotage was added to the list of capital offenses. A long series of "sabotage trials" followed, reflecting the increased activity of Spear of the Nation and the intensified counteraction of the police. In part as a result, 257 Africans were condemned to death in 1963–64, and 164 of them were in fact hanged.†

This kind of atmosphere can easily spawn prison abuses. When

---

* In 1963–64. See page 61.

† In 1961–65, according to United Nations figures, 1,066 people were executed throughout the world. Nearly half of them were hanged in South Africa.

Mr. Strachan and a colleague, also a political prisoner, complained to a warder at Pretoria Central that he was victimizing them, the warder replied, according to Strachan: "As a matter of fact, I am. You are political prisoners, and I am making your life as hard as possible. . . ."

In these years of incipient revolution in South Africa, the then Minister of Justice, B. J. Vorster, now Prime Minister, sought and obtained new powers. In 1963, Parliament gave him authority to jail a man or woman for successive periods of 90 days—that is, indefinitely—in virtual solitary confinement (he would be visited weekly by a magistrate) if the police suspected him of having committed, of intending to commit, or of having information about, political offenses. No charge or trial was necessary.

This law applied to both whites and nonwhites, and was obviously a very serious infringement of due process and the rule of law. Perhaps in part because of worldwide protests, it was suspended in January 1965. But it was not repealed, and shortly thereafter it was replaced by a new 180-day law similar in its effect.

Vorster reported to Parliament that a total of 1,095 persons were detained under the "90-day" act while it was in effect. As of May 1967, 282 persons had been held under the 180-day law. The principal purpose was interrogation. It was generally assumed that torture was used, when necessary, to get the information desired. Indeed, some men who went through the experience and were released signed affidavits swearing they had been tortured—by being made to stand, for example, for 72 hours or more until they collapsed (the "statue" method). Others said they had been beaten and/or given electric shocks. Few were able to withstand the ordeal. Some prisoners committed suicide, turned state's evidence, or cracked. "Torture by mind-breaking," an opposition MP called it.

Albert Louis Sachs, 32 years old, an advocate of the Cape Supreme Court, told the United Nations inquiry how it was accomplished in his case. He described how six interrogators dealt with him in groups of two, working four hours on, eight hours off, around the clock. He related:

At first it was merely a sort of political harangue and pleading, followed by periods of quiet, in which they would just sit

there and watch me. . . . I was told I would not be allowed
to leave that room until I made a statement.

As the night wore on, I got more and more tired, and in
the early hours I was extremely fatigued. Whenever my eye-
lids closed, there would be a bang on the table or my name
would be shouted out, or my body would be touched, tickled
or pushed.

The position got worse and worse. My mind and body became numb, and eventually I collapsed off my chair onto the
ground. [His case was somewhat unusual in that he was allowed to have a chair.] Cold water was thrown on me, but I
lay exhausted on the floor. I was picked up, placed on the
chair, and I collapsed again.

This process was repeated several times. Then the whole
team crowded around me, propping me up with their hands,
holding my head up, and when my eyes closed, Captain Swanepoel pushed them open with his fingers. . . .

Sachs later recovered enough to take a few steps, and as he
did, he said, "I had thoughts of throwing myself over that wall
to either injure or kill myself." The police prevented him, and
eventually he decided "to settle on the best possible terms."
Sachs, a white man, had acted as legal counsel for African nationalists, sometimes successfully, and knew many of them. He
had considerable information the police would have found useful.

Acting on information gained from another 90-day prisoner
arrested earlier, the secret police swooped down in July 1963 on
the home of Arthur Goldreich in Rivonia, a section of Johannesburg. They rounded up seventeen alleged leaders of Spear of the
Nation, including Nelson Mandela, the so-called Black Pimpernel
of the African underground. The widely publicized "Rivonia
trial" followed, resulting in convictions and (in most cases) life
sentences. This effectively decapitated Spear of the Nation and
sharply retarded the wave of sabotage attributed to it. (Intermittent sabotage continued until July 1964, more than two-
hundred acts being committed in all.)

The police also made progress against Poqo. In March 1963,
a few months before the Rivonia raid, the police seized a PAC
courier, a woman, carrying enough information to facilitate a
nationwide roundup and enable the police to wipe out that body
as an effective agency. Whether coordinated or coincidental, this

crackdown was accompanied on April 1, 1963, by a British police raid on PAC headquarters then located in Maseru, Basutoland, now the capital of independent Lesotho. Just before the raids, Potlaka Leballo, the PAC's presumed leader, had boasted in Maseru that his organization was about to stage a nationwide bloodbath in South Africa.

Since underground organizations take years to build, these crackdowns were severe blows. The police were winning the battle of 1961–64, the first major round in South Africa's racial revolution.

That a second round will be fought, even the most self-confident government officials agree, though no one knows just when. Meanwhile, as African underground movements become more desperate, they may well turn, as Leballo threatened to do, from sabotage of property to deliberate attacks on persons. Rivonia has been called "the death knell of amateurism." Whether the next phase of South Africa's race war will be wholly professional —and, indeed, whether the first phase was wholly amateur—is not clear. But few can doubt that the days ahead will be bloodier than those behind.

African nationalism is also turning to the Left. Since 1950, when the Communist Party was made illegal, South African Communists have increased their efforts to penetrate and control the ANC. According to best intelligence estimates, there are about 700 hard-core, card-carrying Communists in the Republic of South Africa, plus some 6,500 active sympathizers, and the number is growing. This is more than enough, of course, to dominate an underground organization. Moreover, South Africa's Communists have the reputation of being unusually capable.

How much influence they have gained in the ANC is hotly debated. Western intelligence sources think it is very considerable; ANC people indignantly deny it. A friend of mine, thoroughly versed in Marxist theory, though not himself a Communist, interviewed members of the Lesotho (Basutoland) Communist Party in Maseru in 1963. He loosened them up with his knowledge of their ideology, and when they were speaking freely, one said: "Since we gained control of the ANC—"

A colleague snapped at him: "Shut up, you bloody fool."

"Since we established liaison with the ANC—" the first man began anew.

The government attempts to equate all underground activity with communism. To get evidence with which to convict suspected Communists, police agents seek to infiltrate the Party. One such agent, Detective Warrant Officer G. G. Ludi, a young man with a goatee whose code identification was Q–018, surfaced in December 1964 as the government's star witness in the trial of Abram Fischer, a prominent advocate, and thirteen others accused of being Communists.

Fischer is a member of a distinguished South African family which included a judge-president and a state secretary of the Orange Free State. He had been in charge of the defense at the Rivonia trial of Mandela and his Spear of the Nation colleagues. He was also a defense attorney during part of an earlier mass treason trial which lasted from 1956 to 1961 and which, unlike Rivonia, the government lost, all 156 of the accused being acquitted.

Secret agent Q–018 told a story worthy of the most lurid detective fiction. He said he behaved as a Communist from 1960 to 1963. Finally, in May 1963, after attending a Marxist study group, he was rewarded with acceptance into the Party. His code name at cell meetings was "Harry." He was carefully instructed, he said, to maintain absolute secrecy at all times, not to address other members by their real names at meetings, and never to admit being a Party member.

The task of his Johannesburg cell, he said, was "to control and infiltrate white youth movements with leftist tendencies." Fischer, whom he described as leader of the Party, welcomed him, he testified, told him how glad they were to have him as a member, and then warned everyone in the cell about the dangers of police infiltration. Ludi said "chills went down his spine" as cell members described their methods of dealing with "traitors" and "informers."

A year before being formally admitted to the Party, Ludi continued, he volunteered to attend a "Festival of Youth and Students for Peace and Friendship" in Helsinki, Finland. He first went to London, he said, where the Soviet Embassy gave him a diplomatic visa and an air ticket to Moscow. He then zigzagged his way across Europe to avoid British intelligence.

Ludi explained that he had secured jobs on two opposition newspapers, the *Rand Daily Mail* and the Johannesburg *Star*.

Fischer showed much interest in the political views of reporters, he said. So, apparently, did Ludi's real employers. While he was on the *Mail,* one of that paper's reporters was arrested under the 90-day detention law. Shortly after Ludi left the paper, a reporter for another publication owned by the same company was also seized.

An impartial observer does not know how much of this to take at face value. Fischer acknowledged in court that he was a member of the South African Communist Party; he may well have been its leader. His prosecution may perhaps have been simply a crackdown on the Communist Party. Many, however, believe that it was also, and perhaps primarily, a reprisal for the embarrassment he had caused the government by his skillful handling of the Rivonia and treason trials. Moreover, it might have represented an effort by the government to prepare the climate for legislation, introduced in 1965, to disbar lawyers suspected of membership, past or present, in underground organizations.

During the trial, Fischer further embarrassed the government by jumping bail and successfully eluding capture for ten months by means of plastic surgery and a beard. (Much of this time he was in Joannesburg under the very noses of the police.) Finally, in November 1965, they caught up with him and got him back in custody. He then was convicted and sentenced to life imprisonment.

The testimony about how Ludi, as a presumed Communist, had worked for antigovernment newspapers was an added bonus for the government. It not only implied (quite unjustifiably) that the opposition papers knowingly hired leftist reporters, but, more important, it tended to intimidate weak-kneed newspapermen. They could be expected to start looking over their shoulders, wondering which of their colleagues was a police informer and guarding more carefully their words and actions. Since in the eyes of the police almost any criticism of the government indicates leftist tendencies, this is a pervasive form of intimidation.

Moreover, it is part of a reporter's normal job to contact people of all political persuasions. The knowledge that at any time the newsman might be seized, questioned, and perhaps tortured into disclosing the identities and views of his contacts could act as a severe inhibition on the sources—and indeed (because he would feel added responsibility) on the newsman himself. Nothing told to or discovered by a reporter could ever again be privileged. The right to "protect his sources," one of a newspaperman's most highly valued prerogatives in a free society, was being abrogated.* Ludi's tale was lurid enough to get maximum play in the South African press, and hence to have maximum psychological effect.

In the face of this developing pattern of conflict, there was one African leader who, throughout his lifetime, clung to the hope of a peaceful solution—the hope, that is, though perhaps not the expectation. He was Chief Albert J. Luthuli, who until 1967, when he was killed in an accident at a railroad crossing, was head of the ANC. (The organization being illegal after 1960, no one officially held that post.) Luthuli was the Zulu chief who, resisting all pressure for violence, held the ANC to a peaceful course during the 1950's and won the 1960 Nobel Peace Prize for it.

For years, Chief Luthuli was under a government banning order, which meant that his movements were restricted to a narrow area and his day-to-day contact with other people limited. (Like most persons under "bans," he could not legally be in the same room with more than one or two people at a time—even for social purposes, as, for example, to attend a wedding or a funeral in the family.) Nevertheless, though out of direct contact, he remained to the end one of the most respected leaders of African nationalism in South Africa.

A devout, soft-spoken Congregationalist who talked in terms of compassion and patience and brotherly love, he wanted nothing so much as a reconciliation of the races and a happily shared society. In order to talk to him alone in 1964, when I was there, one contacted a middleman and arranged a rendezvous, hopefully ducking secret police surveillance. (The government frowned on such interviews and sought to prevent most of them.) Once we were by ourselves, he spoke freely, with much reminiscing of the early days of the organization he had headed since 1952.

He paid a tribute to the United States Government for its

---

* In 1967, a reporter for the Johannesburg *Sunday Times,* Basil William Hitchcock, was given a six-week jail term for refusing to reveal the sources of articles he had written on neo-Nazi activities and anti-Semitism. He could have been given twelve months.

civil rights struggle, but wished America would take a firmer stand on civil rights for South Africans. He put it this way: "To America we say: 'We look upon you as a champion of liberty. Be true to yourself!'

"I do not say this in the spirit of those who say, 'You are going to lose Africa, man.' As for me, I'm not going to drop Christianity if it fails me today. Nor am I going to reject America.

"Some people come to me and say, 'Don't have anything to do with America.' To me, that would be a regretful day. I call on the United States to stand for her ideals." He yearned for UN pressure on the South African Government, and knew American cooperation was essential to that end.

As for the internal struggle in South Africa, Chief Luthuli approved of violence against property, at least in principle, but much preferred, "in order to win men of good will to our side," to emphasize lesser forms of protest. "I would rule out violence against people," he said. "I want to draw the people of South Africa to us. If I kill someone's husband, I am not creating a spirit of friendliness."

Chief Luthuli remained a Christian gentleman while some of his compatriots—albeit understandably—were caught up in a miasma of hatred. He seemed tired, discouraged, and disillusioned; persuasion had shown so few results. Still, he hoped to avoid bloodshed and was willing to compromise. His ultimate objective was a fully shared society; but he believed that if the government, even then, would sit down and "discuss with our people on the basis of a qualified franchise, they would find a goodly number of our people willing, regardless of what certain leaders may say. We would accept any progressive suggestion." His was a voice of common sense crying in a wilderness of confusion and fear. But he was drowned out, as racial moderates so often are, especially when progress is slow, by extremists calling for "action"—in effect, for "black power."

In South Africa, "black power" means immediate universal suffrage—though some of its advocates indicate in private that, as Luthuli said, they would settle for less, at least as a first step. Swept from frustration to desperation, they argue for guerrilla warfare and terrorism, which Luthuli deplored. It is ironic that the "grand old man of African nationalism," a force for moder-

ation all his life, should have been so severely restricted by a
government which stood to gain so much from moderating influences.

Chief Luthuli was very far from being a Communist, but even
he excused the ANC's alliance with the Communist Party. Communists helped to hasten the ultimate goal, he felt, and everyone's help was needed. "We'll start fighting communism on the
other side of the river," he said.

Judging from a sampling of people in touch with the underground, this is, unhappily, a very widely held view. Communists
have managed to sell themselves as dedicated, reliable revolutionaries. They have made deep inroads into the confidence and
loyalties of many, just as they did in Yugoslavia, France, Italy,
and elsewhere during World War II, and in India during its
struggle for independence. Sometimes, as in the case of Mahatma
Gandhi, leaders do successfully reject communism on "the other
side of the river," after the struggle has been won. But often
communist influence remains pervasive. The danger that this will
happen in South Africa is one of the tragic implications of apartheid.

"The ANC is not a political party, it is a liberation movement
of people," Chief Luthuli told me. "I don't say to a man who
wants to help us to freedom, 'You are too much of a rightist';
or 'You are too much of a leftist.' What the Communists have
done in our movement was part of our program.

"If I am hungry and a man comes and says to you, 'That man
is hungry!' are you asking me to say to him, 'Don't say I'm hungry! Shut up, man. You're a Communist!'?"

Luthuli did not confirm it, but it is well-known that the Soviet
bloc is feeding money and arms to the ANC. Mandela said at
the Rivonia trial that during his travel in Africa he had found
that "almost every single one" of the African independence movements—in Angola, Mozambique, Rhodesia, and South Africa—
had received "all forms of assistance from the socialist countries
as well as from the West." He recommended that the ANC do
the same, and no one doubts that it has. African revolutionaries
are much too desperate, and have too limited a range of choices,
to care that communist money compromises their independence
and forfeits much of the appeal they might otherwise hope to
have for Western opinion.

Leaders of the rival Pan-Africanist Congress (PAC) initially broke with the ANC in part to protest its collaboration with Communists (though paradoxically the PAC also wanted to be more activist). In the period 1959–64, PAC literature criticized "communist imperialism" along with the Western brand. If this was an opening for the CIA, however, it was not followed up, except perhaps to the extent of getting money indirectly to certain individuals considered worth encouraging in their orientation toward the West. Not many PAC leaders were in this category after 1964, most of the moderates having been jailed or forced to flee. As a result, therefore, the PAC, too, began to turn to communist sources—to Red China, in its case, rather than to Russia—for money, arms, and training.

Just how deeply the PAC has gone into hock to Peking is hard to say. Its literature now employs terminology the Chinese find congenial; it berates "revisionists," for example, and "communist imperialists" are now "Soviet imperialists." A 1967 visitor to the PAC office in Dar es Salaam asked for a book of quotations from Mao Tse-tung and was told the office had "a bunch" of them. One was quickly produced. PAC leaders insist, however, that "the Chinese don't try to influence our strategy—they say 'revolutions must always emerge from the people.'" And some Westerners believe the leash is indeed fairly loose. The Chinese have been too stingy with their money to buy tight control.

The second-echelon leadership which, since the early 1960's, has been in control of the PAC is hard to characterize. It is an amorphous group, often bitterly quarreling within itself. Some are middle-of-the-road men, ideologically; others, like Leballo, are considered erratic and extreme. They talk volubly of "African socialism"; but in South Africa, as elsewhere in Africa, this is an ill-defined phrase. Cynics translate it "dictatorship plus nationalism."

A study entitled *African Socialism,* edited by William H. Friedland and Carl G. Rosberg, Jr., for the Hoover Institution, Stanford University, describes the phenomenon as "a pragmatic ideology incorporating features of classical socialism, communism, capitalism, traditionalism and African nationalism"—in other words, an ideological corned beef hash. Its objective appears to be to find capital for swift economic development without incurring the risks of "neo-colonialism" (economic influence by an erstwhile colonial power).

The exact extent to which communism has won influence and control in the African nationalist movement in South Africa is, therefore, one of the great unknowns. Despite the South African Government's strenuous efforts to portray infiltration and control as a wholly accomplished fact, the best objective evidence is that this is not yet true.

What the government says today could become true tomorrow if events continue on their present course; this is clearly one of the great dangers of the situation. "I believe that our government's racism is giving communism the greatest opening it has ever had in Africa," a United Party MP, J. D. du P. Basson said in Parliament. G. Mennen Williams, then Assistant Secretary of State for African Affairs, told a House Foreign Affairs subcommittee in March 1966 that "there is no doubt . . . that the communists have had some success in Africa by seeking to identify themselves with African aspirations in South Africa and by identifying the United States with the controlling white minority."

The Soviet Union and Red China are, of course, doing what they can to widen this bridgehead. At least 2,000 African students are known to have slipped out of South Africa for education and guerrilla training, perhaps one third to one half of them going behind the Iron Curtain (Russia, North Korea, and Cuba). How many South Africans go to Red China is not known. The figure for all of Africa—that is, the total number of Africans from whatever country receiving Chinese training in sabotage, terrorism, and political agitation for use in overthrowing black as well as white governments—was, until recently, believed to be approximately three hundred a year. Whether this program has survived intact the upheavals of the "cultural revolution" is not clear. It seems likely, however, that it has. In November 1966, a group of about thirty Africans arrived in Addis Ababa airport, Ethiopia, from Karachi, Pakistan, to change planes for Dar es Salaam. They were wearing uniforms of the Chinese Red Guard, including worker's caps, and Mao Tse-tung badges. (Photographers who tried to take pictures of them were beaten.)

Africans who go behind the Iron or Bamboo Curtains do not always return convinced Communists; some are disillusioned with what they see. But many do, and all have the capability of taking part with some considerable effectiveness in underground violence. These trained operatives feed back, month after month, to South Africa, some—but not all—being caught. Over a period of time they will virtually guarantee a "second round" of attempted revolution.

Most of the refugees leave South Africa via an underground railroad to the long, thinly patrolled border between South Africa and Botswana (which, until September 30, 1966, was Bechuanaland, largest of three British High Commission Territories enclosed by, or adjacent to, South Africa). They return by the same route. There is one point on the Zambezi River, a spot known as Kazungula, at which (although the exact location of the junction is not known) Botswana, Zambia, Rhodesia, and South-West Africa all converge, and it is here that the refugees come.

At this point—a few yards of riverbank—it is possible to cross from the northern tip of Botswana to the southern part of Zambia, and vice versa, without entering Rhodesia. One simply uses the river ferry—a primitive log raft just about big enough to carry an automobile, which is supported by empty oil drums and powered by two outboard motors. Cattle are regularly herded north to Zambian markets, and even to the Congo, via this route. Botswana would like to build a bridge to link its farms with East Africa, and with outlets to the Indian Ocean; but lawyers have not been able to decide where (or whether) pilings could be driven into the riverbed without impinging on Rhodesia or the Caprivi Strip of South-West Africa, or both.

Approached along the Zambian side of the river, Kazungula is a few hours' drive from Livingstone, at Victoria Falls. It is a desolate spot, with no visible habitation, the riverbanks being clogged with rushes. Crocodiles sun themselves lazily in the midday heat, as if waiting for the raft to capsize or disintegrate.

I drove my car onto the ferry and we chugged across. There was virtually no border control at the Bechuanaland frontier, only a hinged wooden pole horizontally across the dirt path a few hundred yards south of the riverbank. There a casual uniformed guard strolled out from an enclosure, glanced at my travel papers, lifted the pole on its hinge, and waved me on. It would have been a simple matter for a man on foot to evade the control, if necessary, merely by ducking into the heavy growth on either side of the road.

Over this route a trickle of refugees passes—mostly north-bound, though there are some returnees. Something like 25 to 50 people cross in some months (the flow varies greatly); there are no reliable figures on how many return. In early 1964 Vorster said 150 had been caught.

In July and August 1967, a band of some eighty guerrillas newly trained, they later said, in Algeria, Cuba, or behind the Iron Curtain, trekked from Tanzania to Zambia and across the Kazungula ferry into Rhodesia (apparently evading the Botswana border guards). They consisted of twenty members of the Zimbabwe African People's Union (ZAPU), a Rhodesian underground, and approximately sixty ANC men, including Zulus and Coloreds. They proceeded southeast some two hundred miles to a point in the wild bush country of Rhodesia between Bulawayo and the Wankie game reserve. There Rhodesian troops, police, and jet fighter planes engaged them, South African police later joining the battle in helicopters, armored cars, and trucks. (Some of the South African "police" were reportedly soldiers in police uniform.) Questioned as to what South Africans were doing fighting guerrillas in Rhodesia, Foreign Minister Müller said the white-ruled countries of southern Africa (plus Malawi, Botswana, and Lesotho) had joined in a mutual-security arrangement—thus acknowledging publicly for the first time what had long been an open secret.

There were several weeks of sporadic fighting, including at least one pitched battle in which the guerrillas drew Rhodesian forces into an ambush and then pinned them down for long periods, preventing them from moving their heavy weapons and evacuating their wounded. There was also some hand-to-hand fighting. White soldiers later said the guerrillas were tough, quite unlike any of the amateur terrorists encountered previously. Rhodesian forces lost seven men killed and at least fifteen wounded; thirty-one guerrillas died and thirty-two of the rest were captured. Some others fled to Botswana. South African casualties, if any, were not disclosed.

It was a hint of things to come, a paragraph of handwriting on the wall. Another incursion led to open fighting in March

1968. Day after day and week after week, the traffic through Kazungula continues—some of it, no doubt, wholly innocent, and some simply appearing to be. The day I crossed over and back, a preacher was heading north. His flock had come out to bid him good-bye, and in farewell he was leading them in singing gospel hymns. They were still singing and waving as the raft chugged away from the muddy bank. If he was a revolutionary, it was a persuasive disguise.

The dimensions of the South African underground are hard to estimate. In 1963, Leballo claimed the PAC had 150,000 members; government investigators divided the estimate by ten. By now, the government figure may be nearer right. No one really knows. In 1960, the ANC also claimed 100,000 to 150,000 members in 1,000 cells. The claim may have been true then, but seems unlikely to be true today, though there certainly are hundreds of thousands of sympathizers, as a huge turnout for Luthuli's funeral indicated. One reason it is difficult to pin down a figure is that to some extent—not as much as the South African Government charges—both the ANC and PAC recruit by means of intimidation.

Neither the ANC nor the PAC maintains a plush front. Typical offices of the two organizations in Dar es Salaam, Tanzania,* are in run-down buildings, the rooms furnished with a simple desk or table and a few chairs. There clearly is no money to spare, the PAC being in particularly difficult straits. All efforts to bring the two organizations together into a common revolutionary front have failed, despite the obvious disadvantage to Africans of two bitterly competing groups, each dissipating some of its energies battling the other.

In May 1963, the Organization of African Unity set up a Committee of Nine (or "Liberation Committee") to channel funds to undergrounds in white-ruled southern Africa. (It is now a Committee of Eleven.) Subsequent OAU meetings are understood to have set a confidential quota as each member's contribution to the committee; but if so, few if any have met it. Still, with a number of African states and some others having contributed a little each, there is said to be a revolving kitty that often runs

---

* ANC headquarters is now in Morogoro, Tanzania; that of the PAC, in Lusaka, Zambia.

into six figures a year—more than $250,000, according to informed estimates in late 1967.

Since this sum must be split at least eight ways (to two undergrounds in South Africa, two in Rhodesia, one each in Angola and Mozambique, and two in South-West Africa), and since it must help pay for weapons, training, and travel costs to such training areas as Algeria, the U.A.R., the Congo (Brazzaville), and Tanzania (the Communists presumably pay for travel beyond), it is not as sizable a sum as may appear at first glance. Nevertheless, it is not negligible. How it is broken down among the various recipients is not known, but both the PAC and ANC are said to be receiving shares. This OAU money constitutes perhaps 25 percent of the income of revolutionary undergrounds in Africa. The rest is received directly from donors (communist governments, for example, making all their contributions directly). Usually the point of contact is a secret London bank account.

The ANC and PAC are still the only two significant underground movements in South Africa. From time to time, however, there are reports of others.

There is a mysterious cloak-and-dagger outfit known as the Yui Chui Chan Club (YCCC). Yui Chui Chan is or was a leader of Communist China's official government trade union organization. He was the head of a Red Chinese delegation to an Afro-Asian "solidarity conference" held in Tanganyika, as it was then known, in 1963. The "club" bearing his name is said to be made up of Africans trained in China, though according to some knowledgeable people they are now more Trotskyite than Peking-oriented.

Dr. K. G. Abrahams, a physician who at one time practiced in South-West Africa among the Rehoboth "Bastards," is understood to have been one of those instrumental in its founding. Ten of its alleged members were arrested in July 1963. Little else, however, is known about it.

Still further underground are the Cape Peninsula Students' Union (CPSU) and the African People's Democratic Union of Southern Africa (APDUSA), a small group whose leader is in Lusaka, Zambia. Some years ago, there was something known as the Black Hand, but this seems to have died out when Spear of the Nation was formed.

Violence begets violence, and injustice begets desire for revenge. It seems likely that one underground organization after another will be spawned in South Africa, many with communist money. Meanwhile the government—one hand creating the grievances, the other trying desperately to check the consequences—goes on telling the world it is a bulwark against communism in Africa.

South Africa is sowing the wind, and one day, as surely as the sun rises over Durban Bay, it must reap the whirlwind.

CHAPTER FOUR

Reform from Within?

The danger of unrest and ultimately of revolution in South Africa being so clear, and the consequences of inaction so potentially disastrous, the obvious question is: Why don't South Africans do something about it?

There is a significant school of thought, both in South Africa and elsewhere, which argues that they are doing something meaningful about it, or that they will do something if they are given time and if outside pressures are relaxed. The late Clarence B. Randall, President of Inland Steel Company, Chicago, was an outstanding American spokesman for this view. "Roaring at South Africa . . . will not help," he wrote in the *Atlantic Monthly* (and *Reader's Digest*) in 1963. "Reform must come from within, and there are clear signs that liberalizing forces are at work: businessmen are organized for the purpose of increasing Bantu wages; new spiritual values are evolving within the Dutch Reformed Church; the wealthy Afrikaner is becoming international-minded; an independent press survives in spite of rumors to the contrary; the Bantu may, and do, buy shares in South African corporations on the stock exchange; and the government-owned-and-operated airplanes are not segregated.

". . . it is my firm opinion that the Republic [of South Africa] is entitled to a fair trial period within which to prove its good faith before it is condemned by outside opinion. . . . Because there is so much in South Africa that is magnificent, combined with so much that we believe to be wrong, I dare to make this plea to my fellow countrymen. Let us lower our voices. Let us drop the tough talk, which will take us nowhere, and adopt instead friendly argument and thoughtful persuasion on a man-to-man basis.

"The white people of South Africa are charged with a great

responsibility toward the black people, and they know it. In the end they will do right. Let us give them a little more time." *

This kind of reasoning sounds persuasive, but is in fact highly debatable. A close study of the South African scene does not encourage hope for self-generated peaceful change. The attitudes and practices to which so much of the world objects are deeply rooted in centuries of searing experience. The now-dominant white man, the Afrikaner, descendant of the original Dutch and Huguenot pioneers, had to fight furiously for virtually everything he values most. The social, political, economic, and religious setting in which race conflict has arisen in South Africa is unique in the world, and militates against constructive change.

Dutch pioneers arrived at the southern tip of Africa, near the legendary Cape of Good Hope, in 1652. Scholars say the Bantu probably had crossed the Limpopo River, coming south into what is now the Transvaal, centuries earlier; the government says the Bantu crossed at about the same time. At any rate, all agree that the more primitive Hottentots and Bushmen preceded white men into the Cape. Regardless of who was first, the European pioneers settled the land and thought of it as their own.

In the 1830's, breaking away from the British who followed them to the Cape, Afrikaner Voortrekkers (pioneers) fought their way north and east against Native tribes in a series of so-called Kaffir Wars. (Actually these wars had begun earlier, and lasted nearly one hundred years: 1779–1877.) These grim and bloody struggles for survival grew essentially out of competition for land, not unlike the American Indian wars. But they were looked upon by the Voortrekkers as crusades against savages, a conflict of church against infidel, with divine sanction. Many Afrikaners emerged from them with a contempt for black men as a race, a feeling which transcends prejudice as love transcends infatuation.

Still later, in 1852 and 1854, the Voortrekkers established two independent republics, free of British rule, in the domain they had won from the Natives. In an effort to perpetuate these republics, with the gold and diamonds which were discovered under the soil, they fought bravely against the British for three years (1899–1902) in the so-called Boer (or South African) War. The Voortrekkers' heroism in that war is still a source of pride to Afrikaners, but they were defeated. They could not cope with the might and firepower of the British Empire. (It was in this war—named by the British after the Afrikaner Boers, or farmers, against whom they fought—that Winston Churchill first won fame as a war correspondent.)

The experience was traumatic. Among other things, some 25,-000 Afrikaner women and children died in British concentration camps. Their survivors and descendants have been seeking retribution ever since. Until roughly 1945, antagonism for South Africans of British descent (now 40 percent of the white population) was a much greater preoccupation for most Afrikaners than any problem of relations with the Bantu. Today, the Afrikaners have their republic once again, having won a plebiscite for its establishment in October 1960. The following year they withdrew from the Commonwealth. In effect they have reversed the results of the Boer War, and as a result, some reconciliation is now taking place with the English-speaking community.

Nevertheless, memories of the Kaffir and Boer Wars are still vivid. Many elderly people are still alive who fought in, or witnessed, the latter struggle. Some are mentally still at war, with both the British and the "kaffirs." On appropriate anniversaries, speeches are delivered which scarcely could be much more impassioned if the fighting were actually in progress today. This fervor, plus pride of language and culture, are some of the ingredients of Afrikaner nationalism, a phenomenon which explains much that the governing party, political vehicle of this nationalism, is doing today.

It is unrealistic to expect Afrikaner traditionalists (as distinct from Afrikaner intellectuals and the English-speaking South Africans, many of whom are more liberal) to alter fundamentally the country's course, however much time they are given and however patient and "understanding" the outside world might be. Only a drastic change in the political balance, removing the Afrikaner extremists from power, could produce peaceful change in a constructive direction. But the Afrikaner nationalists are solidly entrenched.

In the view of these nationalists, they *are* doing something effective about the challenge of racial strife: they are beating back the African hordes, keeping the Bantu "in their place." As the late Adlai E. Stevenson once put it, they regard the disease as the remedy; they prescribe "for the malady of racism the bitter toxic of apartheid." They hope that by the uninhibited exercise of political and police power, the whites can remain indefinitely in control and impose a "solution" on the nonwhites. The "solution" would consist of "separate development"—forced isolation for some nonwhites and forced subordination for the rest.

No power can be summoned, South Africans say, strong enough to divert them from this course. External military force? What can Black Africa muster, they ask, that can hope to challenge their modern, well-equipped armed forces? Soviet intervention would complicate the problem, they acknowledge, but Russia's supply lines would be long, and in any event, the United States and/or Britain, they profess to be confident, would intervene to block Moscow. A domestic underground, perhaps one day buttressed by guerrilla fighters based in a black-ruled Rhodesia, Mozambique, Botswana, and/or South-West Africa? The terrain is ill-adapted for guerrilla warfare, they point out, with little natural cover available. Moreover, the South African army and police have proved themselves highly proficient at breaking up underground forces, and the Africans are psychologically debilitated by centuries of enforced inferiority.

One right-wing Nationalist MP put it to me this way: "Our power structure could be compared to that of the Soviet Union. We, too, are an elite controlling all the mechanisms of power. Can you imagine a successful revolution in the Soviet Union?" I doubt if he would have wished to pursue the analogy too far. It would not, in fact, have been wholly accurate to do so, since South Africa—for all its tragic modifications of the rule of law— is not yet a full-fledged police state on the Soviet model, so far as whites are concerned. Political opposition by whites is free to operate, within limits; many higher courts are independent; and the often-critical English-language press is allowed to publish, though subject to severe pressures, restrictions, and intimidation. Still, the comment reflected accurately an attitude of supreme self-confidence within the government, an attitude which much of the experience of 1963–68 has seemed to bear out.

This structure of self-assurance is fallacious in several key respects—in its estimate, for example, of the potential skill and determination of the nonwhite resistance, and of the probable role of United States military power in a confrontation. Yet it does explain much about the government's policies and actions. The Nationalist Party hopes, and some leaders believe, that they can hold out until the United States, Britain, and even Black Africa come to "see and acknowledge that South Africa is right." Some "Nats" may have private doubts as to their capacity to retain control while the rest of the world "awakens," but these doubts come to the surface only rarely. In any event, the Nationalists feel they have no choice but to try. They admit that total economic sanctions, enforced by a blockade, would upset these calculations, but they dismiss this prospect as a fantasy.

In the meantime, apartheid is an ideology well suited to maintaining the Nationalists' grip on a safe majority of the white electorate. It is, in other words, a useful instrument of domestic political power. The more frightened the whites become; the more South Africa is denounced and boycotted in the outside world; and the more turmoil, upheaval, and bloodshed there are in Black Africa, the more the white electorate tends to vote Nationalist to obtain "protection" from these perils and pressures. Many a white voter, including an increasing number from the English-speaking community, has voted Nat in recent years on the ground that "there isn't much difference between the Nats and the UP [United Party], but at least the Nats are strong. They won't sell us down the river." The very ruthlessness of the Nationalists seems to many to be a commensurate response to the challenge. The willingness of the United Party to ease apartheid, in part to restore South Africa's reputation abroad, has come to seem weakness—in some eyes, even lack of patriotism. And the electorate has moved steadily to the right, the Nationalist Party gaining strength correspondingly. Its hold over the voters has become progressively stronger in each election since it came to power after World War II.*

---

* When the Nationalist Party began its current tenure in 1948, it won 70 seats in the then 150-seat Parliament, a plurality, with only 37.4 percent of the popular vote (less than that polled by the UP). By 1953, the Nats had a plurality of the popular vote as well as a solid majority in Parliament, and in 1958, they had a popular majority. The election of 1961 was less representative, a particularly small number of seats (86 out of 160) being contested; but then, too, the Nationalists continued to show strength. In March 1966, they won an overwhelming 126 of the 166 seats at issue (a 3–1 major-

But the Nationalists have not been satisfied with this accretion of political power. They have sought to make their position totally invulnerable, and they have come very close to succeeding. One of their early steps was to take the Cape Coloreds, who normally vote for the opposition, off the common voting roll, so that the Coloreds could influence the election of only four members of Parliament specially designated as their representatives. This constitutional change required five years of struggle, the climax of which was a measure packing both the court, which had declared the step unconstitutional, and the upper house of the legislature, the Senate, which had blocked the required two-thirds majority. The Nationalists also arranged to seat in Parliament, as regular members, representatives from the mandated territory of South-West Africa. These representatives were usually government supporters.

By far the most significant factor, however, in the government's favor, especially in the early years of its rule, has been a system of gerrymandered election districts, predating 1948, under which rural constituencies could (and still can) legally embrace up to 30 percent fewer people than urban ones. The thinly populated and hence overrepresented farm areas are uniformly the ones where the Nats are strongest.*

Verwoerd, during his lifetime, took full advantage of this "weighted" farm vote, though by the 1966 election he was so deeply dug in he could win without it. He campaigned through farm areas like a George Wallace or an Orval Faubus—pandering to prejudices and inflaming them.

Among rural voters, and among unskilled, poorly educated whites in the cities, apartheid is closest to a sacred creed. Some simple farm homes still today display art dating from the days of the Kaffir Wars. Black savages are portrayed leaping through

---

ity), the United Party capturing only 39 and the Progressives 1. Just what the figures would have been in each national election had all seats been contested (and hence the views of the whole electorate obtained) is a matter for expert conjecture. But all agree the Nats have made steady gains.

   * Thus in 1961, the Nationalists won 105 parliamentary seats to the UP's 49, a more than 2–1 edge, though they polled fewer than half the votes actually cast, and probably would have gotten no more than 52 percent if all seats had been contested. The Nats' 3–1 parliamentary majority in 1966 was built from a margin of only 7–5 in the popular vote: 758,345 for the Nationalists to 482,491 for the UP and 32,803 for the middle-of-the-road Progressive Party. (Complete election results, 1948–1966: pages 201–208.)

Voortrekker windows with a bloody spear, or bashing white children against a wall. The attitude of some farmers toward Natives has not moderated much from the traditional swagger: "Bigawd, when I meet a damned kaffir, I want him to step off the sidewalk and tip his hat." Signs by the roadside read, "Caution: Africans Crossing"—a considerate gesture, it is felt. The inference that Africans are to be regarded as comparable to animals is not very wide of the mark, though many white householders will speak of *their* African servants as though they were unique in that they were human beings.

Nor are these extreme prejudices necessarily always limited to the ill-educated. "What do you want to do?" an Afrikaner diplomat once asked a liberal. "Make us a bastard mongrel state like Brazil?" Asked to characterize the average African, Professor C. F. van der Merwe, leader of the extreme right-wing Republican Party, said in 1966: "He is un-Christian. He has done nothing for himself—no science, no literature, no order. Hate, destruction, and communism—these are the inevitable consequences of the black man's nature."

A letter to the editor of *Die Transvaler*, an Afrikaans-language newspaper which Verwoerd once edited, complained bitterly because nonwhites were allowed to visit the Voortrekker monument in Pretoria, which honors the pioneers. It was not enough that the nonwhites were limited to special hours and carefully segregated: the writer wanted them barred entirely. "It is enough to make one faint," the letter said. "I believe more than one of our heroes honored there would turn in his grave. Why on earth do we still want to drag the non-Europeans [nonwhites] in?" The authorities in charge, to whom the letter was referred before publication, replied in all seriousness that they had looked into the matter and decided that, on balance, there was no reason to alter the practice.

Under different circumstances, it might be logical to look to the churches as an influence for constructive change. However, in South Africa the Dutch Reformed Church (Calvinist), of which a great majority of Afrikaners are devoted members, is a powerful influence for the perpetuation of racial prejudice. All three of its branches, in differing degree, support apartheid, though the largest branch, the Nederduits Gereformeerde Kerk, while championing the principle with some fanaticism as an ideal to be sought, does not always subscribe to every detail of the practice.

This attitude survives despite considerable turmoil and heart-searching in recent years. The old scriptural theses used as a basis for apartheid have been discarded, and new ones are evolving. In the days of the Voortrekkers, ministers and prominent laymen taught that the Bantu tribes were descendants of Ham, one of Noah's sons, and of Canaan, Ham's fourth son. (Ham traditionally was supposed to have been a Negro.*) The Bantu tribes, there-fore, it was said, were God-ordained to be servants, as per Genesis 9:18–27:

"And the sons of Noah, that went forth of the ark, were Shem, and Ham, and Japheth: and Ham is the father of Canaan.

"These are the three sons of Noah: and of them was the whole earth overspread. . . .

"And [Noah] said, Cursed be Canaan; a servant of servants shall he be unto his brethren.

"And he said, Blessed be the Lord God of Shem; and Canaan shall be his servant.

"God shall enlarge Japheth, and he shall dwell in the tents of Shem; and Canaan shall be his servant."

This passage was widely accepted as the theological foundation for white supremacy in South Africa until the 1940's, when it finally succumbed to modern thinking (some of the more en-lightened views being brought to South Africa by ministers who had gone to Holland or Germany for graduate study, and some having penetrated from Presbyterian churchmen abroad). A long doctrinal struggle ensued, as theoreticians sought a substitute. They found what they wanted in biblical injunctions to the Israelites, and to their presumptive descendants, including the white South Africans, to keep aloof from Canaanites (Canaan being not only one of Ham's sons but, as some authorities have it,

---

* According to biblical scholars, the noun "ham" means "swarthy, dark-colored person"; as an adjective, it means "black" (and also "warm"). The "land of Cush" (Cush being Ham's eldest son) is rendered "Ethiopia" by the Septuagint and the Vulgate. But it is not clear that this "Ethiopia" was necessarily the country known by that name today. And the "land of Ham" was Egypt. The theory was closely associated with the traditional assumption that Shem, Ham, and Japheth, Noah's three sons, were the fathers of three major races of mankind, Japheth migrating to Europe and a portion of Asia, Shem—a Shemite, or Semite—to the Arab world, and Ham to Africa. ("Of them was the whole earth overspread." Gen. 9:19)

the correctly translated name for Ham himself). Such injunctions occur frequently in the books of Moses, as for example in Exodus 34:11-14:

"Observe thou that which I command thee this day: behold, I drive out before thee the Amorite, and the Canaanite, and the Hittite and the Perizzite. . . .

"Take heed to thyself, lest thou make a covenant with the inhabitants of the land whither thou goest, lest it be for a snare in the midst of thee:

"But ye shall destroy their altars, break their images, and cut down their groves:

"For thou shalt worship no other god. . . ."

Intermarriage, it was said, was specifically prohibited by Genesis 24:3-4: "And I [Abraham] will make thee swear by the Lord, the God of heaven, and the God of the earth, that thou shalt not take a wife unto my son of the daughters of the Canaanites, among whom I dwell: But thou shalt go unto my country, and to my kindred, and take a wife unto my son Isaac."

The new theses were debated at some length in the synods (church governing bodies) in the 1940's and 1950's. Dissidents pointed out that it was the gods, the false religious beliefs and practices of the Canaanites that the Israelites were enjoined to abhor, not the people as such. Indeed, the peoples surrounding the Israelites were also Semites of the same race and color, it was contended. The Canaanites, specifically, were Phoenicians, it was pointed out.

But the majority accepted the theory of God-ordained separation, adapting it to the particular requirements of apartheid. One must "respect the work of God," they came to say (and say today). God created different peoples, intending them to be separate, and man should not challenge the wisdom of God, nor attempt to reverse His will. To those who cite the command, "Thou shalt love thy neighbor as thyself," the hierarchy replies, "We are doing the nonwhites a kindness to enforce separation; it is a matter of Christian charity to let them develop separately against their own background. When they are drawn into white society, they are uprooted and lose what is their own." To the Golden Rule, "Whatsoever ye would that men should do to you, do ye even so to them," Church authorities say, with varying degrees of sincerity: "Separate development is what we would have them do

unto us." To Peter's statement "Of a truth I perceive that God is
no respecter of persons," they say, in effect: "Equality under God,
yes; intermingling and equal temporal power, no." Finally, to
Paul's sermon on Mars Hill: "God . . . hath made of one blood
all nations of men for to dwell on all the face of the earth," they
quote his further phrase, ". . . and hath determined . . . the
bounds of their habitation."

A visitor is tempted to believe they must be rationalizing a
predetermined conviction; but if so, it is in many cases done
unconsciously. The Church's governing bodies are not at all impressed that they are alone among Christians, at home and abroad,
in their interpretation of the Bible. Churches abroad, they say,
have been infiltrated by liberals and Communists—and they have
unearthed an ultra-right-wing McCarthy-era book *Collectivism
in the Churches,* by Maj. Edgar Bundy, in an effort to prove it.

Some courageous theologians continue to challenge the accepted doctrine, despite immense pressure to conform. In November 1960, eleven of them joined in a defense of the equality of
Christian believers and a plea for racial moderation in the Church
which they embodied in the book, *Vertraagde Aksie (Delayed
Action).* One of the authors, the Reverend Albert S. Geyser, a
professor of New Testament Theology at the University of Pretoria, was actually placed on trial for heresy before the Synodical
Commission of the Nederduitsch Hervormde Kerk and found
guilty. He was deposed as a minister and forced to resign as a
teacher (the Church controlling selection of divinity faculty at the
university). Professor Geyser challenged the decision in the Supreme Court; and the Church, capitulating, paid him compensation and reinstated him as a minister (he obtained a different, and
better, teaching post independently).

In 1963, a group of dissident churchmen came together under
the leadership of the Reverend C. F. Beyers Naude, editor of
the monthly magazine *Pro Veritate,* to form the Christian Institute of Southern Africa, an interracial and interdenominational
body in which all races worship and engage in theological study
together. The institute was subjected to intense attack, including
blasts from Verwoerd and from fellow theologians. The Church
subsequently forbade its members to join and ordered those who
had joined to withdraw. Its offices were raided by the security
police. Members were socially ostracized. "Nothing but liberalist

stepping-stones from which propaganda which suits communism admirably is carried into our churches," said one critic. "McCarthyism!" retorted the institute's executive committee.

In 1967, the two sides fought a climactic battle in court. A leading spokesman for the majority view, the Reverend Professor Adrianus Drost Pont of the University of Pretoria, a disenchanted ex—student of Professor Geyser, had written a series of several long articles in 1964–65 for *Die Hervormer,* an official publication of the Hervormde Kerk. In them he called the Christian Institute a "front" organization, a "medium used to bring leftist and communist ideas into the South African church world." He also accused unnamed liberal theologians "from the Christian Institute" of seeking to overthrow "the existing order." Beyers Naude and Geyser, two obvious targets of Pont's innuendos, sued him for libel and won damages of $14,000 each, half of what they asked, together with costs estimated at ten times that amount. It was the largest libel judgment ever obtained in South Africa. Among the members of a well-financed committee of churchmen and others who had unsuccessfully championed Pont was Dr. J. D. Vorster, brother of the prime minister. It had been a clash of the giants, reflecting the depth and ferocity of differences over the scriptural basis for apartheid. Commented the *Rand Daily Mail:* "In no other sphere is the struggle for the soul of South Africa taking place with such intensity as within the Dutch Reformed Churches." And with good reason, for the Dutch Reformed Churches comprise the single most powerful nongovernmental entity in South Africa—capable, if one day they were to have a change of heart, of bringing about peaceful change in that troubled country.

Many other religious denominations, both Roman Catholic and Protestant, have broken wholly or in large part with apartheid. Every few years the Catholic bishops of Southern Africa have issued joint pastoral letters progressively more outspoken. The one for 1957 rejected apartheid and stated: "There must be a gradual change . . . but change must come, for otherwise our country faces a disastrous future." In 1962, the bishops said: "As Christian people, we dare not remain silent in the face of the injustices inflicted on members of the unprivileged racial groups." In 1966, they denounced apartheid and all forms of discrimination which it engenders.

As early as 1947 and 1948, the Methodist Conference insisted on fundamental human rights for all. In 1952, it rejected apartheid as impractical, undesirable, and inconsistent with Christian principles. In 1963, an African, the Reverend Seth Mokitimi, was elected Conference president.

In 1957, outside the Anglican Cathedral Church of St. George in Cape Town, a block away from Parliament, the then Archbishop of Cape Town, the late Bishop Joost de Blank, placed a sign with letters a foot high: "This cathedral is open to welcome men and women of *all* races to *all* services at *all* times." (The government was furious.) Other courageous Episcopal theologians such as Bishop Trevor Huddleston, Bishop Ambrose Reeves, the Reverend Michael Scott, Bishop Crowther, and many others have hurled themselves into the struggle with extraordinary dedication and self-sacrifice, writing a chapter of Church history in which Christians everywhere can take pride. But all these congregations are much less numerous and influential than that of the Dutch Reformed Church. And in many cases, although churches are open to all races, nonwhites have not in fact been made to feel welcome, and few attend.

Calvinism comes close to being a state religion in South Africa. It has extraordinary impact on the national life. The Church took the defeated Boers to its bosom sixty-five years ago following the Boer War, when many of them were impoverished and broken in spirit. It helped restore their dignity and self-respect, fostered a renaissance of their nationalism, and was a major factor in bringing them to political power. Today, it is reaping the benefits. Along with top government officials and other influential leaders of the community, the highest Church authorities (and, indeed, perhaps 40 percent of the rank-and-file ministers) are understood to be members of a secret society of some 8,000 persons called the Broederbond (Society of Brothers) which has significant influence on government policy. Its goal is "the Afrikanerizing of South Africa."

A measure of the Church's importance in the community is its puritanical impact on social mores. In the largely rural Orange Free State, where Calvinism is strongest, no sports are played on Sunday, no public swimming pools are open, no bathing suits or even shorts may properly be worn on Sunday. No movies or teahouses are open anywhere in the country on the Lord's Day;

some *dominees* even consider it a sin to read a Sunday newspaper. Churchmen conduct periodic forays against gambling, sex, and bikinis. Newspaper stories and pictures of bikini-wearers are deplored, among other things, because they "humiliate our women and daughters in the eyes of nonwhites"—the ultimate, it would seem, in humiliation. An album of records offered for sale in Johannesburg and elsewhere in 1967 was taken off the market by the government's Publications Control Board until a picture of a draped nude on the cover had been rendered more presentable by black adhesive strips in the shape of a bikini. (Sales clerks showed customers how the strips could be removed.)

The town council in Brakpan, near Johannesburg, went so far as to enact a law requiring women to wear either a one-piece bathing suit or "a two-piece, the upper garment of which conforms to the style of a fully cut brassiere with fastening at the back, and the lower garment of which extends upwards from the crotch to within one inch of the navel." This was too much for one councilor, Gerald Kalk, who complained that the law "imposes on the suffering male superintendent of the swimming pool an obligation to study styles of brassieres and to determine if and when a particular cut lacks fullness. It imposes on him, too, the need to measure the one-inch gap between navel and garment without stating whether the inch is curvilinear or as the crow flies." Mr. Kalk's protest was popular with many women, but was unavailing. A majority of the town council insisted on the law.

The influence of the Dutch Reformed Church is vastly greater among the Afrikaners than among the British. The latter are widely regarded by *dominees* as sinning unbelievers, and the light regard is often reciprocated. When an Afrikaner preacher in Cape Town rebuked English-speaking students at the local university for wearing women's panties during a campus shindig called "Rag Time," a Durban newspaper ran the story under the headline "Pantie Pirouetting Pains Parson."

A poster on one of the dormitory bulletin boards at the university screamed *SEX!* in red letters a good ten inches high. In normal print at the bottom of the poster was the footnote: "Now that we have your attention, please don't forget the meeting of the Student Council. . . ." Nor would sex seem to be wholly an academic interest. A woman teacher complained to a pastor that, as he later recounted in a sermon, she had been invited to a

University of Cape Town party among the sand dunes and told,
when she arrived, to "undress and take part in the nude." He
dropped the story at this point, but it is clear the Church has its
work cut out for it among the errant ones.

Similarly, the Church has succeeded in "selling" its extreme
views on white supremacy primarily to the Afrikaner population,
although, for different reasons, some English-speaking people
have of late been approximating some of the same points of view.
Racial doctrines are often propagated with evangelical fervor
and equated with devotion to God. Opposition to apartheid is
regarded as heresy.

It is also viewed as a serious secular aberration. The government and the Church have combined in recent years to promote
a wave of McCarthyism, in which advocacy of even the most
moderate steps toward a multiracial, shared society is made to
seem tantamount to communist sympathy. This has the effect of
powerfully discouraging the expression of liberal opinion and
minimizing pressure for significant change. It never seems to
occur to the government that racial integration could be an important blow against, rather than for, communism.

The attitude that serious resistance to apartheid makes a man
a "comsymp" has been enshrined into law (though South Africans
have not yet caught up with that acronym for communist sym-
pathizer, popular with the American right wing). Under the
"Suppression of Communism Act" of 1950, the word "communism" is defined as (among other things) "any doctrine or
scheme which aims at bringing about any political, industrial,
social or economic change by the promotion of disturbances or
by unlawful acts or omissions"—a definition that could make
virtually any active supporter of racial integration a Communist.
Moreover, the severe penalties of the law—including part-time
house arrest—apply to anyone who "is deemed by the Governor
General . . . to be a Communist on the ground that he is ad-
vocating, advising, defending or encouraging, or has at any time
before or after the commencement of this act, whether within or
outside the Union [of South Africa] advocated, advised, defended
or encouraged the achievement of any of the objects of communism or any act or omission which is calculated to further the
achievement of any such object. . . ." Among the "objects of
communism" is, in the government's view, an integrated South

Africa. "In this country," Archbishop de Blank once commented, "Christ would quite likely have been arrested under the Suppression of Communism Act."

"Liberalism" is considered "the next step to communism." The word has come to have unfavorable connotations in South Africa. The Orange Free State Synod of the Church unanimously passed a resolution condemning "Youth for Christ," an international and nondenominational group, as "liberalistic-humanitarian," a label obviously considered highly derogatory. The Minister of Education, Arts and Sciences, Senator Jan J. de Klerk, announced that a new university would be founded in Johannesburg to "eliminate humanism, root and branch." Along with liberalism and communism, humanism must be destroyed, he said, to preserve white civilization and the Afrikaner way of life. The Johannesburg *Star* commented editorially that the new university promised to be a unique institution.

The "poison" of liberalism is seen as primarily an external peril. James Fouché, then Minister of Defense, said in a tone of alarm in 1964 that South Africa "lies in the middle of a universal flood of modern liberalism. The results of the British and American elections show clearly that this flood of liberalism is uncontrollable. [This was the nearest Pretoria came in public to regretting the defeat of Senator Barry Goldwater.] We must, therefore, accept it as a fact.

"Now, does this mean that we must allow ourselves to be pushed into this stream . . . ? No, we will not commit national suicide."

This curious suspicion of liberalism is explained in part by the fact that for generations, Afrikaners who did not read English, French, or Dutch were cut off from the mainstream of European and American liberal thought. The works of Thomas Paine, Jean Jacques Rousseau, and the great English liberals have never been translated into Afrikaans. Such concepts as government by the consent of the governed, the inherent dignity of individual man, the rule of law, and much of what the Western world knows as human rights are thus strange and suspect. It is only since World War II that genuine liberalizing movements have sprung up in South Africa.

There have, of course, been notable exceptions over the years. Jan Christiaan Smuts drafted the preamble to the United Nations

Charter, which proclaims that the peoples of the United Nations, among other things, "reaffirm faith in fundamental human rights, in the dignity and worth of the human person, in the equal rights of men and women and of nations large and small. . . ." Smuts, however, was less liberal at home, and in any event his party was thrown out of power soon thereafter.

The curtain against "dangerous" outside ideas is drawn with much care. Many books may not be imported and sold in South Africa. The censorship is often done by incompetent customs officials, and is carried to ludicrous extremes. Censors have actually rejected (temporarily) such books as *The Return of the Native* by Thomas Hardy, apparently out of belief that the "native" was an African; *Caribbean Mystery* by Agatha Christie, because the Caribbean is suspect as a multiracial area; and *Soviet Russia in China* by Generalissimo Chiang Kai-shek, because it dealt with communism. *Hitler—A Study in Tyranny* by Alan Bullock was barred, perhaps because theories of racial superiority were not treated sympathetically. Even James Bond has run afoul of South Africa's censors. Ian Fleming's *The Spy Who Loved Me* was banned, perhaps because it was considered salacious. (No official reason is ever given.) Book-banning is encouraged and urged by the Morals Committee of the Dutch Reformed Church, which contends that, despite all vigilance, much objectionable material still enters the country.

So far as the ruling Nationalist Party, the dominant church, and their supporters are concerned, therefore, there is no visible likelihood of self-generated reform. No doubt if it became necessary for the Nationalists to moderate their practices in order to stay in power, ideology would be bent to the requirements of politics. "We Afrikaners are so motivated by self-interest that we'd even be *liberal* if we though it would help us," a leading intellectual told E. J. Kahn, Jr., of *The New Yorker* magazine. But there is no such necessity at present; on the contrary, the Nats appear to have a solid grip on the electorate—because, not in spite, of the policy of apartheid.

This is not to say there is no dissent. Moving leftward in the political spectrum—from black, as it were, to dark gray—the next most enthusiastic backers of apartheid, after the Afrikaner farmers and lower-class city workers, are the better-educated, more sophisticated Afrikaners in the cities. They, too, have a profound attachment to their language, their culture, and the Republic which they now have firmly established. Afrikaner nationalism is to them, too, a real and living thing. But some of them are not fighting the Kaffir and Boer Wars today with quite the same fury as their rural brethren. Many, if not most, are bilingual (in English and Afrikaans), and their racial prejudices are less extreme, though they, too, are likely to believe they have a God-given mission to preserve civilized standards. Some of them, though not many, may even vote for the United Party, as some of the wealthier Afrikaner farmers may do. Many of these "de-tribalized" Afrikaners have shaken off the haunting inferiority complex which still seems to bedevil others of their community and which causes them to behave in aggressive ways, insisting vigorously on their superiority over nonwhites.

Right-center in South African politics (though of late more right than center) is occupied by the United Party. Since Sharpeville, at least, the UP has been drifting steadily toward the government point of view, until today its differences with the Nationalists are primarily of degree and method. It might permit the urban African to put down roots, to have a family life, and in many cases to take jobs for which he is qualified, but it would not give him the right to vote on the common roll. It would set up what it calls a "racial federation," which means separate representation in Parliament for each race, or "nation," the number of representatives for each being determined in such a way as to assure majorities for the white "nation." Seeing his support steadily fade, Sir de Villiers Graaff, the party leader, has become less and less moderate in recent years, hoping to woo the left wing of Nationalist support. On some issues, such as the Bantustans ("little Cubas," he called them) and on support for whites in Rhodesia, he has even tried to out-flank the Nationalists to the right—not an easy thing to do. He concentrated so largely on winning conservative votes that the left wing of the UP broke away in the 1950's and formed the Liberal and Progressive Parties.

The Progressives, at the left-center of the political spectrum, embrace much of the active white opposition to apartheid—the people who, like the ladies of the Black Sash and the intellectuals of the Institute of Race Relations, feel strongly enough about government folly to try to do something about it. They are ordinary people with a conscience; people offended by flagrant injustice and inhumanity, or afraid of its consequences; businessmen who are restive under the economic inefficiencies of apartheid—the unavailability, for example, of needed labor because of job reservation. By far the largest proportion of the protesters are drawn from the English-speaking community.

They are in an unenviable position. I talked at some length with a highly successful industrialist who was preparing his annual report to a stockholders' meeting. He regarded apartheid as a ton weight around the company's corporate neck, and felt it would lead, one day, to bloody disaster for the country, which he passionately loved. But he found the task of drawing up his report anguishingly difficult. How much to tell the stockholders? How much would they believe? Surface manifestations were favorable; how could the real state of affairs be made credible? Was it worthwhile to try? I do not know how he resolved his dilemma, but I do know that many others share it with him.

There is a dilemma involved just in deciding whether to vote Progressive at all. One expresses his real views with such a vote, but knows he is having little or no effect on the outcome of an election, his party having little or no chance to win. He is "throwing away his vote" on a splinter party. If he votes for the United Party, he might at least help prevent the election of a "Nat" MP. Many progressively inclined whites resolve the dilemma in favor of supporting the UP—so many, indeed, that observers believe the actual election results are not a faithful reflection of Progressive strength. The "Progs" got 69,042 votes (less than 10 percent) in 1961, their first election, and 32,803 (less than 3 percent) in 1966.

It is considered surprising that they elect even one Member of Parliament. The successful candidate, both in 1961 and 1966, was Mrs. Helen Suzman of Johannesburg, a brilliant, indefatigable, and fearless woman with a wit as fast, and on occasion as sharp, as an adder. She has been a formidable gadfly to the government. In 1966, as she faced an all-out battle to keep her seat, Nationalist MP's would stop her in the parliamentary lobbies and say in mock concern, "Shame we won't be seeing you around anymore, Helen." To which she would reply, "What? You're not standing this year?" In her heart, she may perhaps have doubted, at times, her ability to withstand the onslaught; but she fought it out and emerged with a 711-vote margin out of a total of 10,881

votes cast. Since she was bucking not merely her immediate opponent, a UP man, but a massive drift of the country to the right,
this was a very remarkable accomplishment. It suggested that
opponents of apartheid who are courageous and outspoken
enough, and who have a fighting chance to win, can muster majority support in some constituencies.

The Progressive program, a qualified franchise for all, would
be classified right-center, if not conservative, in almost any other
country in the world. But many South Africans consider it dan-
gerously liberal, desperately radical, or even crypto-communist.
Under the qualifications which the Progressives would establish
for the franchise, it might be something like fifty years before
Africans had enough voters to constitute a majority. Yet the
Nationalists (and the UP) have persuaded many people this would
be getting on a "slippery slope"—that the qualifications would be
progressively lowered, and presently the terrible day of majority
rule would be upon them.

The "Progs" are having an uphill battle persuading the country that a shared society would represent stability rather than
peril. It is of course true, they acknowledge, that nonwhites, given
a political voice, would agitate for an ever-broader electoral base,
just as they did in Rhodesia when political agitation of this kind
was feasible. But South Africa is *sui generis,* they point out. To
grant South African nonwhites an honorable and respected minority role in the governing of a genuinely shared society would be
regarded by most of them as such sensational progress that they
would accept it gladly for the time being. Chief Luthuli's comments on willingness to compromise would appear to bear this
out.

Political agitation is not something to be feared in a stable
democracy. If the demand for an ever-broader franchise, leading
to one-man-one-vote, were given a legitimate outlet, it is at least
possible that this kind of protest would be the only, or certainly
the principal, form which unrest would take. If this constructive
channelizing of discontent were to be looked upon as getting on
a slippery slope, at least it would be one with a higher coefficient
of friction than the slope South Africans now are on—the slope
called apartheid, at the end of which is disaster. As nonwhites
grew in maturity and education, whites might well discover that
a qualified franchise was a slippery slope to salvation.

Until mid-1968, there was a party for which, under conditions of free political activity, many Africans undoubtedly would have wished to campaign and vote. It was the Liberal Party, which stood at the far left of the political spectrum, calling for universal adult suffrage, regardless of race. Many Africans did in fact work for the Liberal Party, until the government enacted legislation that prevented it. Unable to be a multiracial entity, it decided to disband.

Whites in this party were likely to be idealistic and totally dedicated, or else members of the outlawed Communist Party (or perhaps, in some cases, both). They were few—not much more than a large handful.

At their head was the world-renowned novelist Alan Paton (*Cry, the Beloved Country*). This superb master of the written word— better known outside South Africa than any of his countrymen, with the possible exception of golfer Gary Player—is respected for the brilliance and artistry of his writings, his intense patriotism, and his courage, which is considerable seeing that a government banning order could, among other things, halt the sale of his books in South Africa (though it might give them a resurgence of popularity abroad). Politically, however, he was a "prophet without honor. . . ." The Liberal Party, contesting few seats, polled exactly 2,461 votes (less than one third of one percent) in 1961, and ran no candidates at all in 1966.

Years of frustration and seemingly futile effort to move his countrymen have left Mr. Paton saddened and a bit crusty— a fact that seems anomalous to a visitor who knows only the poetry and compassion of his work. I drove out to his attractive country home a few miles from Durban and asked him if he saw any prospect of a national change of heart. "I don't believe in the change of heart of nations any longer," he told me. "Americans go on hoping. You have both idealism and a strong practical streak. One can appeal to an individual to do what is morally right; you can't appeal to a group of people. They want security first and foremost."

Mr. Paton did not believe his Liberal Party could come to power by the normal electoral process. There would first, one infers, have to be some major crisis—perhaps an incipient or actual revolution, perhaps sanctions combined with a blockade, perhaps a dramatic intervention by the United States and Britain. Convinced that majority rule must come, however, he has lent his prestige to the cause.

As with many other South Africans I met, Mr. Paton diagnosed the principal cause of South Africa's disease as *fear*. Other causes, he said, include the *material advantages* of apartheid, "which have seduced so many British" South Africans; *prejudice:* "A man is very easily prejudiced against another when he is afraid of him"; *greed:* "desire for a good life; for cheap labor; for political power"; *the legacy of history:* "Black opposition to the white man's advance; war, murder, families being wiped out; retaliatory missions by the Voortrekkers, ten eyes for an eye"; the *"certainty of one's superiority."* Above all it is fear, he said, attracting to itself other motives. Fear of having one's throat cut; fear of losing "civilized standards."

The core of the problem, Mr. Paton said, is "how to offer a man a chance to do what is right, and security at the same time." Thinking aloud, he said, "You can't offer security to whites in this country." Later, he mused that perhaps it might be done if the United States and the Commonwealth combined to tell South Africa: "There are certain things you've got to do; and we will guarantee you the right of opposition, the rule of law, if you do them." The Nordic nations, which have proposed United Nations guarantees of "law and order"—that is, protection for the whites —during and after a transition period, "are on the right road," Paton said.

Perhaps because of failure fully to understand South Africa, perhaps because of what Mr. Paton would consider an excess of idealism, I myself did not come away despairing of a change of heart, at least among that part of the political spectrum which ranges from light to dark gray. Several things, however, which are not now on the horizon, will have to take place.

The first necessity will be a transformation in the white man's estimate of the nonwhite. At present, white South Africans are absolutely certain the black man cannot exercise responsibility, and are terrified of majority rule as a result. The very phrase, "responsible Native," sounds to them like a solecism, a contradiction in terms. The Africans they have come in contact with seem irresponsible, childlike, near-savage—and, of course, some of them are. Few have had much opportunity to discharge responsibility. Those who are able, cultured, and intelligent rarely come in contact with whites. It is one of the great tragedies of South Africa that there is so little constructive communication across the color line. It sometimes seems that the government is deliberately keeping the ablest nonwhites isolated from the white community in order to perpetuate the illusion of white superiority. Deliberate or not, such a large number of talented nonwhites are in jail, in exile, or silenced by official "bans" that many whites genuinely believe they do not exist and cannot be produced.

There is even an insidious myth that an educated "Native" invariably reverts to savagery if he is temporarily returned to primitive surroundings. "My houseboy went back to his *kraal* for the holidays, and when he returned, he began putting dung on cuts and going to witch doctors all over again," a housewife will tell you. It does not occur to her that the fault might be with the depth and efficacy of the education he has been permitted to obtain.

Unlike white education, which is free until the end of high school, African schooling is subject to fees. The cost to parents varies from place to place, and from grade to grade; but a "conservative estimate," according to the Institute of Race Relations, is 17.25 rand ($24.15) per child per year in each of the first four grades. This represents thirteen days' pay for an average African worker, the average monthly wage * being 40.75 rand ($57.05). In the fifth through seventh years of school, it costs a parent 28 rand ($39.20), or more than three weeks' pay, per child per year. For the few pupils who reach secondary school and high school, the estimated cost is, respectively, more than five weeks' and nearly fifty days' pay per child per year. These are very sizable sums, especially if a man has a large family—the mean African household in 1965–66 was 6.4 persons—and a bare-subsistence income. In point of fact, many African parents cannot afford to

---

* In Soweto (Johannesburg), November 1967. The absolute minimum monthly cost of living for a family of five (for food, clothing, rent, fuel and light, transportation, taxes, cleaning materials, medical expenses and education) is figured at 53.52 rand ($74.65) by the Johannesburg Non-European Affairs Department. About 68 percent of African families in Soweto are below this subsistence level, and have been since 1962 despite a 14 percent rise in wages, the Department acknowledges. Rises in the cost of living have negated the effect of the wage hikes. One result is that hundreds of thousands of African children suffer from malnutrition.

give their children an education. No fewer than 26 percent * of African children, according to the Minister of Education (October 1966), never attend school at all—and most of them would desperately like to do so. Of those who do, according to figures presented in Parliament by Mrs. Suzman, half drop out before the fourth year. Only one in 83 reaches secondary school (the eighth year), and one in 500 stays in school more than ten years. Only 1,880 Africans, out of a total African population of 12,750,-000 and a total African school enrollment of more than 2,000,000, were university undergraduates in 1967. (Of these, at least 431 were taking correspondence courses.) This made an African's chances of getting a college education in South Africa less than one in 1,000. (One out of every twelve white students goes to a university.)

Most Africans must now be taught, the government has decreed, not in English or Afrikaans, the languages which make contact possible with modern life, but in the native dialect, which imprisons the children in their own milieu. And the quality of education is very elementary. In 1966–67, the government spent approximately 11.50 rand ($16.10) per primary-school pupil per year for African education and approximately 52.58 rand ($73.61) per African pupil in secondary and high schools. This totaled less than two-fifths of one percent of the 1966 gross domestic product † (and only about half of this came from white taxes, the rest being proceeds from taxation of Africans). Roughly twenty times as much is spent, per pupil, on white education. (The United States spends $503.) African pupils have been crammed into double and even triple sessions ‡ in order to economize on costs and maximize enrollments. Most (some 95 percent) of school lunches have been eliminated, although surveys cited by the In-

---

* Government literature now (1968) speaks of one in five (or, variously, 17 percent); but children classified as incapable of utilizing education are apparently left out of consideration.

† Gross domestic product (GDP) is considered a better measure of overall activity for South Africa than the more restrictive (and elsewhere more common) gross national product (GNP). The GDP includes payments to the rest of the world—dividends, interest, wages, salaries, etc. In 1966, the GDP was R8.756 billion ($12.258 billion) and the GNP R8.528 billion ($11.939 billion).

‡ There was, in 1965, an average of 52 African pupils per teacher. Of 7,222 schools, 4,057 were holding double sessions.

stitute of Race Relations show 60–70 percent of African school-children "recognizably malnourished," and almost 10 percent—some 200,000 (in 1967)—in need of hospitalization as a result. A private nonprofit organization called Kupugani is trying to fill the gap.

Propose to the housewife that the quality of African schooling be improved and the opportunities made universal, and she will reply: "Think of the taxes we would have to pay!"—not realizing, it seems, that the taxes she pays to enable the South African armed forces and police to defend her from "savage" Africans are also very great. The 1966–67 defense budget was $358,190,-000, or six times as much as the last one before Sharpeville ($55,787,200). The difference, roughly $300,000,000, would give something like 700,000 African children—some 40 percent of the total 1966 enrollment (1,705,116 *)—an education of the same quality white children get. It would give every African child an education roughly six times better than the average African school child gets today.

Thinking of Africans as incapable of bearing responsibility, most South Africans see in majority rule a formula for the same chaos they believe prevails in all of Black Africa. The popular image of Black Africa is almost as distorted in South Africa as is the popular image of South Africa in the rest of the continent. The able, rational, and statesmanlike things done north of the Zambezi are almost completely lost sight of, swamped with horror stories told by white Belgian, British, and other refugees from the Congo, Kenya, and other areas—where disorder resulted, not from the "mistake" of majority rule, but from failure to prepare African majorities for that rule and from the behavior of white minorities during the period when they held power.

The government and its supporters take care to guarantee that breakdowns of law and order in Black Africa—uprisings in the Congo, communist infiltration in East Africa, civil war in Nigeria, the ruthless suppression of dissent under such dictators as former President Kwame Nkrumah in Ghana, and intermittent military coups—are widely publicized for maximum impact.

---

* Exclusive of the Transkei. With the Transkei it was 2,039,426. The total expenditure for African education for 1967–68 was estimated at 29,754,000 rand ($41,655,600).

"There but for the grace of apartheid go you," the message reads, implying or asserting that the only choice is between chaos and white supremacy. And many believe it. One-man-one-vote, they are persuaded, would mean the destruction of all they have built up so laboriously over the years—the advanced industrial society, the skyscraper cities, the booming prosperity, the gracious country-club living.

If this conviction is to change, South Africans will have to discover that there are "Natives" capable of helping preserve "civilized standards," of participating constructively in the management of the country. If there could be, elsewhere in Africa, a notably successful multiracial society with whites and non-whites sharing power harmoniously, the example would be of great value. At one time, there was hope that Rhodesia might be such an example, but events took a very different course. Perhaps Zambia will qualify, or Kenya or Swaziland.

The second essential precondition to a national change of heart will be a political vehicle in which common sense can have effective expression. This means—difficult as it will be—that the moderates, now splintered and politically impotent, will have to unite.

There has not been any serious effort in this direction in recent years. It is doubtful that it can happen while Graaff is leader of the United Party. Despite the utter failure of his move to the right, he persists in seeing it as his only course. He is like the skipper of a sailboat, steadily losing position in a race, who adamantly refuses to switch from starboard to port tack. Graaff regards the idea of a coalition with the Progressives (let alone the Liberals) as political death. He resents their breakaway from the United Party, and they in turn have scarcely concealed contempt for him. Perhaps a deputy leader of the party, S. J. Marias Steyn, or a previous leader, J. F. K. Straus—both able men of more moderate bent—would be capable of bringing the various factions together and hammering them into a significant political force. After all, the party of Jan Christiaan Smuts should not be beyond rescue. But it clearly needs an injection of new blood, new ideas, and new backbone. Even if all the people who voted for the UP, the Progressives, and the Liberals had united in support of a single ticket, they could not have defeated the Nationalists in 1966.

The third essential precondition to a change of heart is an awakening to the real implications of apartheid. Many whites simply do not know what is happening around them. A kindly lady took me by the arm after church one Sunday and purred: "Look around you. Our blacks are content." A man prominent in a denomination whose basic tenets include the Golden Rule told me, in perfect seriousness, "We *are* blessing the Natives." This paternalistic attitude, of course, infuriates the Africans, and would infuriate them even if it bore any resemblance to the truth. But the real point is that many whites believe it, and if they did not believe it, they would not support apartheid.

Paton said they were "seduced." Diplomats stationed in South Africa sometimes call it "brainwashed." The East London *Daily Dispatch* wrote that the government had "mesmerized" the whites in the Transkei. I like the latter word; it could be applied more generally. A great many South Africans have been mesmerized— not just subconsciously by fear and by material prosperity, but quite deliberately by a government highly skilled at propaganda distortion. Its thesis: that the end justifies the means. The result: a virtually universal conviction that South Africa is misunderstood abroad, that it is on the right track, that the world will awaken one day and see this to be the fact.

The means employed to mold popular thought are familiar to anyone who has observed a power "elite" in action. The government, with control of the only radio network, uses it for incessant news-slanting and "interpretation." * Furthermore, the government virtually controls much of the Afrikaans-language press and seeks to intimidate and discredit English-language newspapers. It mans the ramparts resolutely against the advent of television; TV is "too expensive," an "unnecessary luxury," the "greatest destroyer of family life in the Western world," the government says. Moreover, and much more to the point, tele-

---

* The director of the South African Broadcasting Corporation, Dr. Piet J. Meyer, reportedly also head of the Broederbond, was so enamored of Hitler in the 1930's that he named a son "Izan"—Nazi spelled backward. Others of the ruling hierarchy also have been and are suspected of having pro-Nazi backgrounds. *Die Transvaler,* when edited by Verwoerd, objected to South Africa's participation in World War II on Britain's side. Vorster, the Prime Minister, was confined to an internment camp for alleged pro-Hitler activity. Anti-Semitism breaks to the surface intermittently, even today, in parliamentary debate.

vision would bring in too many dangerous liberal ideas, not all
of which could be filtered out by censorship, since many programs would be dependent, especially in the early stages, on
English-language tapes. It would also popularize the wrong language.

Dr. Albert Hertzog, Minister of Posts and Telegraphs, says
TV is the instrument which "overseas money power" seeks to
use for "the destruction of white South Africa." British and
American films which would be shown on TV, he says, are
"drenched with liberal and demoralizing propaganda," including
propaganda for "internationalism," an ideology whose purpose,
in Verwoerd's words, is "to make people lose respect for what
is their own." The "little black box," to Dr. Hertzog, is a "deadly
weapon" which has been used to "undermine the morale of the
white man and even to destroy great empires." Mrs. Suzman,
the Progressive MP, said the "empire" in danger was that of the
Nationalist Party. "If the leading members of the government
front bench had to appear on television, three-quarters of them
would lose their seats," she jibed.

The government information service spends hundreds of thousands of rand a year attempting to mesmerize people, at home
and abroad. In September 1966, it started operating a powerful
$5,600,000 radio transmitter—a Voice of South Africa—which
reaches the United States and many other countries. It periodically takes full-page newspaper advertisements in foreign newspapers, lauding the beauties and advantages of the country. These
ads point to immigration, both legal and surreptitious, claiming
that "hundreds of thousands" (or, variously, "over a million")
Africans have crossed the border illegally in recent years "to enjoy the higher wages and better living standards in South Africa."

One advertisement then asks: "Why are so many people of
different backgrounds eager to go there?" and answers:

"Because there is stability, peace and progress. . . . Because
the opportunities are vast and free enterprise is taken for granted.
. . . Because South Africa's people are uniformly and consistently
anti-communist. . . . Because South Africa has in the past stood
shoulder to shoulder with the United States and other western
powers. . . .

"It is a stable and prosperous land, a reliable western country
in Africa with the promise of a bright future. Here any individ-

ual can, within his own community, rise to the top of his profession and become a business executive, cabinet minister and a leader among his people." The observer who knows what conditions actually are like wants to send out an emergency call to *New York Times* columnist James Reston for "Uniquack," Reston's propaganda-deflating "machine" which translates fantasy back into fact.

Since 1960, the efforts of the South African Information Service have been seconded by the South Africa Foundation, a semi-independent group which harnesses private capital (reputedly more than $1,500,000) to much the same end. The foundation concentrates on foreigners visiting South Africa, and indeed frequently provides expense-paid trips to influential and hopefully susceptible visitors, guiding them with much skill and exposing them to just enough opposition opinion for the pro-government pitch to seem honest and candid.

With some tourists, little or no effort is required. They virtually brainwash themselves. South Africa is a lovely country, and the contrasts with the rest of Africa, which many of them have visited en route, are sharp. They enjoy being called "master" and "boss"; the blacks are so very polite and deferential. One's vanity and sense of superiority are pleasurably inflated. Everything seems surprisingly tranquil. (Some come expecting Sharpeville massacres on every other street corner.)

The visitor sees colorful native dances on the gold mines and decides that Africans really are savages, unfit to share in the government. Whites are pleasant, hospitable, and persuasive, and the tourist is beguiled. Businessmen, too, are ready converts; you can make between 15 and 26 percent of your investment! Must not apartheid be all right if you can amortize your capital in four to seven years? And (so long as you hire nonwhites) no worry about difficult labor unions!

The effectiveness of this mesmeric spell is enhanced for the domestic audience by the government's very considerable success in muffling contrary views. As we have seen, this is accomplished by a variety of police measures which succeed strikingly in overawing the average man-in-the-street, white and nonwhite alike. Those who express opinions critical of the government take care to do so away from possible listening devices. They are constantly aware that their phones may be tapped; that their homes can be entered and searched without warrant; and that various forms of confinement, such as house arrest, restriction, banning, and jail itself, can be imposed without court proceedings. They assume that mail is opened, telegrams read, associations watched.

In 1965, the government virtually acknowledged it had intercepted some mail. It advertised in the newspapers that persons who had attempted to send money abroad to gamble on the "Rhodesian Sweep" (sweepstakes) could get their money back by writing to the South African Post Office, which had not forwarded letters containing such bets. (Lotteries are illegal, and all gambling is frowned upon.) There was no apparent way for the post office to have known the content of the letters without having examined them; the address on the envelope would not have been sufficient.

An acquaintance of mine, Prof. Gwendolen M. Carter of Northwestern University, discovered her briefcase mysteriously missing from a locked hotel room. When the police "found" it a day or two later, the papers in it had been reshuffled—a process wholly unnecessary if the purpose had been merely to identify the owner. One important document was missing. There was no proof the police had gone through it, but it contained notes on conditions among the Africans and names the police might have considered useful. The police may also have thought the experience would inhibit her. She was later refused a visa to return.

Those few critical foreign newsmen who manage to gain admission are sometimes harassed and expelled, as from Iron Curtain countries. In December 1964, a correspondent of *The New York Times*, J. Anthony Lukas, had his papers seized by police at the airport as he sought to leave the country. Agents complained that one manuscript was "full of propaganda against South Africa." They also took an address book and questioned him about telephone numbers on a scrap of paper. The papers were returned a day or two later.

The net effect of the government's one-two punch—propaganda plus suppression of dissent—is a successful manipulation of the public consciousness, a mesmeric spell packaged with great skill and sold to an audience conditioned for it by circumstances external to South Africa. Boycotts and wildly exaggerated criticism of the country in the United Nations enhance the effectiveness of the government campaign, stirring South African patriotism, and making it seem un-South African to oppose apartheid. Unrest and communist infiltration in Black Africa, seemingly suggesting that western interests are in peril where Africans rule, encourage the belief that "America and Britain will come around." Soviet and Red Chinese propaganda blasts lend verisimilitude to the theory that communism and opposition to apartheid are synonymous.

At the same time, the Nationalists' pitch is often made in terms of high morality. "The finest blend of cruelty and idealism ever devised by man," Paton has called it. "The cruel man stomachs the idealism for the sake of the cruelty; the idealist stomachs the cruelty for the sake of the idealism." Nationalist followers will be found speaking proudly of the fine hospitals built for "our blacks"—unaware, it would seem, that ward after ward is filled with African children suffering from malnutrition and tuberculosis as a result of the submarginal wages paid their fathers.

Thus, many South Africans have been lulled to sleep. They do not know anything serious is wrong; they are sure others are misinformed about them. They will entreat a visiting newsman to "go home and tell the truth about us," the obvious implication being that few others have. This yearning for vindication is at once touching and tragic. Anyone who suggests that perhaps they themselves are misinformed is dismissed as prejudiced or ignorant.

Even pro-government circles sometimes acknowledge the extent of this aberration. The Nationalist newspaper *Die Transvaler* said in an editorial, "Every white person will have to be made to recognize that there is a race problem. How this knowledge can be brought to the whites is a problem nobody has yet solved. The time has truly come for thousands of whites who are in ignorance to wake up."

In some respects this state of mind is reminiscent of the Germany of the 1930's. Some Germans knew the meaning of Hitlerism and condoned it; but many more were genuinely ignorant of what was happening in Belsen and Buchenwald. Anything that would contribute to opening up South Africa to a freer exchange of ideas and fuller knowledge of itself would be immensely beneficial.

There is little or no likelihood of this happening without ex-

ternal intervention. The chances of spontaneous change springing from within South Africa are minimal. This is not to dismiss
the conscientious work being done in that direction by thousands
of dedicated people. It is simply to say they need help.

They are divided among themselves and are up against a government that has entrenched itself with the army, the police, and
the civil service; that crushes active opposition; that could hold
power even if its popular vote were cut by one-third, thanks to
a gerrymandered system of election districts; that skillfully uses
many instruments of thought control; and that has had an inordinate number of "breaks" externally.

Those who contend that merely by a "lowering of voices" in
criticism of South Africa, by patience and "understanding" of
her "special problems" (though this is needed), the outside world
can encourage or bring about peaceful change, are deceiving
themselves. Of the three essential preconditions for change—discovery that nonwhites are capable of sharing power, cooperation
among white opposition parties, and escape from the government's mesmeric spell—only the second (unity among moderates)
is practical without outside help.

Many times during my visit to South Africa, liberals and moderates said to me, "Give us time. Give us understanding." On
each occasion, I asked what would happen if the United States
and Britain did fend off serious external pressure—that is, sanctions and a blockade—for, say, five years. Would the situation
be essentially different at the end of that time? Would any change
for the better have taken place? Not one of my friends said confidently that it would. Each conceded that things might well
have become worse (and, indeed, in the four years that have
followed, they have become worse). If anything in South Africa
is self-evident, it is that apartheid is not going to erode sponta-
neously any more than the communist state will wither away.

Harold Macmillan, then British Prime Minister, went to South
Africa in 1960 to deliver his famous "wind of change" speech.
He had a long, private session with Verwoerd. At the end of it,
he commented privately to a friend: "You might as well talk to
the southeast wind." Others who have sought to reason with the
government—Secretary of State Dean Rusk, for example, who
has had many long sessions with South African officials, and the
late United Nations Secretary-General Dag Hammarskjöld, who

went on a peace mission to South Africa in January 1961—have had a similar experience.

If the outside world wants peaceful change in South Africa in the direction of the twentieth century's single most compelling secular precept—that a man is to be judged by what he is and what he does, not by the color of his skin—it will have to raise, not lower, its voice. And it will have to do more than talk. It will have to act, with supreme skill.

CHAPTER FIVE

Penetrating the "Golden Curtain"

On July 8, 1853, Commodore Matthew Perry sailed into Uraga harbor, Japan, and, training his guns on the startled military authorities, jolted them out of their isolation from the United States and the world. Thus began a process that lifted Japan from centuries of feudalism into today's modern, industrialized country—one of the five or six most advanced industrial nations of the world.

South Africans would not care for the analogy, but in the mental realm, what really is required in Pretoria today is a Commodore Perry. Much more than they realize, Afrikaner nationalists are isolated from the present-day world.

Some of this isolation is consciously and deliberately self-imposed. Scorning "liberalism," they have retreated into a mental fortress, shutting out the world as their Voortrekker ancestors shut out hostile tribes by arraying ox-drawn covered wagons in an improvised rectangle (*laager*). Much of South Africa is as modern as tomorrow in its physical plant, its business acumen, its industrial techniques; but ideologically its dominant faction is still in the era of the Kaffir Wars.

Just how much international intervention would be helpful in ending this mental isolation, and what form the intervention should take, is a problem of great complexity. There are many who would update and employ the Perry approach—using superior, decisive force, either economic or military or both. They argue that lesser measures of persuasion and pressure have been shown to be futile. This is true, but there is also a very real danger that major external intervention would merely drive South Africa deeper into its *laager*. What is needed is a mixture of pressure and persuasion—just enough of each to encourage indigenous reform, helping moderates to unite and gain strength and tipping the balance of domestic political power. An all-out assault would simply make right-wing extremists out of many present moderates and provoke last-ditch white resistance.

Before any course of action can be adopted, a prior question must be disposed of. Is international intervention legal and proper at all? Or are South Africa's race relations the business of South Africans and no one else?

This issue has been argued exhaustively in the United Nations and elsewhere, South Africa frequently citing Article 2, Paragraph 7 of the United Nations Charter which begins: "Nothing contained in the present Charter shall authorize the United Nations to intervene in matters which are essentially within the domestic jurisdiction of any state. . . ." Friends of South Africa have repeated this argument in many guises, legal and practical, contending that the country's problems are unique, that it alone is qualified to deal with them, that the outside world—certainly the western world—has no interest or justifiable concern.

This domestic-jurisdiction argument has been largely discredited. By now, the consensus is strongly against it. On the legal level, intervention by the United Nations is clearly justified by Article 10 of the Charter, which empowers the General Assembly to deal with "any questions or any matters within the scope of the present Charter," and by Articles 55 and 56, which bring human rights well within that scope, pledging all member states to take "joint and separate action in cooperation with the organization" to promote "universal respect for, and observance of, human rights and fundamental freedoms for all without distinctions as to race, sex, language or religion." Article 14 further authorizes the Assembly to remove impediments to "the general welfare or friendly relations among nations. . . ."

On the practical level, virtually the entire international community agrees that the common interest of mankind is involved. An offense against a man on the basis of his color causes anguish to others of his color, not merely in that country but everywhere. "Any man's death diminishes me," said John Donne, "because I am involved in mankind." Some of the deepest convictions and aspirations of man are affected. The injury is no less painful for being mental rather than physical, and it can provoke physical reprisal. In this interdependent world, in which ideas are not insulated by political walls, it is no answer to say, "You have no right to be concerned. It is not taking place in your area of political jurisdiction." Still less is it a satisfactory response to say, "You are making the issue international by your protest; be silent, and all will be tranquil." Or, "There are unsolved problems in your own backyard; do you regard this as a precedent for their discussion in an international forum?"

A man may burn leaves on his lawn if he wishes, and the law permits; but if he risks setting his neighbors' houses on fire, they have a right to intervene. Apartheid has caused profound upheaval in Africa, and the shock waves have spread far. Attitudes toward it have a considerable bearing on dealings with the governments of Black Africa. The course of the cold war in Africa is affected; so is the direction and volume of trade. To say that the implications of apartheid are international is merely to state an obvious fact. In the language of the United Nations Charter, it not only "might lead to international friction or give rise to a dispute" (Article 34), but has done so; it is, indeed, the wellspring of a dispute the continuance of which is "likely to endanger the maintenance of international peace and security" (Article 37). The Security Council has formally so found. There is no sound or reasonable basis for doubting that apartheid is a proper subject of international concern.

Many who agree that South Africa's race relations transcend domestic jurisdiction do not take the next step and acknowledge that at this time they constitute a "threat to peace" within the meaning of Chapter VII of the United Nations Charter. This is the chapter which, in the event of a "threat to the peace, breach of the peace, or act of aggression," authorizes the fifteen-nation Security Council to compel compliance with its orders. Such compulsion may take the form of "complete or partial interruption of economic relations and of rail, sea, air, postal, telegraphic, radio, and other means of communication, and the severance of diplomatic relations." If those steps are considered inadequate, the compulsion may also involve "such action by air, sea, or land forces as may be necessary to maintain or restore international peace and security. Such action may include demonstrations, blockade, and other operations by air, sea, or land forces. . . ." In other words, compulsory economic, diplomatic and military sanctions.

To be sure, this compulsive power exists very largely on paper.

The United Nations has rarely made use of it. Even the Korean war (1950–53) and the struggle to suppress Katanga's secession (1962–63) were fought pursuant to "recommendations" rather than binding "decisions" of the United Nations Security Council. Similarly, first steps in response to Rhodesia's unilateral declaration of independence in November 1965 called for voluntary cooperation by the world community. Only when such cooperation broke down were Britain and the United States willing to resort to compulsion.

The question of whether South Africa is a proper target for Chapter VII compulsion has been a subject of bitter controversy. Washington and London have argued that sanctions should be invoked only in a dire emergency—normally, that is, only in circumstances involving actual, or immediately threatened, warfare. (Rhodesia is obviously an exception.) Black Africa has been extremely impatient with this "legalistic" view. Eager to see sanctions imposed, Africans have urged a broad reading of the words "threat to the peace." A revolution inside South Africa, aided from the outside (as it surely would be) would imperil the peace, they say; and the fact that such a course could develop makes apartheid a "threat" today. To contend that a "threat" is not a "threat" until the emergency is so severe as to be virtually unmanageable is to rule out sanctions as a measure of preventive diplomacy, they point out—with persuasive logic. They could add (and in private some do add) that the Anglo-American stand is also a formidable incentive for them to create a war situation—that is, to provide (insofar as they are able) an immediate and clearly recognizable threat to the peace, as defined by Washington and London.

There is, on all sides, a tendency to interpret the law to suit a predetermined view of what is desirable politically. As in so many other fields, diplomats are certain the United Nations Charter authorizes what they want to do about apartheid and forbids what they do not want to see done. Their view of the legalities, moreover, is likely to change as their political judgments change. The only area of general agreement is that the world community has some proper role to play; its extent and character remain in dispute.

An independent effort to define the proper role of the world community would have to begin with a definition of the objective. Except for the Soviet Union—which undoubtedly would prefer turmoil and revolution, leading to communist intervention—there is wide agreement outside South Africa that an ideal solution would be a well-planned and carefully executed transition from white supremacy to responsible majority rule by way of graduated steps, taken slowly enough to preserve political and economic stability but surely enough to remove any rational reason for disillusion and desperation on the part of the blacks. In short, a political decompression chamber.

There can be no doubt that this is the right answer. But it is far more easily said than done. Even in the United States, where the rule of law is rooted in nearly two hundred years of tradition, it has not been possible to bring about a bloodless and peaceful transition from segregation toward integration, and the distance being traversed in the United States, while great enough, has been short by comparison with that in South Africa. Moreover, in the case of South Africa there is no central authority which is determined to force integration, comparable to the United States Justice Department and Supreme Court. The United Nations falls far short of such a role, though it may have to try to simulate it. Thus South Africa is one of the toughest challenges diplomats have ever faced—so tough, indeed, that much effort to date has been expended to avoid facing it.

Most white South Africans are determined not to change their way of life. As we have seen, they are absolutely persuaded that they are right and the world is wrong. Even some white South Africans who criticize apartheid among themselves, or have reservations about it, will leap to its defense if foreigners attack it. Many are unaware of its real nature and significance. The problem, therefore, is to awaken South Africans of goodwill and create greater receptivity for change.

One possible instrument of awakening might be an Afrikaans-language newspaper expressing a moderate point of view. There is today no anti-apartheid paper in Afrikaans (unless *Die Beeld,* which occasionally has some reservations about the government's omniscience, and *Weekblad,* a kind of house organ for the United Party, are so considered). Virtually the whole Afrikaans-language press, reaching the people who are the backbone of the government's support, is uncritical, although *Die Burger* of Cape Town, an organ appealing to intellectuals, sometimes wants apartheid carried out more rationally. To be sure, the hostile English-language press is read by many of the government's urban supporters. But they heavily discount it, as the government encourages them to do, and the fact that it is in the "wrong" language is a handicap. There is overwhelming need for a respected voice of reason in the language of the Afrikaner nationalists.

Such a paper has, from time to time, been tried and abandoned because it was not a paying proposition. It should not be expected to be—certainly not at first. It should be subsidized, preferably by a progressive South African of great wealth such as Harry Oppenheimer, John Schlesinger, or Dr. Anton Rupert. If local South African financing were not to be available, then as a second choice (a poor second choice) outside money could come in. Foreign financing would render the paper more vulnerable to xenophobia; but if it were locally edited and written, and particularly if it were of high quality, the charge of "outside interference" could be shunted off. Perhaps, although it would be extremely difficult, the real source of the financing could be successfully concealed behind a corporate front ostensibly South African.

There are not now any national newspapers in South Africa with the prestige of a *New York Times* or a *Guardian* of Manchester. The one I am proposing should aspire to this status. Its tone and constructive approach to the news should be like that of *The Christian Science Monitor*. Since the Transvaal elects nearly one-half the members of Parliament, it should be based in Johannesburg or Pretoria. It should attempt to build a circulation throughout the country. Like most other major newspapers in the world, it should seek to syndicate its contents; its market would be South Africa's 150-odd "district" newspapers, primarily those in Afrikaans but also the English-language papers if they chose to buy and translate the material. The paper should invest in correspondents of major stature, both locally and overseas, and in short, seek to become a national institution with authority and prestige. It could not then be ignored, and might be better able to fend off the assaults to which it would certainly be subjected—the government pressure, the advertising boycotts, the labor union difficulties, perhaps even the proscription by authorities of the Dutch Reformed Church.

The initial investment required for such an undertaking would be great, and the day-to-day subsidy might have to continue for some years. But the potential impact would also be great. A newspaper of this stature could hope eventually to influence the whole mental climate of the country. If it were financially secure, it could survive and even thrive on persecution, as courageous publishers and editors in many countries have done. The stakes would be high enough to inspire dedication.

Also useful would be an independent radio station, a "Voice of Reason," operated by South African moderates. Because of the government monopoly on radio in South Africa, it would have to be located in neighboring territory to the north, presumably in Lusaka or, if conditions change sufficiently to permit it, in Bulawayo or Salisbury, Rhodesia, or in Lourenço Marques, Mozambique. Alternately, it could be located on board ship, beyond the three-mile limit, like the pirate radio stations that once operated off Great Britain.

Its programs would be useless—indeed, counterproductive—if they consisted of abusive harangues. They should not be influenced by South Africa's emotional critics. They should consist of high-quality entertainment, factual news, and quasi-religious material of high moral content, primarily in Afrikaans but also to some extent in English. Calm and rational news analyses, with interpretation, along the lines of an Edward R. Murrow, would be desirable. Afrikaners of a progressive bent, moderate journalists, and exceptionally qualified and responsible nonwhites would be ideal commentators. The South African Institute of Race Relations has a number of such people on its staff.

It would be very difficult politically for Black Africa to permit such an operation on its soil without seeking to influence the content; but for them to interfere would be fatal. Once the station were to become associated in South Africa with the Black African "propaganda line," it would be finished as far as influence on white South Africans was concerned. Its only purpose thereafter would be to arouse nonwhite South Africans, which is not what needs to be done.

Perhaps the 1,500,000 kilowatt Voice of America transmitter in Monrovia, Liberia, could be used a few hours a day. As of this writing, ten and three-quarters hours of VOA programs in English are audible each day in South Africa, and have some limited popularity; but nothing is broadcast in Afrikaans and little is said about apartheid. ("We're awfully tired of Vietnam and de Gaulle," a listener remarked to me. "Can't you make at least as much effort to penetrate the Golden Curtain as you do the Iron Curtain?") The South African Government could jam the proposed transmissions, but to do so would be to put itself on a par, in the world's eyes, with the Soviet Union of the Stalin era.

There are other possible means of opening the mental doors of South Africa.

• The United States Government and private agencies might expand exchange programs, enabling a much larger number of South African civil servants, business leaders, churchmen, teachers, and others—of all races—to see at first hand how an integrated society can be built. The South African Government has shown itself concerned over the "liberalizing" effect of such exchange programs.

• Something analogous to the South African Foundation—a Freedom Foundation, as it were—could be set up in the United States to increase travel by influential South Africans to areas other than the continental United States which also are, or are en route to becoming, successfully integrated: Hawaii, Puerto Rico, Brazil, Jamaica, and Hong Kong, for example. There is very little understanding in South Africa of just what racial integration really involves.

The Freedom Foundation might also finance public relations activity, like newspaper advertisements, lectures, and drama with a "message," in South Africa. Funds might be obtained from existing philanthropic and public-spirited foundations, and from American businesses which are involved in South Africa and hence have a special stake in peaceful transition there. Some businesses now accused of supporting apartheid could minimize the damaging impact of this complaint by contributions. Such contributions could even be made tax deductible.

• A wide variety of steps could be taken to dramatize for South Africans the deep and sincere disapproval most Americans feel for racial prejudice. This would help combat the widespread impression that "Americans will come to see we are right" and that "we are just like the American South."

The first step to this end would be to arouse public and official opinion in the United States on apartheid—as it has been aroused, for example, in Sweden and Denmark. There should be an Anti-Apartheid Movement in Washington, as there is in London, equipped to supply news media with balanced, factual, up-to-date information on apartheid and its implications. The President could call periodic White House conferences on South Africa, and speak out himself more often and more persuasively. So could members of Congress. (Some Senators and Congressmen —Senator Edward Brooke of Massachusetts and Congressman Barrett O'Hara of Illinois, for example—are already interested in the issue, but more could awaken to the political advantage to be gained.) Civil rights groups could assist materially by making known their interest, and by directing it to the right targets: the White House, the Secretary of State, the Secretary of Commerce, and Congress rather than the Africa Bureau of the State Department, which is already convinced. Some groups are already doing so, but they could do a lot more. They could also remind business firms more frequently and more persuasively that there are American customers to be lost if they wittingly or unwittingly strengthen apartheid. (Most firms care very much about their public image. It can have very practical implications. One bank which has been pressured by anti-apartheid groups, Chase Manhattan of New York, is understood to have lost two major trust accounts, running into at least seven figures, as a result. First National City Bank, New York, lost a $10 million investment portfolio, that of the Methodist Board of Missions, because the Board objected to its participation in credits to South Africa. A New York-based "Committee of Conscience Against Apartheid," headed by A. Philip Randolph, has organized individual withdrawals from these two banks, running, the committee says, into the tens of millions.) Newspaper editors in the United States could catch on to the fact that racial conflict in South Africa is one of the most dramatic human interest stories in the world, with a massive potential reader audience. It gets a big play in Canada. They could kick up more of a fuss when independent and outspoken correspondents are forced out of the country.

From this solid basis of awakened conscience, Americans could seek to project their convictions more vividly to South Africa. Many more theatre groups, musicians, dancers, and other performers could refuse to appear before segregated audiences in South Africa, as some, including officially sponsored groups, have already done. (It could be made a condition of the issuance of a passport valid for travel there.) Sports teams could be dissuaded from, or forbidden to, play against segregated South African teams.

A number of American and British playwrights and composers already have refused to let their work be performed before segregated audiences, with the result that the South African theatre and concert stages have suffered from a shortage of top-flight material. At least one theatre in South Africa has been offered for sale as a result, and one producer has predicted that the South African theatre "will be set back some fifty years." More such pressure could have telling effect. (In response, the government now has, in effect, legitimized piracy through a new Copyright Act which permits usage of dramatic material without permission in cases where the refusal is for ideological reasons. But royalties still are supposed to be paid, and these could be contributed to funds which assist victims of apartheid.) With-holding of motion pictures until they could be shown before multiracial audiences would have still greater impact.

In this same category—demonstrating disapproval—the United States Embassy in South Africa could make all its diplomatic receptions, cocktail parties, and other group entertaining multiracial. At present, only two major parties a year—on the Fourth of July and Washington's Birthday—have racially mixed guest lists; it is considered progressive, even daring, to have this many, in the face of government objections. Smaller mixed parties are held from time to time, and there is some social contact (lunches, for example) with nonwhites by themselves; but the great bulk of the entertaining is for whites only, in "deference to the customs of South Africa" and because many whites will not attend other-wise.

This deference is all too easily confused with approval, or at least acquiescence. Another way of making American attitudes clear would be to assign Negroes to the embassy staff and to other American installations such as the NASA tracking station near Pretoria, defying the unofficial South African Government pro-hibition. If such personnel were refused admission to the country, as they presumably would be, this fact could be widely publicized, with resulting embarrassment to Pretoria which might eventually have an impact on the policy.

A special presidential emissary—someone like former President

Dwight D. Eisenhower—could be carefully briefed and sent on an education mission armed with speeches and press statements. The visit of the late Senator Robert Kennedy in 1966 had very considerable impact—and Verwoerd, though foreseeing this result, did not dare bar him.

When the government refuses, as it did in 1965, to permit the public showing of a film such as *Years of Lightning, Day of Drums* (on the career of President Kennedy) without civil rights passages deleted, the United States Embassy could screen it uncut in the embassy compound, under protection of diplomatic immunity, and invite South Africans to come and view it. Similarly a videotape of President Johnson addressing Congress on civil rights, as he did, for example, in the wake of the Selma crisis, could be offered. This would do much to indicate how Americans really feel about racial injustice.

The United States might send as its ambassador to South Africa, not a professional diplomat, but a "presence" whose statements would make major news. An outstanding Negro such as Dr. Ralph Bunche could even be named.

South Africa would not sit still for this kind of thing. The cabinet would boycott multiracial embassy entertainment, as they do now (sometimes complaining publicly about diplomats "who do not honor South African customs"). Social contact between the embassy and the government would be reduced. Nonwhites named to the embassy staff, including a nonwhite ambassador, would— if admitted to the country at all—be declared *personae non gratae* (that is, expelled) as soon as there was a pretext. Installations seeking to introduce nonwhite personnel into the country might be ordered out or restricted. There certainly would be increased tension between Pretoria and Washington, further reducing American influence on the South African Government.

However, the effect on the white population, while mixed, ought to be on balance good. Many Afrikaners say they don't know what American policy really is. They would then know. It would be made clear that the United States was not "awakening" to the "justice and equity" of South African policy; that American criticism of apartheid in the United Nations was not just a cynical effort to "court kaffir states."

South Africans care what is said and thought about them; their indifference is a cultivated pose. The Afrikaner particularly wants to be loved and "understood." He admires and consciously emulates much that is American, looking to the United States as his country's first friend abroad. Thus American disapproval, if expressed tactfully and compassionately, without venom, could make a profound impression. At the very least, many South Africans might begin questioning theses they now take for granted. The utter conviction of their own rectitude might be undermined.

In the rest of Africa, the results of such action would be sensationally good for the United States. No longer would Communists be able to smear Washington so readily by identifying it with Pretoria. The United States would be demonstrably on the side of racial justice.

• Britain and the rest of the Commonwealth could take parallel action to demonstrate the genuineness of their disapproval. With English-speaking South Africans, this would have even greater impact than American disapproval. If, for example, England, Scotland, Wales, Ireland, Australia, and New Zealand were to refuse to send champion rugby and cricket teams to South Africa unless the stadium crowds were integrated, the blow to South Africa would be comparable to cancellation of the World Series in American baseball. New Zealand's refusal in 1965 to remove nonwhites from its top rugby team, resulting in cancellation of the team's scheduled series in South Africa, had very considerable impact on South African opinion, giving useful ammunition to government critics.* In 1967, Vorster capitulated and agreed to admit racially mixed teams from South Africa's "traditional" opponents.

• There could be a massive campaign of letter-writing—tens of thousands of Americans, Britons, and others sending polite, friendly, hopefully persuasive letters to opposite numbers in South Africa, the lists of potential recipients being drawn up with some care by South African moderates. No doubt many recipients would reply with an effort at self-justification, and a dialogue could ensue, both sides benefiting. The government could intercept such letters, but not without damage to its image at both

---

* In an effort to counter the criticism there were even suggestions, apparently serious, that Maoris (Polynesians) on the New Zealand team, whom the South Africans sought to bar, might be designated "honorary whites." (New Zealanders, dismissing the idea, quipped that they could be classified "honorary Japanese.")

ends. South Africa is itself encouraging supporters of apartheid to write letters abroad.

• Restrictions could be imposed on travel to South Africa, thus affecting both her tourist income and her highly cherished objective of increased white immigration.

• The United States, Britain, the World Bank, and other sources of capital could launch a comprehensive program to develop Botswana, Lesotho, and Swaziland. The beginnings of such a program already exist. To the extent that it was successful, it would reduce some of the dependence of these enclaves on South Africa, thus making them less vulnerable to influence and correspondingly more useful centers of pressure in the opposite direction. It would also improve their bargaining power when they sold their labor across the border, and make them—as islands of black prosperity and stability—examples of successful racial integration. Discovery of diamonds, nickel and copper in Botswana suggests that the task is by no means hopeless.

• Money available for scholarships to refugees and other South Africans abroad could be multiplied at least tenfold. In 1965–68, the United Nations was able to raise $729,480 * for its Education and Training Program for Southern Africans, of which the United States contributed $75,000 (10.2 percent). The Johnson Administration asked Congress for $150,000 for this and other South African relief and refugee projects in 1967, but only $50,000 was appropriated.† With money collected up to March 20, 1968, the United Nations gave 350 South Africans ‡ scholarships to institutions in Britain, India, Ireland, the United States, Germany, Canada, Norway, Switzerland, and East and West Africa. (Czechoslovakia had offered five scholarships.) This modest, though encouraging, beginning compares with rival, often communist-inspired, programs outside the United Nations under which hundreds, perhaps thousands of Africans are taken behind the Iron

---

* As of March 20, 1968. $118,888 more had been pledged. The 1966–68 target was $2,000,000.

† Half of this was pledged to the Education and Training Program, and half to the UN Trust Fund for South Africa (see page 121). The United States promised to contribute $40 for every $60 which was pledged by other countries during 1968 and paid by Dec. 31, 1970.

‡ Also recipients of UN scholarships were 31 South-West Africans, 250 refugees from Portuguese Africa, and at least 10 Rhodesians.

and Bamboo Curtains, and many more go to Algeria, Tanzania, Congo (Brazzaville), the United Arab Republic, and (according to Pretoria) Ghana and Ethiopia for "education" and guerrilla training.

There are many things that might be done to counter communist influence in the South African underground; but surely one of the most obvious steps would be to alter the heavy imbalance in favor of communist-sponsored education. Hundreds of thousands of South African nonwhites yearn for elementary or secondary learning. Others, though not as many, are qualified for college-level training. These are people who must one day share responsibility for the political and economic life of South Africa. Money invested now in their training will profoundly affect the kind of country there will be a generation hence. It is little short of criminal to let their immense hunger for education be harnessed to ideological ends by the Soviet Union, Red China, and their camp followers. It should not be necessary for these South Africans to accept guerrilla training and communist indoctrination in order to satisfy that hunger. The free world can, and should, offer healthier alternatives. As of this writing, however, in addition to the United Nations program, only 113 South African and South-West African nonwhites are pursuing peaceful studies in American institutions of higher learning with American government help, and very few are there on private scholarships.

Possibly an American- or United Nations-sponsored institution should be set up near South Africa—say, in Botswana (if that country dared risk South African reprisal) or in Zambia—to offer proximate education. There is a privately owned institution of this kind, the Waterford School near Mbabane, Swaziland, fourteen miles from the South African border, to which some one hundred South Africans have fled for education. It is a small-scale model of the kind of thing I am proposing, and it is seeking to expand.

One by-product of offering education "on the spot" would be the reduction or elimination of costs of transporting students great distances to existing schools and colleges. The effect of providing educational opportunity near at hand might be to encourage a flood of South African refugees—as from Castro's Cuba or the Hungary of 1956 or East Germany before the Berlin wall. The impact on South Africa, under these circumstances, would be a similarly embarrassing form of pressure and a vivid demon-

stration to the world that conditions are not as idyllic as the South
African Information Service is fond of portraying them. The
spectacle of refugees by the thousands fleeing the country for
education might even shame Pretoria into providing less inadequate schooling itself. The reaction of many South Africans
probably would be "good riddance," but others might ponder the
implications more seriously.

• Much greater assistance in other areas could be provided to
victims of apartheid. The United Nations has established a Trust
Fund for South Africa which is intended to be a clearinghouse
and central collection agency for such assistance. Specifically, according to the General Assembly resolution which established it
in December 1965 the fund covers:

"(a) Legal assistance to persons charged under discriminatory
and repressive legislation in South Africa;

"(b) Relief for dependents of persons persecuted by the Government of South Africa for acts arising from opposition to the
policies of apartheid;

"(c) Education of prisoners, their children and other dependents;

"(d) Relief for refugees from South Africa."

The Committee of Trustees of the Fund estimates that there
are "in the order of 8,000" persons in South Africa eligible for
such aid, and "several hundred" outside the country. Some are
persons charged with political offenses, such as distributing ANC
or PAC literature, or membership in these organizations. They
may face trial without legal help of any kind. (In South Africa,
the court is not required to provide defense counsel except in
cases of capital offenses.)

Earlier efforts to aid political detainees have met with strong
government resistance. A Defense and Aid Fund set up by liberal
South Africans to furnish legal help was banned in March 1966,
the South African Government raiding the home of Alan Paton,
among others, and seizing funds. This was just before 161 persons
who had served sentences for supporting African nationalist
causes were brought up for retrial and resentencing for their
original offense. It was a particularly blatant case of double jeopardy, but few of the accused could afford counsel, and lawyers
who did take the cases could face disbarment or worse. South
Africa denounced the Defense and Aid Fund, seeking to link it
to "Communists" and to the African National Congress, but no

persuasive evidence was offered to buttress the charge. Meanwhile an International Defense and Aid Fund in London, which says it is separate from the South African Defense and Aid Fund, has continued in being, seeking to circumvent government restrictions on the distribution of funds in South Africa. Some Americans also are privately getting money to South African lawyers courageous enough to represent political detainees.

This is the kind of activity which American Government money could support with great effect—both the direct effect of encouraging South African liberals and the indirect effect of demonstrating American concern over apartheid. A contribution to the International Defense and Aid Fund after its domestic South African counterpart had been declared illegal would be an especially dramatic gesture which could not help but stir thought and debate in South Africa, particularly if it were accompanied by an explanation that the United States was dedicated to the rule of law and the right of every accused to be represented by counsel. The humanitarian aspect of the fund—its help for the wives and children of political prisoners, many of whom are destitute— could also constructively be highlighted. If South Africa refused to let the money into the country through legal channels, that fact, too, would be eloquent.

The South African Government has shown considerable sensitivity to pressure of this kind in the past, especially when the criticism was accompanied by a tangible demonstration that it was not just words. Money does talk. As of this writing, however, the United States Government has contributed nothing to the International Defense and Aid Fund, and has pledged only a token $25,000 (on a 40–60 matching basis) to the Trust Fund. Private contributions from Americans have been limited almost exclusively to one $50,000 contribution to the Trust Fund by the African Aid and Legal Defense Fund, of which George M. Houser of New York, Executive Director of the American Committee on Africa, is secretary. Thirty-seven countries, including even the Soviet Union ($15,000), have brought the Trust Fund to a total of $532,102.*

---

* As of March 26, 1968. The four largest contributors were Sweden ($148,-380), Denmark ($119,125), Britain ($40,000), and the Netherlands ($27,584). Pledges totaled $107,234 more.

Many Africans and some others have urged that, as a further source of pressure on South Africa, she be expelled from the United Nations and from other international organizations of which she is still a member. South Africa has already been ousted, or withdrawn under fire, from UNESCO, ILO, and FAO (the United Nations Educational, Scientific and Cultural Organization, the International Labor Organization, and the Food and Agriculture Organization) and has all but cut her ties with the World Health Organization and the United Nations Economic Commission for Africa.

There are two major objections to such exclusion. The first is that, like severance of bilateral diplomatic relations, it removes a pressure point which can be used to influence South Africa. Moreover, United Nations sessions provide a useful opportunity for many private contacts with South African officials. Despite the scant results from such contacts, more intercourse of this kind, not less, is needed. Commodore Perry would have accomplished little if he had turned around and retreated from Uraga harbor in a huff.

The second reason for questioning the wisdom and effectiveness of expulsion proceedings is that they would not have the desired effect on white opinion in South Africa. Many South Africans care deeply about their country's reputation abroad, but they are not prompted to blame the government when South Africa is rebuffed in international forums. They blame the external critics, and rally round the government as a kind of patriotic duty. Exaggerated and intemperate criticism is especially counterproductive; and when it brackets all South African whites into one monolithic camp, it tends to produce exactly that state of affairs.

Thus expulsion from the United Nations, although it might have temporary shock effect, would be likely to be damaging, not helpful, over the long run. If South Africa were not now in the United Nations, advocates of constructive change might rationally seek means of luring or summoning her there. Some African delegates have shown they realize this by urging South Africa to attend sessions of United Nations organs which she has chosen to boycott. Nevertheless, a practice of challenging the credentials of South African delegates on the ground that the government is not representative of the people sprang up at the 1965 General

Assembly and continued in subsequent years, prompting Pretoria
to threaten withdrawal.

Penetrating the "Golden Curtain" by means of persuasion,
education, and enlightened propaganda should not be expected
to have immediate or dramatic effect. The process of awakening
supporters of apartheid and influencing the climate of opinion in
South Africa must necessarily be gradual. Active outside intervention should have begun at least a generation ago.

It will, therefore, be necessary to apply, in addition to persuasion, pressures which are sufficient to nudge the process forward,
and if this does not work, to give it some forced momentum. The
race between reform and revolution must not be lost if it can
possibly be won.

The most sensitive single pressure-point may well be South
Africa's pocketbook. As with most people, South Africans welcome, and if necessary rationalize, that which makes for comfortable living. Whatever brings stringency is distasteful, regardless
of its theoretical advantages. This may not be strictly true of the
more zealous and puritanical of South Africans; in their eyes,
ideology may take precedence over purse, "the Volk over the
Volkswagen." But to students cavorting in the nude on sand
dunes, ideology is certainly a secondary consideration.

Apartheid does unquestionably provide comfortable living for
its beneficiaries. The South African economy is booming—less
so in 1966 than in some previous years, but still at a remarkable
5.6 percent growth rate, one of the fastest in the world. Servants
are available at every hand for wages of five or six cents an hour.
Mine laborers may be had for less than ten cents an hour. Add
large dividend checks and leisure time for the country club, and
it is hard to persuade a man the system should be modified. An
employer who never has to worry about strikes by an African
labor union; a housewife who almost never has to open so much
as a window by herself; an ill-educated white cab driver whose job
is protected from nonwhite competition by "job reservation"—
these do not want to be told apartheid is immoral.

Moreover, there is something insidiously corrosive about
baasskap. It flatters the ego to be treated with deference and
servility, to feel that one is a superior being. "Don't speak to me
like I was a damned kaffir," an ill-educated white said in my

hearing when rebuked. The implication was that it would have been perfectly all right, indeed normal and natural, to speak sharply to an African.

Over a period of time, such people might be made to see, by persuasion, that the dangers and disadvantages of apartheid outweigh its advantages. But to persuade them in time to avoid an explosion, the advantages must be undercut or removed. To do this by means of outside pressure will be incredibly difficult. But it will have to be tried.

The ideal form of economic pressure would be one which would hurt South Africa much more than it would the country applying the leverage—or would not hurt the latter country at all. Then there would be little motive to evade or shirk the task. Experience has shown that this kind of pressure is rare, if indeed it exists; but it may perhaps be approximated.

One possible device would be to put pressure on the South African gold industry, which may well be the country's economic Achilles' heel. Gold is a billion-dollar-a-year industry in South Africa. It represents 40 percent of tangible exports and 10 percent of the gross domestic product. South Africa produces 50 percent of the world's output. (Russia is the other principal source.) Still, there are many marginal producers. At one point in the recent past, rising costs rendered an estimated $1,400,000,000 worth of South African gold uneconomic to mine. Some mines were kept in operation in the hope and expectation of a price increase, depending on uranium, a by-product, for solvency in the meantime. Then, in March 1968, speculative buying forced the lid off prices in the private field; and to some extent the gamble paid off. But the volume involved in private sales is not such as to render South Africa's gold industry invulnerable to pressure. Governments, which have agreed to continue paying $35 an ounce, still have great leverage if they choose to use it.

It would not be necessary to organize a total boycott of gold purchases, as some observers suggest (and others vigorously oppose for its disruptive effect on international financing). Quotas for purchases from South Africa might be agreed upon, and progressively reduced as further leverage was desired. (The side effects of a reduced supply would have to be cooperatively controlled.) Or, gold purchasers might even agree to reduce the price they paid (again, cooperating to cushion the probable backlash).

Any such steps, disturbing the patterns of international financing, are likely to be highly controversial, especially at times when gold is in great demand. Careful advance planning would be required, along with joint execution by a large number of countries—a very difficult thing to pull off. But the predictable impact on South Africa would be heavy enough to justify a lot of effort. Her boom could be converted to recession very quickly, with extensive side effects, both tangible and psychological. Moreover, once the machinery was established, the international community would be in a position to increase or decrease the pressure in accordance with South Africa's response. There would thus be a continuing source of leverage.

Also difficult but likely to have substantial impact if taken would be a decision by the United States and Britain to discourage or prohibit further private investment in South Africa, including the reinvestment of current earnings.* As of the end of 1966, the most recent date for which figures are available, some 260 American companies and thousands of individuals had plowed $630 million into the South African economy in direct and portfolio investment. The corresponding figure for Britain was $2.7 billion. This money, though only 1.1 percent of total foreign investment (in the case of the United States) and roughly 10 percent (for Britain) was nevertheless a significant part—respectively 14 percent and 59.8 percent—of total foreign private investment in South Africa ($4.5 billion). †

Foreign investment is not a large element in overall South African capital formation; domestic capital is much more significant. But foreign money is important for other reasons. It helps the South African balance of payments; it brings in machinery, licenses, copyrights, and the know-how resulting from research and development.

Most important of all, it is psychologically significant. The fact that hard-nosed American and British investors continue to ex-

* In January 1968, as a temporary measure to help redress the balance of payments, the Johnson Administration prohibited new direct investment of American capital in a number of places, including South Africa. However, reinvestment of current earnings, which accounts for as much as 30 percent of private direct foreign investment in South Africa, was not prohibited, nor was borrowing from South African sources.

† Total foreign investment in South Africa from all sources, private and governmental, worldwide, was $5.355 billion.

press confidence in South Africa's future is a reassurance to supporters of apartheid, as well as a contribution to the atmosphere of confidence so important to any business community. When foreign capital started fleeing the country after Sharpeville, the impact was so great that the government clamped tight controls on the flow.

Foreign capital is also highly visible. American firms are in evidence nearly everywhere in South Africa, their trademarks mingling with such non-Madison Avenue names as "Hubbly Bubbly," a soft drink, and such slogans as "It freshivates." International Harvester, del Monte, Esso, Mobil, and Caltex are a few names familiar to Americans. Some streets in Johannesburg and Durban have so many American goods displayed they might almost be corners of Detroit or Miami.

Two American manufacturers, General Motors and Ford, together sell roughly half the new cars purchased in South Africa each year. On assembly lines in the Port Elizabeth area, whites get six times as much pay as Africans for essentially the same work; thus Ford and GM stockholders benefit from this aspect of apartheid. (Ford fell into official disfavor in 1964—indeed, was subjected to an unannounced government boycott which lasted three years—because it failed to bid for a contract to supply trucks that could be fitted out with machine guns. The United States Government had said it would deny export licenses for necessary components. When Ford of Canada became interested, Ottawa—in consultation with Washington—adopted a similar policy, both governments cooperating with a United Nations arms embargo. A British affiliate of GM got the contract.) In 1963 and 1964, Ford and GM invested in engine assembly plants which would enable South Africa, in an emergency, to build tanks from the ground up. Only twelve countries in the world have this capacity.

Dr. Henry P. Van Dusen, President Emeritus of Union Theological Seminary, put the case against such investment in a letter to *The New York Times* from Johannesburg a few years ago:

Of course this is not the first occasion [he wrote] when American commercial practice has defied the conscience of the American people. In 1937, at the height of Japan's subjugation of China, a representative of one of the largest United States oil companies, when asked how he justified his sale of gasoline

. . . to the Japanese government to power planes engaged in bombing Chinese civilians, replied with a wry smile, "Oh, you know the answer. We'd sell to the Devil himself if he paid cash."

But there seldom has been a more flagrant instance of American business' disregard of national conviction. Let there be no underestimate of the importance which the ruling minority in South Africa attaches to American financial support. I know from first-hand testimony that it is their strongest single encouragement to pursuit of their present policies. . . . One of the foremost statesmen of South Africa remarked to me in personal conversation, "So long as United States banks and business back us, we can go ahead."

As in most public questions, the issue is both ethical and practical, i.e., economic. It is an issue in which the United States citizenry are deeply involved. Every American who is a stockholder or depositor in commercial firms doing business in South Africa is indirectly a participant in the cruel repression of the majority of the South African populace, in the aggravation of violence, bloodshed and brutality which daily increase, and, it may well be, in the ultimate loss of American financial investment.

To say that every stockholder is an indirect "participant" in the cruelty of apartheid is overstating the case. But there is no question that he is a beneficiary of it and that he is helping to perpetuate it by encouraging its sponsors.

He is also doing a disservice to the United States. The existence of massive private investment in South Africa is a severe handicap to American and British diplomacy, an albatross around the necks of Washington and London. It makes the United States and Britain to some extent hostages of the South African Government, in that South Africa has a weapon of reprisal for use if they join in international pressure for an end to apartheid. It subjects the United States and Britain to frequent and intense, if often irrational, criticism in the United Nations and elsewhere.

Communists rarely pass up a chance to insinuate or charge that the dollar stake is the principal motive behind British-American inaction on South Africa. Washington and London, Moscow says, are really hand in glove with Pretoria, insincere in their opposition to apartheid. A business lobby in Washington is portrayed as pulling the strings. In March 1968, for example, when the United Nations Security Council was demanding the release of South-West African guerrilla fighters whom Pretoria had captured, tried (under a retroactive law) and imprisoned, Soviet delegate Platon D. Morozov professed to see the evil hand of western "imperialists" behind South African behavior. "The Pretoria racists," he charged, "would never have dared to act in such defiance, had they not continued to enjoy wide support from certain imperialist powers, principally the United States of America, Great Britain and the Federal Republic of Germany, the political and military allies and the principal economic and trading partners of the so-called Republic of South Africa. These countries continue to give full assistance and support to the Pretoria racists, doing the bidding of the international monopolies that stand behind their backs and that are interested in the exploitation of the vast natural wealth of South-West Africa. The interests of these monopolies are served by the racist régime of Pretoria in the southern part of the African continent. . . ."

This modern application of economic determinism has far more currency than it deserves. The idea that American business is engaged in a sinister conspiracy to keep South African non-whites in bondage for the sake of exploitation and profit making is nonsense. The old saw about Wall Street being Washington's puppeteer went out with the Charleston in the twenties. But there is an uncomfortable element of truth in the statement that influential and articulate business leaders, persuaded, perhaps too willingly, that apartheid is wise and constructive, or if not, that it is "evolving"—and in any case, that nothing can or should be done about it from the outside—contribute a share to American policy-formulation and legislation. A great many Africans and others move easily from this fact to the view that American policy toward South Africa is dollar-oriented, and that the United States and Britain are two-faced, professing to oppose apartheid but in fact supporting it. Even as moderate and pro-western a leader as Dr. Kenneth D. Kaunda, President of Zambia, told the United Nations General Assembly in November 1966: "I would like to emphasize that the accelerating fanaticism of apartheid would not have made the successful but deadly strides which it has made in South Africa were it not for the overt and open support, the confidence which the white totalitarian regimes have received from certain powers and their financiers who have poured investment capital in thousands of millions of pounds, as well as expanding their trade."

The fact that American business operates almost wholly independently of the government in most areas, including foreign investment, and is motivated by totally nonpolitical aims, is not understood or believed. Thus the spread of communist influence on the African continent is assisted. African leaders find themselves under pressure to adopt an anti-western posture and to accept the "friendship" and "aid" of the communist bloc. Prospects of stability on a deeply troubled continent are further reduced.

It would be a substantial contribution to the national interest to be relieved of this handicap. Until pressure on the balance of payments forced Washington's hand, however, the American Government did not even attempt to discourage investment in South Africa. When potential investors sought advice, as a number of them did, officials were instructed to explain the opportunities and hazards, but not to make a recommendation for or against.* The weight of evidence as presented may have tended to the conclusion that investment in South Africa would be speculative, but no direct effort was made to fend it off.

The existence of major American financial involvement in South Africa being such a manifest disservice to the national interest, it is hard to understand this policy. Elements within the State Department did, in fact, urge that it be reversed; but others, backed by the Commerce Department, successfully resisted change. Commenting on the 1968 executive order which at least

---

* In testimony to the House Foreign Affairs Committee, March 1, 1966, the then Assistant Secretary of State for African Affairs, G. Mennen Williams, defined the policy as follows: "The Government neither encourages nor discourages investment in South Africa. Potential investors who seek our advice are briefed on the political and racial situation, the outlook, and American policy and interests. The decision about whether to invest remains with the individual or company."

He added: "The Government encourages both new and old companies to maintain high standards in the treatment of personnel employed in South Africa. We believe American companies abroad should lead in such respects as fair wages, non-discrimination, pension systems, and the like. . . . American companies operating in South Africa are obliged to abide by South African laws; nevertheless, we are encouraged by their generally progressive record."

temporarily resolved the issue, Ernest A. Gross wrote in *Foreign Affairs* (July, 1968): "We may discern here a parable of priorities: measures to redress the balance of justice, no; the same measures to redress the balance of payments, yes."

United States citizens cherish their freedom to act independently of the government, even when their acts run contrary to what the government considers the national interest. At the same time, however, Americans are not permitted to invest in or trade with Cuba or Red China, the national interest taking precedence. The day is fast approaching when trade and investment in South Africa will similarly be seen to be so injurious to the country as a whole that the interests of the many will make it necessary to limit permanently the freedom of the few.

This would at least keep the problem from getting any worse. What can be done about the existing financial stake is less clear. It would be no simple task to turn back the clock. If American producers were to shut down local plants voluntarily and/or cease distributing in South Africa (a step hard to envisage), no doubt someone else would offer a substitute for their product—though if there were one which was equally good and equally popular, it would be on the market now. Perhaps the government would seize the plants and put them in operation. If the United States Government required the companies to sell out, it would have to reimburse stockholders for losses sustained, and it is hard to imagine Congress appropriating the money.

There would certainly be disputes over the extent of the loss. Not only might it be difficult to appraise existing property and intangible assets, but what of the possibilities for expansion? For how many years would profits be adjudged to have been lost, and what would their amount be? Would it be possible, under present South African law, to repatriate any of the proceeds of the sale? The United States might well have to reimburse the companies for the full $630 million value of their property, plus indeterminate derivative losses.

To be sure, this would be less expensive than involvement in another Vietnam, if it would indeed tip the balance against such a disaster. But as a preventive measure, ahead of a crisis, it is certainly well beyond the range of practical possibility. What the United States Government might do is to require (not merely encourage) American-owned firms in South Africa to adopt, so far as possible under South African law, fair labor practices: equal pay for equal work, a decent minimum wage (scaled to the cost of living), employee-safety provisions, disability insurance, retirement allowances, and so on. The United States having power, under its authority to regulate foreign policy, to prohibit companies from doing business in a foreign country, it could properly establish the conditions under which such business would be permitted. Or, if direct action of this kind were to be considered unconstitutional—the enforcement of American law on American citizens abroad being an uncertain and highly contentious area of jurisprudence—the same thing could perhaps be accomplished indirectly by requiring firms to meet certain standards in all their operations, including foreign subsidiaries, as a condition of doing business with the United States Government. (Many, if not most, of the major firms involved do seek to deal with the Government.)

Fair labor practices, as known in the United States, would be sensational novelties for most nonwhites in South Africa; with rare exceptions, they are utterly unheard-of today. The fact that they were suddenly available, or might be available, at American-owned plants and their American-operated subsidiaries would produce something approaching a revolution in the outlook of workers (and employers) at other plants. Indeed, though it would be explosively unpopular with nonwhites, the South African Government might well step in and forbid such benefits; it lays down wage scales, now, in most major industries and discourages special fringe benefits, sometimes threatening reprisals if employers depart from "generally accepted practices." Some American businessmen in South Africa are so afraid of government disfavor they keep their pay scales below approved levels. (Some even join government officials in boycotting racially mixed receptions at the American Embassy.)

If, as a result of obeying American law, the companies were penalized by the South African Government, the United States could legitimately provide compensation, either directly or through insurance coverage. If American properties were seized, the amount of compensation could be a subject for proper intergovernmental concern, and though stockholders might suffer, the American national interest would benefit greatly from the economic (and political) disengagement that had resulted. Indeed, some Machiavellian strategists and policy planners have suggested it might be good tactics deliberately (if subtly) to provoke South Africa into seizing American properties, thus getting the United States onto a safer and, from the national point of view, much more advantageous wicket without suffering a domestic political backlash in the process.

In any event, the psychological impact on South Africans of American pressure for decent wage scales and fair labor practices would be formidable, whatever the South African Government's reaction and whatever the outcome of the resulting dispute. The worldwide publicity given to the extraordinary labor standards the South African Government was attempting to preserve would delight Africans, inside South Africa and out. It is even possible the government would feel obliged to modify these standards.

Many other miscellaneous forms of pressure, short of total sanctions, might have a discernible effect on South African attitudes and pocketbooks.

The United States could, for example, transfer equipment and personnel from space tracking stations outside of Pretoria to the manned-space-flight station in the Malagasy Republic, thus helping to dissociate itself from South Africa and depriving Pretoria of some of its leverage on American policy.

The United States could cancel South Africa's sugar quota.

International airlines and telephone and telegraph companies could increase the price of service to and from South Africa. (If cable costs for news media were increased, however, it would have the undesirable effect of cutting down on the flow of information. In the case of air fares, international agreement would be required.)

Intergovernmental lending agencies, as well as large private banking institutions, could deny loans to South Africa. The United States and Britain have decisive influence in the World Bank, which, as of August 1966, had made eleven loans to South Africa totaling $241,800,000. After one which was announced in July 1966, Achkar Marof of Guinea, chairman of the United Nations Apartheid Committee, expressed on behalf of the committee "profound indignation at the complicity of the Bank with the torturers of the African peoples."

Stocks and bonds of South African concerns could be barred from the New York and London stock exchanges.

The arrangements by which South African diamonds are marketed through London could be made less advantageous.

Britain could treat South Africa as a "nonscheduled" country, denying her the imperial tariff preference which she now shares with members of the Commonwealth.

Firms doing business in South Africa could be declared ineligible for United States Government guarantees on investments which they make elsewhere in Africa. Some of the risk these latter investments incur derives from the fact of parallel dealings with South Africa—a risk it is scarcely appropriate for the United States to help underwrite.

The United States could expand its present arms embargo to include prohibition of trade in strategic commodities, including notably machine tools, sheet steel, and engine blocks. This would, in effect, classify South Africa (for this purpose) with the Soviet Union. Other countries could be encouraged or pressured to do likewise, especially Switzerland and the NATO allies, some of whom are selling fairly extensive quantities of arms to South Africa. The NATO Council could usefully be asked to adopt an arms embargo.

It is considered fashionable to brush aside such measures as these as pointless and ineffectual on the ground that apartheid is so deeply rooted in South African tradition, practice, and prejudice that nothing short of all-out pressure or force would dislodge it. This thesis may be true. Certainly the kind of partial measures that have been tried to date have had little constructive effect. However, the proposition has yet to be given a real test. It could equally be true, as other astute observers believe, that much support for the Nationalist Party is like sand driven against a piling. Change the wind direction, it is said, and sand will drift elsewhere. Make apartheid as injurious to the pocketbook as it now is beneficial, and there would be demands for change.

Whether this is so or not, it would seem obvious that the world community ought at least to try enlightenment, persuasion, and moderate pressures before calling in the steamroller. A modern Commodore Perry needs a wider and more sophisticated range of weapons than those used at Uraga harbor.

CHAPTER SIX

Sanctions—The Ultimate Weapon

The most difficult single issue in the whole catalogue of problems posed by South Africa is this: Should the world community, seeking to force peaceful change, dip into its heavy arsenal for the most drastic power it possesses—military and/or economic sanctions? Is it necessary, in order to avoid the ultimate tragedy, to employ the ultimate remedial weapon?

Eager to come to grips effectively with the challenge, opponents of apartheid long have sought to bring sanctions into play. They have grown impatient with the hesitancy of those who could give economic pressure real impact, the United States and Britain, and have tried to initiate the process themselves with partial measures of economic denial. These measures have been singularly ineffective. They have produced minor distortion and strain in the South African economy, but have done little serious damage. In some cases, they have hurt the sanctioneer more than they have hurt South Africa, while third parties, willing to step in and relieve the pressure, have benefited. This in turn has given rise to still more strident demands for total sanctions, and to still further resentment over Anglo-American caution.

It is in the United Nations that the campaign for intensified pressure on South Africa has come to focus. The United Nations has debated some aspect of apartheid virtually every year since 1946. The General Assembly and Security Council alone have passed more than thirty resolutions, while other bodies such as the Special Committee on Apartheid have produced dozens of reports and recommendations. Many scores of hearings have been held for complainants; hundreds of thousands of impassioned words have been spoken.

Yet, while all this has had some constructive effect in awakening world opinion, it has had little or no visible impact on South

Africa in the direction intended. "It is only stating a fact of life," the late Adlai Stevenson observed in the Security Council in August 1963, "to say that the visible result of all these discussions and resolutions in the United Nations and all diplomatic activity so far is zero. . . . There has been no forward motion; indeed, there has been retrogression [in South Africa]—calculated retrogression."

Even as an exercise in public information, United Nations debates on apartheid have long since reached the point of diminishing returns. They are normally held before virtually empty press galleries. The amount of space they command in most American newspapers is usually not more than a stick—a couple of inches —if that. This is not because civil rights is not a newsworthy subject, nor is it primarily because apartheid is not a "local" story, though that fact is obviously part of it. Sharpeville got a big play. It is essentially because most speeches on apartheid contain little that is new, and efforts by Africans to make repetitive statements newsworthy by the use of ever more extravagant language have tended to reduce their credibility and impact.

Nor is it solely newsmen who are unimpressed. Many United Nations delegates, if the truth were told, also are bored with the subject, referring to it privately as one of the United Nations' "hardy perennials." They stay away from debates if they can, discounting much of the perfervid oratory as an effort to impress a home audience—which, of course, some of it is.

Demands for action against South Africa nevertheless are deadly serious, and are intensifying. The influx of more than thirty new member countries from Black Africa in the years 1957 to 1968 has forced the subject to the fore, since it is a matter of passionate interest and supreme importance to them. Along with colonialism and economic development, it is in their eyes one of the most important items on the United Nations agenda.

Almost immediately after the new African states began to enter the United Nations, they made clear they would not be satisfied with the relatively mild exhortations on apartheid (and on the treatment of Indians in South Africa) which previously had been passed, year after year, by the General Assembly. In March 1960, they brought Sharpeville to the Security Council. Apartheid had never previously been before this most potent of United

Nations organs. They demanded that the Council exercise its powers of compulsion under Chapter VII of the Charter. The Council majority declined to do this, but ruled that the situation, "if continued, might endanger international security" and asked the then Secretary-General, Dag Hammarskjöld, to undertake a mission to South Africa. Like many others, Hammarskjöld came back empty-handed.

One of the first General Assembly resolutions the enlarged African bloc had a hand in drafting, the one adopted on April 13, 1961, requested "all states" to begin considering sanctions, hinted at possible expulsion of South Africa from the United Nations, and found that South Africa's policies had "led to international friction and that their continuance endangers international peace and security."

That fall, on November 28, 1961, the Assembly for the first time used the word "condemn" in relation to apartheid policies. It urged all states to "take such separate and collective action as is open to them in conformity with the Charter to bring about an abandonment of those policies." It also nudged the Council once again. (A tougher resolution, calling for sanctions, failed of adoption.) When South African Foreign Minister Eric Louw presented his views in the "general debate," outraged African delegates reacted with a vote of censure. This was the first (and probably the last) use of this unusual procedure in an organization of sovereign states where every delegate has, and nearly all exercise, the right to present unpopular views.

Despite the Assembly's recommendations, the Security Council was unwilling seriously to consider sanctions. (The voting balance in the two organs was very different.) On November 6, 1962, therefore, the Assembly took matters into its own hands and attempted to invoke them. It requested member states voluntarily to take "the following measures, separately or collectively. . . :

"(a) Breaking off diplomatic relations with the government of the Republic of South Africa or refraining from establishing such relations;

"(b) Closing their ports to all vessels flying the South African flag;

"(c) Enacting legislation prohibiting their ships from entering South African ports;

"(d) Boycotting all South African goods and refraining from exporting goods, including all arms and ammunition, to South Africa;

"(e) Refusing landing and passage facilities to all aircraft belonging to the Government of South Africa and companies registered under the laws of South Africa."

The vote was 67–16, with 23 abstentions. This was more than the two-thirds majority necessary for formal adoption. However, the countries voting "no" included all of South Africa's principal trading partners except Italy. Among the countries abstaining there also were many with substantial trade, so that the 39 countries declining to support the resolution purchased 79 percent of South Africa's exports and provided 60 percent of its imports. It was clear from the outset, therefore, that the recommendation was not going to be accepted and carried out willingly by the governments to which it was primarily directed. Sponsors of the resolution knew this before they proposed it, but they apparently hoped they could bring enough pressure on South Africa's trading partners to force a change of policy.

In one respect, some of the pressure did take effect. During the debate, the United States announced it would no longer sell South Africa weapons useful in enforcing apartheid. Other results, however, were scant. Even in Africa, there was evasion and heel-dragging. Ghana reportedly continued to buy South African steel and mining machinery, Tanzania pilchards (fish), and Zambia mealies (corn), though in each case the product was ostensibly from a source other than South Africa, having first been transshipped by a middleman. Uganda celebrated its independence in October 1962 with brandy and fireworks obtained indirectly from South Africa.

This is not to say there was no reduction in Black African trade with the hated enemy. Some African countries, including Uganda, greatly reduced it at considerable sacrifice, beginning even before the Assembly resolution. (Major reductions began in 1961.) Denial of overflight and landing privileges forced South African Airways to reroute its European flights by way of Portuguese and Spanish airstrips, lengthening the route by perhaps 1,000 miles and increasing the cost. African treasuries lost millions of dollars in airport landing fees. But contacts were not eliminated, and increases in trade by some African countries tended to counterbalance reductions by others. This indicates that even where political and emotional motivation is extremely high, economic pressures and the simple desire to "make a buck" sometimes take precedence. Where there is less motive to sacrifice economic interest, the incidence of evasion is higher.

Even communist countries, which habitually make a dramatic show of opposition to apartheid at the drop of a gavel, continued and increased their trade with South Africa, direct or indirect. A report to a committee of the Organization of African Unity, submitted by Kenya in January 1965, charged that communist countries were increasing such trade faster than the West. Red Chinese commerce with South Africa, the report declared, was growing at a faster rate than that of any other country in the world. Red China indignantly denied it, but figures obtained from South Africa by the International Monetary Fund, a United Nations specialized agency, bore out the charge. The Soviet Union made a similar accusation against Peking.

To help cultivate sales to China, South Africa stationed a trade mission in Hong Kong headed by a Z. Swanepoel who, presumably to build goodwill, used a Chinese form of his name: Swan-Po. As testimony to Swan-Po's efficiency, one intelligence report places Peking's purchases from South Africa at $15,750,000 in 1962 and three times that figure in 1963.

In Europe, East Germany actively imported fish meal and hides from South Africa, soon becoming, next to Great Britain, South Africa's biggest customer for fish meal.* Czechoslovakia and Poland also increased their trade following the United Nations crackdown, and Albania began trade for the first time.† Yugoslavia and Hungary continued to trade on a reduced scale. Business apparently is business—even to followers of Marx and Lenin.

Outside the communist bloc, compliance was similarly spotty or nonexistent. The United States, Britain, West Germany, and Japan continued to be South Africa's principal trading partners,

---

* East Germany bought 29,400 metric tons in 1963 at a cost of $2,940,000. (The corresponding figure for 1960, before the United Nations sanctions move, was 5,300 metric tons.) An East European trade mission even offered, according to one report, to sell East German rifles and small-arms ammunition to South Africa in return for the meal.

† Czechoslovakia sold approximately $2,800,000 worth and Poland, $700,-000. Albania imported $900,000 worth of goods in 1963.

Britain and the United States accounting, together, for 46.7 percent of South Africa's 1963 imports and taking 39 percent of her exports (exclusive of gold). On a smaller scale, at least seven countries which, like the Black Africans and the Communists, voted for the United Nations sanctions appeal, also fell short of full compliance. They were Ceylon, Iraq, Israel, Mexico, Pakistan, the Philippines, and the United Arab Republic. Some of these countries had actually sponsored the appeal. In March 1967, Malawi even signed a formal trade agreement with South Africa.

As the United States has discovered in the case of Cuba, and Britain in the case of Rhodesia, it is very difficult to block channels of trade. Each trader is reluctant to forego advantage, believing—usually correctly—that if he does forego it, someone else will step in and fill the vacuum. So, under this "lowest common denominator" theory of international morality, everyone does what he believes someone else, given the opportunity, will do. To cover his tracks (and perhaps to circumvent his own government) the trader may consign the goods to a third party and have them transshipped—insisting, if exposed, that he knew nothing of the transshipment. Scarcely a single Afro-Asian or communist country involved has not denied vehemently that there has been any trade, the Communists first denying there had ever been any and then insisting it ended in 1964.

"The principal result of the boycott," Kenya told the OAU, "has been to impose great economic hardships on Afro-Asian countries which put it in force, to the profit of other countries— especially in the Eastern and Western blocs and some in South America—which have replaced them and increased commerce with South Africa." Whether this is an accurate summary or not, someone obviously must have been trading with South Africa, since her 1963 exports, by comparison with 1962, increased 10 percent to a record high, and her imports increased 18 percent.*

Widespread noncompliance with the 1962 sanctions resolution had a sobering effect on some African United Nations delegates. It demonstrated clearly the futility of paper resolutions as a source of meaningful diplomatic pressure, and focused attention

---

* Exports went up from $2,017,400,000 in 1962, before United Nations sanctions, to $2,219,600,000 in 1963, after sanctions. Imports rose from $1,-436,500,000 in 1962 to $1,696,700,000 in 1963.

on the potential value of mandatory sanctions imposed by the Security Council—where a resolution can have legal force and practical meaning, since key countries can block the proposal unless they are prepared to carry it out. Whipped on by extremists, however, Africans continued to make fiery speeches and pass sweeping Assembly resolutions (by this time they had the votes to do the latter virtually at will), hoping for leverage on the United States and Britain but succeeding, in most instances, in devaluing the currency of Assembly decisions.

One decision which got partial results was a call, in November 1963, for all states voluntarily to refrain from supplying arms, military equipment, or "any petroleum or petroleum products" to South Africa. Since the 1962 resolution had already called for a ban on intercourse of all kinds, this measure seemed redundant; but African delegates considered it useful to single out the proposed arms and oil embargoes, perhaps as a device to annoy (and hence, hopefully to pressure) the West. The call for an embargo on oil was almost completely ignored by countries whose actions mattered. The arms ban, however—followed as it was by pressure in the Security Council to the same end—elicited from the United States an announcement that as of January 1, 1964, unless some major overriding consideration of national security intervened, no further arms or military equipment of any kind would be sold to South Africa. Britain's new Labor government followed in late 1964 with a similar action,* though after a considerable flap, it did agree to follow through with delivery of a number of Buccaneer low-level attack bombers previously ordered. Pretoria had issued what the South African Information Service called a "clear ultimatum" to Britain that if the bombers were not forthcoming, British vessels would be denied the use of Simonstown Naval Base, important for refueling and repairs. (Later, in November 1965, when Prime Minister Ian Smith of breakaway Rhodesia was able to discourage a British invasion

---

* In December 1967, with Britain under great pressure to stabilize the newly devalued pound, Prime Minister Harold Wilson was very hard put to maintain the ban. South Africa had offered to buy a reported $500 million worth of frigates, fighter planes, and other heavy items, and several cabinet members favored accepting the bid. So did the Confederation of British Industry, which protested the decision to reject it as a "blow to the whole of our export trade with South Africa and to confidence in the realism of Government policies."

in part because of military strength Britain herself had earlier supplied, the case of the Buccaneers to South Africa was recalled. Would they ever be used to thwart a British-supported blockade? Or to attack a fleet of United Nations submarines enforcing an oil embargo?)

One immediate effect of the ban was to spur domestic South African arms production. By May 1965, the then Defense Minister James Fouché was able to boast that South Africa was practically self-sufficient in arms. Some doubt was cast on this, however, when word leaked out in Washington that Fouché had sought unsuccessfully to buy $100,000,000 to $150,000,000 worth of American military hardware, including electronic equipment for an advanced marine patrol aircraft, the Atlantic 1150.

Unlike other sanctions moves, the 1963 arms and oil embargoes were aimed primarily at securing independence for the mandated territory of South-West Africa, rather than at apartheid itself. "South-West" is an issue of which the world is now hearing, and is likely to go on hearing, a great deal. It could even be the trigger for a climactic showdown between Black and White Africa.

The international community has a legitimate interest in South-West Africa. Conquered by South Africa from the Germans in World War I, this desert frontier, rich in diamonds and other minerals, fell under the League of Nations mandate system and was assigned to South Africa. South Africa considered the territory hers by right of conquest, and only reluctantly accepted the responsibility of reporting to the League. When the League died, South Africa wanted at long last to annex the territory. From time to time she tried to persuade the United Nations to keep hands off. Failing this, she went ahead and treated the territory almost as if it had been annexed.

The United Nations did not agree the mandate had lost any of its force or relevance. All other League of Nations mandates had been placed under the United Nations trusteeship system, and the United Nations majority could not see why "South-West" should be an exception. The issue was taken to the International Court of Justice (the World Court). In 1950, in an advisory opinion, the Court decided the United Nations was the League's successor, that the mandate did still exist, and that South Africa could not modify its terms unilaterally. South Africa was not obliged to put the territory under the United Nations trusteeship system, the Court said, but could not have any rights deriving from the mandate without corresponding obligations. While this did not dot all the *i*'s and cross all the *t*'s, it left the United Nations with a strong case for continuing responsibility, which, in fact, it sought unsuccessfully to assert.

The struggle is still in process. In late 1960, some seven months after Sharpeville, Liberia and Ethiopia, as former members of the League, haled South Africa before the Court on charges that the terms of the mandate were being violated. A former American diplomat, Ernest A. Gross of Curtis Mallet-Prevost Colt and Mosle, New York, represented the plaintiffs. On behalf of all the independent African states, they asked the Court to find:

1. That South Africa was under an obligation to submit to the supervision and control of the General Assembly with regard to the exercise of the mandate.

2. That the territory could not legally be incorporated into South Africa, nor could South Africa take any other action "inconsistent with the international status of the territory" or hinder its "orderly development" toward self-government.

3. That by applying apartheid to South-West Africa, South Africa had, in the light of "applicable" international norms and standards, "failed to promote to the utmost the material and moral well-being and social progress of the inhabitants of the territory" as it was obliged to do under Article 2 of the mandate; and that consequently, South Africa had "the duty forthwith to cease the practice of apartheid in the territory."

There were other requests, including the submission by South Africa of annual reports to the Assembly and the transmission of petitions from inhabitants. Liberia and Ethiopia did not ask the Court to cancel the mandate.

South Africa chose to appear and contest the action, a decision which surprised many. First Pretoria challenged the Court's jurisdiction, and when it lost on this point, remained to argue the substance of the case. The Court decision assuming jurisdiction, in 1962, was by the narrow margin of 8–7 *—a circumstance which was subsequently to prove significant.

In July 1966, after hearing four years of argument and sifting

---

* Judges from the United States, the Soviet Union, Japan, the United Arab Republic, and three Latin American countries ruled affirmatively, while those from Britain, France, Greece, Italy, Australia, and Poland were in the minority. Judges appointed by the appellants and by South Africa joined the majority and minority respectively, making it an 8–7 decision.

mountainous volumes of evidence, the Court in effect reversed itself. With one judge (from Pakistan) disqualified by the Court President over the judge's protest, a second (from the United Arab Republic) having died, and a third (from Peru) too ill to participate, the 1962 minority had the votes to overturn the previous ruling. (Certain other changes in the composition of the Court compensated for the loss of two of the votes.) The Court decided that although Liberia and Ethiopia had been within their rights to bring suit, they had insufficient standing—"legal right or interest"—to obtain a judgment on the merits. The majority therefore threw the case out of court without ruling on the substance of the complaint. The margin was again 8–7, or rather, it was a 7–7 tie, which entitled the Australian President, Sir Percy Spender, to vote a second time, employing his "casting" vote.*

The decision was explosively unpopular with Black Africans, and surprised a great many other people. It was widely criticized. The African bloc at the United Nations, then 36 in number, expressed "dismay and indignation," and called it "incredible." "Doubts" had even been created regarding the Court's "integrity," the African delegates stated officially. Privately, in the first flush of anger, some pointed to the fact that the majority had been comprised of Europeans and an Australian—all white men—and hinted melodramatically at a "racist conspiracy." The chairman of the African bloc said no African country would vote to reelect any of the seven judges who made up the majority. Other delegates insisted there would have to be better "geographical distribution" of the fifteen judgeships, a phrase which sounded, in this context, like a euphemism for court-packing. When the next election to the Court took place, during the 1966 General Assembly, all judges who had voted with the majority and whose terms were expiring did in fact either retire or withdraw their candidacies. The Australian who sought to succeed Sir Percy Spender failed to be elected. All judges who were elected were considered "safe" on racial issues.

---

* The lineup was Britain, France, Greece, Italy, Australia, Poland, and South Africa in favor and the U.S., U.S.S.R., China, Japan, Mexico, Senegal, and Nigeria dissenting.

An aerial view of Johannesburg.

A backyard in Johannesburg. According to city authorities, roughly 68 percent of African families in Soweto (Johannesburg), earn less than the absolute minimum ($74.65 a month) necessary to maintain a family of five. (MAGNUM PHOTOS)

A view of Cato Manor—a former African shanty town in Durban from which 7,000 families were moved to two townships.

Another view of a South African township. Such areas are isolated from white residential districts in order to give the army and police room to use tear gas and heavy weapons in case of emergency.

Some older townships, like this one near Durban, are themselves near-slums (MAGNUM PHOTOS)

Most working nonwhites commute by bus, bicycle, train or on foot. Here Africans struggle to force their way onto a crowded train.

(CAMERA PRESS-PIX)

A view of the inside of an African commuter train. (CAMERA PRESS-PIX)

Organized protests against the pass laws came to a climax in 1960 with public burnings of the hated passbooks (now officially called "reference books"). One pass-law demonstration led to the Sharpeville massacre (March 21, 1960). (MAGNUM PHOTOS)

Government housing developments in South Africa serve the dual purpose of slum clearance and population control. Separate "locations" or "townships" are provided for Africans (Negroes), Coloreds (mulattoes), and Asiatics (Indians and Pakistanis). Usually the area is surrounded by a fence (Orlando Township, for Africans, near Johannesburg).

Despite the improvement, Africans sometimes consider it a tragedy to have to move from slums. Some have resisted the change, and been dumped in a primitive rural Reserve. This young man from Besterspruit, in Natal, is disconsolate over a forced transfer. (CAMERA PRESS-PIX)

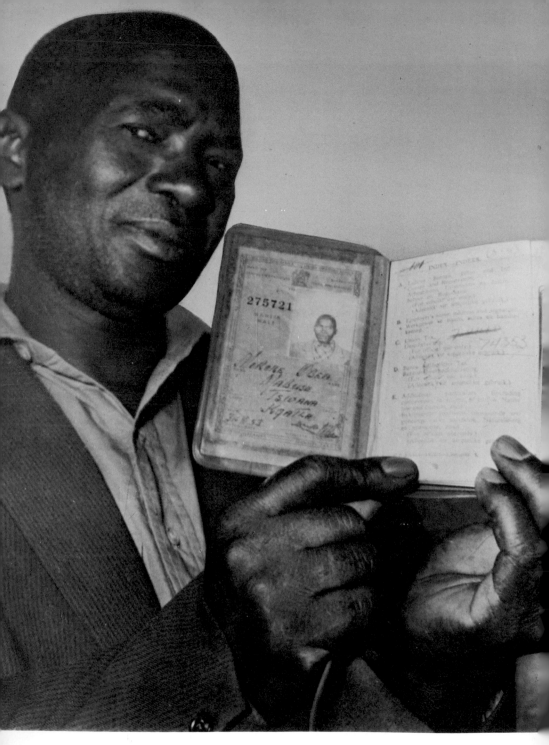

The *dom pas* (stupid passbook), displayed here, is part of a popula-
tion-control system which requires every South African black to live
and work under Government control. More than 1,000 persons a day
are prosecuted for violations of pass laws.

Many African mothers work to supplement their husbands' meager pay checks. Hours are long, and children rarely supervised. Sometimes, however, as in this picture, the youngest are cared for.

African schoolchildren in South Africa are crowded into classrooms with a ratio of 52 pupils per teacher. (CAMERA PRESS-PIX)

Africans provide the bulk of the labor force for South Africa's gold, diamond, and coal mines. White recruiters portray a stint in the mines as a badge of manhood for a young African. (MAGNUM PHOTOS)

Fear of revolution and other violence pervades much of South African life. Here a mother and daughter in Johannesburg engage in pistol practice with an instructor (right).

South African women, seated in their car, buy vegetables from a street vendor and his children. (MAGNUM PHOTOS)

Each Sunday, African mine workers perform tribal dances. Here Zulus dance at a gold mine on the outskirts of Johannesburg.

(MAGNUM PHOTOS)

A majority of white South Africans have chosen to deal with possible revolution by repression rather than conciliation. Here a group of opposition women, members of the "Black Sash," mourn the "death" of the Constitution. The scene was enacted some years ago.

(MAGNUM PHOTOS)

South Africa's daily average prison population is one of the largest per capita in the world. Here, in a rare picture of prison labor, convicts work under armed guard on the rock garden at the Voortrekker Monument in Pretoria. The monument honors Afrikaner (Dutch and Huguenot) pioneers. (MAGNUM PHOTOS)

Afrikaners—descended from the original Dutch and Huguenot settlers —have only recently begun to tolerate the English, who defeated their forefathers in the Boer War. The poster in this picture calls for "white unity," presumably in the face of potential revolution by nonwhites. (MAGNUM PHOTOS)

A street scene near Johannesburg. (MAGNUM PHOTOS)

The Court decision was an unpleasant surprise, for a very different reason, among African specialists in the United States and Britain. They had hoped the Court would supply a constructive and useful fulcrum for pressure on South Africa in the direction of peaceful change. A World Court order to cease the practice of apartheid in South-West Africa could have been made into such a fulcrum—one relatively invulnerable to domestic critical backlash.

Court rulings in contentious cases are, under the UN Charter, enforceable. Article 94 provides that "if any party to a case fails to perform the obligations incumbent upon it under a judgment rendered by the Court, the other party may have recourse to the Security Council, which may, if it deems necessary, make recommendations or decide upon measures to be taken to give effect to the judgment." The phrase "decide upon measures" clearly refers to decisions under Chapter VII, which authorizes sanctions of all kinds up to and including military action, although some authorities contend that a finding of threat to the peace would still be necessary. And UN member states are required to "accept and carry out" such decisions (Article 25). Had the Court cracked down on apartheid as a violation of the obligations under the mandate, a majority of the Security Council might well have favored sanctions to uphold the Court's authority. Under such conditions, the United States and Britain, which have a high regard for the rule of law, would have had little choice but to cooperate. To do otherwise would have been to undercut seriously all efforts to build world order.

Those within the government who wished to act in any event would have been glad to have had this powerful additional impulse to action. Those opposed would have found it more difficult to build a public backfire against sanctions. Friends of South Africa in the country at large, including many right-wingers and detracters of the United Nations, would have had to paint the Court with horns and a pitchfork—a formidable undertaking, even for the redoubtable American right wing, in a country with deeply ingrained respect for the rule of law. The argument that the United Nations was "interfering in domestic affairs of states" would have collapsed. South Africa, on the contrary, would have been misgoverning a mandated territory it had received in trust from the international community. In such circumstances, South Africa might have been thoroughly isolated, except from Portugal and possibly from France.

All this, however, the Court made impossible by refusing to give the Security Council a verdict to enforce. Leverage for which the Africans had worked six years, and which some segments of the American government had hoped they would win, was denied. It was a shattering disappointment.

Washington suggested to the Africans that it still might be possible to take earlier advisory opinions of the Court and make them the basis of pressure on apartheid. The State Department pointed to opinions in 1950, 1955, and 1956 which had established the continuance of the mandate and defined some of South Africa's obligations under it. The Court, however, had decided in effect that the matter was political, not legal, and Africans in the UN resolved to press ahead in the strictly political arena. They demanded that the 1966 General Assembly revoke South Africa's mandate and set up a commission to govern South-West until early independence.

Looking ahead, they expected South Africa to resist the turnover. In that event, the Africans wanted the Security Council to force Pretoria out, using economic sanctions and, if necessary, military force. Indeed, the hope of precipitating just such a showdown with South Africa lay behind much of the Africans' planning. They proposed to equip the governing United Nations commission with a police force from the outset—ostensibly to preserve "law and order" in South-West, but in fact to help prepare the United Nations for the trial of strength they foresaw.

This route to a showdown with South Africa was by no means as palatable to the United States and Britain as enforcement of a Court decree would have been. Indeed, it was not acceptable at all as a shortcut to a confrontation. If revocation of the mandate was ever to be considered as a fulcrum for pressure on South Africa, much preliminary underbrush would first have to be cleared away. There would, for example, have to be a serious effort to negotiate with South Africa on an agreed transfer of power.

Many other considerations also played a part in their reluctance to start down such a road. The legalities were muddy; it was not clear beyond challenge that the General Assembly had power to revoke the mandate. Britain, especially, had serious doubts on this point. Moreover, as a practical matter it would be difficult to get American and British public opinion aroused to do or die for South-West, a part of the world which many had scarcely heard of. Defending the rule of law in the world would have been one thing, but enforcing a political decree by the Afro-Asian majority of the United Nations General Assembly would be quite another, especially when the Afro-Asians had been rebuffed in Court.

Most important of all, Washington and London had too much else on their minds to want a showdown with South Africa at that time. The United States was totally preoccupied with Vietnam, and the British pound, then $2.80, was in much too precarious a position for London to risk the loss of South African trade.

So, as South-West came up for debate in the Assembly, the lineup once again was America and Britain against the Afro-Asian majority—Washington and London heel-dragging while the majority fumed and stormed for action. What emerged was a compromise in which South Africa's mandate was declared forfeited, on paper, and a committee was set up to try to decide how to displace the South Africans in fact. The committee reported to a special Assembly in the spring of 1967, which in turn wrestled inconclusively with the problem and ended by setting up still another committee (or "Council"), this one theoretically empowered to administer South-West and prepare it for independence. An acting administrator also was named. The West fought to have included in the Council's terms of reference an authorization to negotiate with South Africa, but got only a very restricted mandate to "enter immediately into contact with the authorities of the Republic of South Africa to lay down procedures . . . for the transfer of the territory with the least possible upheaval."

The widespread assumption among Africans is that South Africa will never negotiate under any conditions—preferring, if necessary, a direct, climactic confrontation with the United Nations. If this assumption is valid, it dates from the Court decision. Conversations with South Africans prior to that time did not uncover a defiant, die-before-surrender attitude toward retention of

South-West Africa. Even all-out Nationalists who had a sentimental attachment to the territory like the one they might have
had for an adopted child, and who realized the territory's potential riches, nevertheless did not seem to regard it as a life-
or-death matter. After all, many of their fathers opposed the
declaration of war against Germany in 1914, and some even went
into rebellion rather than join the invasion of the territory.

I had a long talk in Cape Town with a group of far-right Nationalist MP's. I asked them what the government would do if
the World Court verdict went against South Africa. Their reply,
in substance, was that, although bowing to the Court would be
extremely distasteful and unpopular, the only thing they would
want the government to insist upon was the permanent demili-
tarization of South-West Africa.

They were afraid the territory might be used as a base for
guerrilla operations against the Republic. (Sea routes would be
used for most of the actual infiltration, presumably, since the
land frontier between South-West and the Republic is very difficult desert terrain.) Short, therefore, of permitting "kaffir states"
to by-pass Angola in their historic sweep southward from Black
Africa to the "white redoubt," certain "adjustments" to the loss
of South-West seemed within the range of possibility.

All this appears now to have changed. There were no indications from South Africa in 1966–68 of a willingness to negotiate
with the United Nations. On the contrary, Vorster seemed to
feel he held all the aces, and did not need to bargain. "South
Africa is administering the territory in the spirit of the mandate
entrusted to it by the League of Nations," Foreign Minister
Müller wrote the United Nations on September 26, 1967, "and
has no intention of abdicating its responsibilities towards the
peoples of South-West Africa." Pretoria clothed this statement
with practical meaning by clamping down ruthlessly on incipient
terrorism in the territory—seizing accused guerrillas who had
returned to South-West from training, holding them in jail in
South Africa while Parliament passed a law applying, retroac-
tively, to their offense, and then requiring them to try to prove
their innocence, rather than the prosecutor their guilt. The
United Nations fulminated helplessly in the face of such defiance,
and exploded when, in February, 1968, 30 of them were sentenced to long prison terms—19, indeed, to life.

Nor was there any readily apparent basis for a negotiation on which the two sides could agree. Both wanted the same territory, and the Africans, at least, were quite unprepared to divide it.

South Africa seemed to be hinting at possible partition when, early in 1967, Vorster offered to set up a new Bantustan similar to that in the Transkei, giving the principal tribe in South-West Africa, the Ovambos (45 percent of the population), a limited form of self-rule. This simply infuriated the United Nations Africans, partly because they do not want to partition South-West, partly because they scorn all Bantustans as frauds, and partly because it meant South Africa was proposing to dispose unilaterally of the territory after the mandate had been revoked. The United States and Britain urged Vorster to reconsider, and he did not immediately go ahead with the plan.

The net effect of United Nations efforts to deal with South-West Africa was thus to leave everything *de facto* just as it had been before the issue was raised. South Africa continued to govern the territory; the United Nations' gestures toward terminating the mandate had had no practical meaning; no confrontation with South Africa had been precipitated, and the Afro-Asians were furious with the United States and Britain. It was obvious the diplomatic struggle would go on, and perhaps get more acute, but no other result was likely.

Meanwhile the Soviet Union had taken a line that surprised many, including Africans who previously had hoped the Kremlin was in their pocket. Moscow demanded immediate independence for South-West Africa (which even the Africans recognized was impractical) and deplored the whole idea of a United Nations interregnum. "Independence or nothing" was tantamount to nothing, since everyone in the United Nations knew independence could not get 20 votes (out of 122, the total at that time) and could not be carried out, even if voted unanimously. The practical effect of this Soviet stand was to portray the Africans as "soft on Pretoria," making it more embarrassing for them to adjust their stand in the West's direction. This was an understandable tactic, perhaps, for Moscow, but a transparent one, and one not designed to advance *de facto* self-determination for the people of South-West Africa. Moderate Africans resented the pressure to be rigid, and speculated that Russia was deliberately holding aloof, waiting for the Africans to pay a higher political "price" for genuine, and effective, Soviet support.

Meanwhile Soviet heel-dragging sabotaged the African plan to prepare a United Nations police force for use in case the long-sought confrontation with South Africa developed. Russia argued that any enforcement action that was necessary could be undertaken through the Organization of African Unity (an assignment the OAU would have much preferred to shift to the United Nations). In part this attitude was an extension of across-the-board Soviet efforts to kill the development of United Nations peacekeeping "teeth." It may also, however, have been a warning to the Africans that they could not count on automatic Soviet support. At any rate, Moscow's opposition forced the Africans to shelve the project.

Although this Soviet heel-dragging surprised and disquieted the Africans, they were much angrier at the United States and Britain for having blocked a showdown with South Africa than they were at Moscow for its independent approach. Their bitterness showed up in what would normally be thought to be unrelated matters. Whether for this reason or not, Africans frequently refused to cooperate with Western diplomacy in the Security Council before and during the Mideast war of June 1967. At one point, just before the outbreak of war, they even declined to vote for a modest Danish resolution calling on parties to the dispute to sit tight and not rock the boat. (The necessary majority was therefore not available, and the plan was not offered publicly.) Much of the world was astonished at the West's failure to control the pace and timing of Council diplomacy in that crisis, and at the frustrating inability of western diplomats to pressure the Soviet-Arab coalition at key points. This weakness was directly traceable to the unavailability of key African votes.

Much of the history of apartheid diplomacy in the United Nations since 1960 has followed this same pattern, the theme being American and British efforts to restrain the Africans—and then, having restrained them, to avoid their backlash. For a time, it was a fairly satisfactory dodge to say, when pressed for a showdown, "Let's wait for the World Court decision." When this wore thin, the United States and Britain took to saying, "Let's study the whole question." There was valid basis for contending that the subject needed study; the idea of sanctions, particularly, had never really been thought through carefully, the practical obstacles fully weighed, and all the probable results, good and bad, realistically anticipated. But to Africans, proposals for "study" seemed to be stalling tactics, and to some extent this was exactly what they were. There seemed to be good reason to delay until the Court acted.

A reluctant Africa acquiesced in the establishment of first one, and then a second expert committee to study apartheid and its implications. The existing Assembly Special Committee on Apartheid having long since become, in Western eyes, merely a pressure group, the two new expert committees were established by the Security Council.

The first of these groups was in part the outcome of a remarkable speech to the General Assembly on September 25, 1963, by Per Haekkerup, then Danish Foreign Minister, in which, for the first time, a United Nations diplomat expressed concern publicly for the plight of the white minority in South Africa during a period of transition from white supremacy to majority rule.

> The approach of the United Nations to the question of apartheid in South Africa, [Haekkerup said] has so far been, and rightly so, that apartheid must be abolished as contrary to the principles of the Charter and to human rights. Recently most of us have felt that if persuasion was not sufficient to induce the South African Government to change its policy, other means would have to be resorted to. . . .
>
> The Danish Government is in agreement with this policy. I repeat: Denmark supports this line of action and feels that it should be pursued and pressure gradually increased. What we desire is not mere words or recommendations of a general nature, but measures the effects of which have been carefully studied beforehand and discussed thoroughly with a view to providing sufficient support from member states. . . .
>
> I must, however, ask myself and ask you a question which many members of this Assembly have certainly for some time been asking themselves quietly. That crucial question is this: is that limited line of action through pressure sufficient in itself to bring about peaceful developments towards a solution of all aspects of the South African question?
>
> I am very much afraid that that is not so. I am very much afraid that a policy of sanctions alone—I repeat alone—may well defeat its own ends, aggravate the present state of tension in the area, and bring the possibility of tragic events closer.

Apartheid today causes misery to millions of people. Its abolition will, however, pose other problems. It is the duty of the United Nations to show the way forward in solving these problems. . . .

We must face the fact that the great majority of the European population in South Africa wrongly assume that abandonment of white domination means abandonment of their own existence. It is our duty to prove to them that that is not so. It is our duty to demonstrate that there is an alternative to catastrophe and that the only road to this alternative goes through the abolition of apartheid. It is our duty to give all groups in South Africa hope and confidence that after abolition of those inhuman and abhorrent principles by which the Republic of South Africa is now guided, there will be a happy and prosperous future for everybody who has his roots in and wishes to continue his life in South Africa.

In other words, if the approach of the United Nations has so far followed a single line, we feel that it has now become necessary for the Assembly to formulate a supplementary policy, to make clear to the world what we would like should take the place of the present set-up—a truly democratic, multiracial society of free men, with equal rights for all individuals, irrespective of race.

Changing a society so deeply rooted in apartheid and dominated by a minority into such a free democratic, multiracial society may well prove to be a task which cannot be solved by the people of South Africa alone. I feel convinced that in such a process of development the United Nations will have to play a major role if we are to avoid a tragic disaster.

We must consider how, if necessary, we can in a transitional period contribute to the maintenance of law and order and the protection of life and civil rights of all individuals. We must likewise consider how the United Nations can best assist South Africa in laying the foundation of its new society.

In our opinion it is high time for the Assembly to give thought to the positive policy to be pursued in South Africa and to the role which the United Nations should play in coming developments. Careful studies to this end should be initiated now. If not, we may one day be taken by surprise and have reason to regret it.

Many governments, including—interestingly enough—that of South Africa expressed a willingness to pursue this suggestion.

The key passage was Mr. Haekkerup's proposal that the United Nations "contribute to the maintenance of law and order and the protection of life and civil rights" during a transitional period. The "careful studies to this end" which he urged were, in large part, what the first expert committee was established to conduct. The Security Council, creating the body on December 4, 1963, directed it to "examine methods of resolving the present situation in South Africa through full, peaceful, and orderly application of human rights and fundamental freedoms to all inhabitants of the territory as a whole, regardless of race, color, or creed, and to consider what part the United Nations might play in the achievement of that end."

The committee was headed by Mrs. Alva Myrdal of Sweden and had as its rapporteur Lord Caradon (then Sir Hugh Foot), a British diplomat with wide experience in the field. Other members were Sir Edward Asafu-Adjaye of Ghana, Dey Ould Sidi Baba of Morocco, and Josip Djerdja of Yugoslavia. (Djerdja later resigned.)

Even before the group met, it became abundantly clear that Africans did not want attention shifted from the plight of nonwhites to the possible needs of whites. Nor did they want any official public analysis to spring from the assumption that African majority rule in South Africa might be anything but orderly, responsible, stable, and competent, with full protection for the rights of all.

"It is not true that the enfranchisement of all will result in racial domination," Nelson Mandela later said at the "Rivonia trial" in an eloquent statement of the African view. "Political division based on color is entirely artificial, and when it disappears, so will the domination of one color group by another. The ANC [African National Congress] has spent half a century fighting racialism. When it triumphs, it will not change that policy. . . . During my lifetime, I have dedicated myself to this struggle of the African people. I have fought against white domination, and I have fought against black domination. I have cherished the ideal of a democratic and free society in which all persons live together in harmony and with equal opportunities. It is an ideal which I hope to live for and to achieve. But if needs be, it is an ideal for which I am prepared to die."

So strongly did the Africans feel on the point that even

Haekkerup felt obliged to retreat. He instructed his United Nations delegate to explain (on October 9) that "we are not implying the concept of special protection for racial minorities. . . . It would be contrary to the very concept of multiracialism to give special protection to minorities just on the basis of race."

This view, no doubt, is unassailable in logic but it has little relevance to the actual state of affairs in South Africa. It makes the unpersuasive assumption that South Africa, under majority rule, would as a matter of course be a true democracy because most Africans wished it to be—or because they now wish it to be (white resistance being quite capable of breeding demands for all-out "black power"). It concedes more to African pride than it does to reality, and does not go very far toward breaking the vicious circle of fear, repression, and counteraction.

Perhaps it is true that the first break in the circle should come at the point where whites refuse to consider any liberalizing change whatsoever in the present scheme of things. Until they do, talk of protection for them in a transition period is necessarily academic. But an assurance of security would greatly contribute to acceptance of change. The unwillingness of many Africans to concede even that white South Africans do have genuine fears— for example, of political chaos, economic disruption, and racial violence—let alone that the fears might under some circumstances be justified, is a severe obstacle to progress.

As Francis T. P. Plimpton of the United States commented during the 1963 debate, the way to bring about change is to provide viable and acceptable alternatives: "It is a basic lesson of life not to push a man against a closed door." Alan Paton, one of the most liberal of South African whites, held that the core of the problem is "how to offer a man a chance to do what is right, and security at the same time."

The Myrdal Committee treated the African view with deference and did not attempt to map United Nations guarantees for a transitional period, though it did say in its report that "if the necessity should arise," the United Nations could "contribute to the maintenance of law and order" as Haekkerup had suggested. The group focused primarily on "the early stages of the 'peaceful and orderly' transformation"—confident, it said, "that when the transformation is started and a fully representative system of government is introduced, a wide range of international assistance can be readily made available at the request of the Government of South Africa."

Among the committee's comments on the "early stages" were suggestions for constitutional safeguards which could offer some reassurance to anxious whites: a federal system of government with firm local autonomy; a powerful Supreme Court; a bill of rights; special legal status for a (white) Opposition; and an Ombudsman similar to the one in Scandinavian countries and elsewhere—that is, a widely respected individual of national stature, appointed by Parliament to watch and guard against infringement of established rights, with extensive power to provide relief in cases where they are violated.

A national convention with whites alone in attendance led to formation of the Union of South Africa in 1910, when the country gained its independence within the Commonwealth. Since then, many moderates, liberals, and African nationalists have urged that a new convention be summoned, embracing representatives of all South Africans. The United Nations group endorsed this idea. "The future of South Africa," it said, "should be settled by the people of South Africa—all the people of South Africa—in free discussion. There can be no settlement and no peace while the great majority of the people are denied the fundamental freedom to participate in decisions on the future of their country." The committee even outlined a possible agenda for the convention. It also suggested steps which could constructively be taken in the educational, social, and economic spheres.

The committee's report was discussed by the Security Council in June 1964. The Council endorsed its recommendation for a popular "consultation" (constitutional convention); established a United Nations–financed education and training program for South Africans; and "noted" with "appreciation" the other recommendations. It did not set a deadline for action by South Africa (other than to "submit its views") nor did it decide to institute sanctions if rebuffed, as the committee had proposed. Instead, it created a second expert committee, this one to study the "feasibility, effectiveness, and implications" of sanctions (though the word "sanctions" was avoided out of deference to Britain).

The new committee was intended to consist of eleven experts, one from each of the countries represented in the Security Council as it was then composed, but France refused to participate.

The ten remaining members set about their work in July of 1964. In the eyes of the United States and Britain, one of their major purposes was to introduce a note of skepticism into talk of sanctions.

Pressure to invoke them was gaining momentum without, in the view of Washington and London, adequate appreciation of what they involved. An International Conference on Economic Sanctions Against South Africa, held in London three months earlier, had resulted in widespread publicity for the view that sanctions would not severely injure the British or American economy. In fact, the conference suggested, any negative effects could very largely be offset. Furthermore, if sanctions forced an end to reliance on gold for international liquidity, they might to that extent actually be beneficial.

Washington and London regarded these conclusions as highly unrealistic, and set out in the expert committee to put the facts in more somber perspective. To back up the United Nations study and facilitate American participation in it, the United States established an interdepartmental "sanctions committee" within the government to coordinate and evaluate available data.

The United Nations group set out to make a thorough survey of the strengths and weaknesses of the South African economy: the extent to which it was vulnerable to outside pressure, the devices that could be employed in South Africa to alleviate such pressure, the effect sanctions might have on countries imposing them, and the problems involved in making them airtight—including notably the problems and costs of a naval blockade.

The United States and Britain offered an array of facts and arguments to support the thesis that while sanctions clearly would injure South Africa, they would be neither quick nor decisive if—as expected—South Africa chose to go all out in resistance. Moreover, they would have important recoil effects on the American and British economies. The Soviet Union scorned this thesis, and others criticized it; but no one wholly rebutted it.

The United States told the United Nations, in response to a questionnaire sent to all member countries, that its imports from South Africa in 1963, were valued at $259,000,000—1.5 percent of total American imports from all sources ($17,140,000,000). Of the $259,000,000, something over one fifth, or $55,000,000 worth, could be obtained readily from other sources or were luxuries that could be done without; the rest—including especially certain ores and minerals—would be hard to get, causing "shortages in particular industries which would necessitate the use of less desirable substitutes and result in decreases in production. . . ." Other buyers who normally depend on South Africa would be competing with Americans for scarce substitute supplies, it was pointed out.

American exports to South Africa in 1963, the Washington account went on, totalled $276,000,000, or 1.3 percent of total American exports to all countries ($22,920,000,000). Alternative markets could not be found for most of these goods, it was said. Particularly hard hit would be the machinery and transport-equipment industry, which sells South Africa more than $120,000,000 worth of goods a year. The textile industry ($30,000,000) would also be dealt a heavy blow.

Assuming that necessary imports could be replaced, but that most of the export business would be irredeemably lost, the "initial adverse effect" on the American balance of payments would be "about $250,000,000 annually," Washington estimated. Add the loss of "invisibles," including investment income, and the total impact would be "about $300,000,000 a year," it was said.

Considering that the overall total of United States international transaction was in the vicinity of $40,000,000,000 a year, a loss of $300,000,000 (or three quarters of one percent) would not be "large," Washington acknowledged, but would be "significant in relation to the present deficit in the United States balance of payments." It was also obvious, though the Washington report did not say so, that both the textile and the machinery and transport-equipment industries would regard the loss as highly significant, and would be likely to make a good deal of noise if it seemed imminent.

Britain, which has even more extensive trade with South Africa, presented a still gloomier picture. She, too, estimated that she "could not expect to find alternative markets for anything like" the $560,000,000 worth of exports (4.8 percent of Britain's worldwide total) sold to South Africa. In one area alone—shipyards and ancillary marine industries—15,000 jobs would be "at risk" as the result of lost markets, it was said. Replacing imports ($321,-160,000, or 2.4 percent) "would involve extra cost, inconvenience and dislocation," London said. "All in all," it was concluded, "the

effect of stopping British trade with South Africa might be to
worsen the British balance-of-payments position by something of
the order of 300,000,000 pounds ($840,000,000) in the first year."
And there would be damaging secondary effects as readjustments
were made in the pattern of world trade.

Both Washington and London implied that sacrifice and disruption of the economy on this scale might be bearable for a short
time if the desired result—abandonment of apartheid in South
Africa—could be achieved. But that result, they argued, could
not be confidently anticipated. The South African economy is,
or can readily be made, self-sufficient, it was said, in all but a few
commodities: oil, ball bearings, spare parts, farm machinery,
transport and communications equipment, textiles, rubber, alu-
minum, chemicals, and electrical equipment (including such advanced equipment as electronic computers). Many of these things
are not absolutely vital, or can be stockpiled, or are susceptible
to substitution, Washington and London continued. Moreover,
short of a comprehensive international system of rationing and
inspection, sanctions would probably be evaded by transshipment,
they said—a surmise which experience with Rhodesia has tended
to bear out. (One of the features of the Rhodesian experience has
been "Mr. One Percent," the man at the apex of triangular trade
who takes a commission of at least one percent, and often more,
for acting as middleman in the transaction.)

The commodity which South Africa most needs to import is
oil.* Even if domestic production of oil from coal is being doubled, as some reports indicate, South Africa will still have to get
more than 85 percent of its oil from the outside. If this outside
supply were cut off completely, the effect would be very severe
indeed, unless or until oil is discovered in South Africa. Extensive
exploration and drillings, heavily subsidized by the government,
are under way.

The Rhodesian experience suggests that total interruption of
oil shipments could not be accomplished short of a naval blockade, since opportunities for evasion are great. Iran, which supplies

---

* In 1965, according to a study conducted for the United Nations by Walter
J. Levy of New York, South Africa had the capacity to produce oil from coal
at rate of only 7,000 to 8,000 barrels a day, or 6 to 7 percent of the 111,400
barrels (16,000 tons) consumed. There were no natural sources of petroleum
known.

most of South Africa's oil, has said it would not cooperate in an embargo unless assured that all other suppliers were also doing so. This condition was largely met in the Rhodesian case. It still has been possible, however, by elaborate devices, including dummy ownership of vessels and falsification of ships' papers, to get tankers as far as Beira and Lourenço Marques, Mozambique, with oil for rebellious Prime Minister Ian Smith. The British have successfully blockaded Beira under the authority of the United Nations, but enough oil has reached Rhodesia by rail from Lourenço Marques and by truck from South Africa to meet her rationed needs.

South Africa has been stockpiling oil for years. As early as January 1964, the government ordered that all available storage tanks be filled to capacity and kept filled. Moreover, more than one hundred huge additional tanks have been and are being built. Exactly how much is on hand today is hard to determine, but estimates start at a year's normal consumption, and it is obvious that in an emergency, rationing would be imposed quickly, reducing consumption by at least 25 percent without serious damage to the economy.

In addition, these other countermeasures are also available to South Africa:

It can bring in oil from overseas in its own tankers. A small tanker fleet is being purchased, and one oil company in Cape Town reportedly set out in 1966 to buy an entire oil field in Venezuela.

Oil could be imported from Portuguese Angola, which produced 631,319 metric tons in 1966 and is still prospecting for new supplies. The crude oil could be shipped by sea in friendly territorial waters, provided South-West Africa remained in South African control. On the same condition—indicating some of the strategic importance of "South-West"—a railroad or pipeline might be built across eight hundred miles of desert and jungle from Tsumeb, South-West Africa (the northernmost terminus of existing railroad lines) to Luanda, Angola. South Africa is self-sufficient in refining capacity.

Available supplies could be stretched by the admixture of alcohol. South Africa had an estimated 900,000 metric tons of sugar available for export in 1967, the equivalent of 368,000 metric tons of alcohol. Maize and fruit are also potential sources.

Some vehicles could be converted (though not without cost and difficulty) to the use of coal as a fuel. Coal is abundant and cheap. Wood could also be used; it powered vehicles in Germany and Scandinavia during World War II.

Not all the emergency measures would be taken on the South African Government's side. Opponents of apartheid would certainly attempt to sabotage fuel-storage tanks, refinery facilities, and the production of oil from coal. Isolated instances of small-scale sabotage, like water and/or sand in gas tanks, would also unquestionably be tried. The railroad from Lourenço Marques to the Transvaal, over which much bootleg gasoline would undoubtedly be shipped, could be blown up by saboteurs. Whether the police force would have enough mobility to curb these measures is impossible to predict. Presumably, the police would enjoy very high priority in the distribution of available fuel and would do their able best.

Guessing how long South Africa could hold out in the face of an oil embargo is therefore a highly speculative venture. If there were no naval blockade, she could undoubtedly hold out indefinitely, provided the police retained control of the nonwhite population and of other opponents of apartheid. Even with a blockade, South Africa might be able to get along for a period of years.

And a blockade is no small undertaking. South Africa has 1,800 miles of coastline and six major harbors. South-West Africa would also have to be patrolled, and so would Mozambique, since Portugal is a close partner of South Africa. On the broader assumption that a total ban was in force on all trade to and from South Africa, Britain told the United Nations expert committee in 1965 that four aircraft carriers and eighteen escort vessels would be required for a blockade, with another fleet, similar in size, to allow for rotation. The total cost would be more than £70,000,000 ($196,000,000) a year if South Africa alone were patrolled and more than £130,000,000 ($364,000,000) if "adjacent territories" were also covered. Some of this expense would be unnecessary if the task were simply to spot oil tankers, which are easily identified, but the operation would still have to be on much the same order of magnitude.

To guard against shipments by air, "very massive additional expenditure for an air-control system" would be needed, the

British delegate pointed out. Other estimates, as for example in a study by the Carnegie Endowment for International Peace, have come up with figures on a similar order of magnitude. Carnegie's estimate was approximately $331,000,000 a year for an air and sea blockade of South Africa (not including South-West Africa and Mozambique). By comparison, the four-week American blockade of Cuba in 1962 during the missile crisis (October 23 to November 20) covered 2,100 miles of seacoast, involved 180 warships, including at least eight aircraft carriers, and cost $183,259,048. The Pentagon had to assume possible active resistance by a great power.

South Africa is not a great power, but it would be unrealistic to expect her countermeasures to be wholly passive. If Pretoria sent its air force and submarine fleet to attack the blockading force, the United Nations might have to be reinforced, at considerable additional cost. It is even possible that response to South African attacks would plunge the United Nations into something approaching active warfare—the bombing of airfields, aerial dogfights, antisubmarine patrols, and other operations which would be costly in lives, equipment, and property. Unthinkable though it would be to everyone but South Africa's most virulent opponents, a blockade, actively resisted, could escalate into a full-scale land invasion by United Nations troops. In addition to all its other elements of tragedy, such an invasion would cost a great deal—$94,537,000 for each thirty-day period, the Carnegie study estimated, with four months likely to be required for victory. South Africa's first atomic research reactor, set up with American assistance under the Atoms-for-Peace program, "went critical" in March 1965. And if she were ever to develop ABC (atomic, biological, and chemical) weapons, all previous calculations would go out the window.

The Congo operation, the United Nations' most ambitious effort to date, cost roughly $110,000,000 a year, or less than one-third of what an unopposed sea blockade of South Africa, South-West Africa, and Mozambique would involve. In the light of the financial crisis that followed the Congo action, it seems out of the question, at first glance, to envisage new United Nations expenditures on the order of $1,000,000 a day.

However, the United Nations can do, or provide the umbrella for doing, almost anything its member countries want to do. If enough countries felt strongly about ending apartheid and were willing to make major sacrifices to that end, it could be done. The "financial crisis" springing from the Congo operation was not really financial; it was and is political. The reason that the Soviet bloc and France refused to contribute to the Congo Army was essentially that (for varying reasons) they did not regard the operation as in their national interests. And they wanted to be in a position to block, through the power of the purse, any future action of which they similarly disapproved. Were the United Nations majority, including the great powers, to regard a blockade of South Africa as desirable, money would not necessarily stand in the way.

The conclusion which the majority of the United Nations expert committee drew, after seven months of study, was that although South Africa "would not be readily susceptible to economic measures . . . she was not immune to damages from such measures." The effectiveness of such pressures "would directly depend on the universality of their application and on the manner and the duration of their enforcement."

The kind of thing that would be damaging, the majority said, included a total blocking of trade; interdiction of communications; an embargo on oil; and a halt in emigration to South Africa. But because of the availability of "means of alleviation" such as "substitution, rationing and redeployment of resources," it was "not possible to draw precise conclusions as to the degree to which these measures or a combination of them might affect South Africa's economic activity, or as to the length of time it would take for their effects to be felt."

United Nations documents normally need a certain amount of translation to get at their real significance. Long, difficult negotiation often goes into their drafting, with compromises and straddling of differences distorting the text. What this report undoubtedly meant was that the United States and Britain remained strongly opposed to sanctions and had been able to carry four other members of the committee (China, Norway, Bolivia, and Brazil) along with them. On the committee's report the vote was 6–4. The Soviet Union and Czechoslovakia submitted a minority report, as did the Ivory Coast and Morocco. Each of these reports took a view of the feasibility and effectiveness of sanctions which paralleled that country's political judgment as to desirability and its views as to optimum tactics. Just as the Anglo-American majority may have exaggerated the difficulties in order to discourage the action, so the minority unquestionably minimized them in order to encourage the action.

An independent observer (if anyone is genuinely independent on this subject) is led to conclude that a total stoppage of trade would be very difficult—indeed, probably unattainable, short of war, and perhaps not even then. However, a fairly substantial degree of compliance, even assuming unenforced sanctions, could undoubtedly be had if the key countries involved really tried. Considering that in the first six months of sanctions on Rhodesia, despite all loopholes, that country lost some 60 percent of its exports,* it is not unreasonable to estimate that South Africa might lose at least 30 to 60 percent of hers. The argument of the British and American Governments that they would suffer grievously from a 1 to 5 percent loss or dislocation of their trade, but that South Africa could manage reasonably well with a loss of perhaps one third to two thirds of hers, is not persuasive. Moreover, many factors which have enabled Rhodesia to absorb economic injury and meet her critical oil needs might not be present in South Africa's case. South Africa herself has been a major cushion for Rhodesia, and this is a favor the Rhodesians would not be in a position to reciprocate effectively, even if whites were still in power in Salisbury.

Thus to say that South Africa, while not "readily susceptible" to economic pressure, is "not immune to damages," is to back into the facts, with more emphasis on her powers of resistance than seems justified. Surely the real truth is not that Britain and the United States could not, but that they do not wish to, do critical injury to the South African economy.

There is another vitally important element in the equation: the psychological effect of sanctions or the threat of them. The United Nations committee mentioned this aspect, but came to no agreement on its importance. One can only speculate on the reac-

---

* By (perhaps optimistic) British estimates. Rhodesia herself, however, acknowledged that in 1966, by comparison with the previous year, her exports dropped £60 million ($168 million at 1966 exchange rates), or 36 percent, and her imports £35.5 million ($99 million), or just under 30 percent. Rhodesia's gross national product fell by some 11 percent in 1966, the British believe.

tion of human beings to a hypothetical set of circumstances. Much, though, is known of the South African mental outlook.

Sanctions are the one external pressure South Africans really fear. At the outset, the government and its more extreme supporters would react belligerently, seeking to rouse the country to all-out resistance. Some government leaders, including Vorster, the Prime Minister, have appeared at times to have a martyr complex. The tougher things get, the more they seem to relish the battle. "Just as God stood by the Voortrekkers in their time of adversity, so He would stand by us in our time of greatest need," they say. Some of them would appear to prefer an oxcart republic with white supremacy to prosperity with multiracialism.

For a time, they might carry the rest of the whites with them. There might well be a great wave of patriotic indignation. The country might rally to the government and sacrifice—as in wartime—to meet the common peril. On a more modest scale, this has been the effect of minor boycotts and embargoes imposed to date. They have strengthened the government, hardening public opinion against a policy change and embarrassing moderates by placing them in unpopular foreign company. This was the initial effect of sanctions in Rhodesia, also.

As time wore on, however, and the inconvenience and disruption of life continued, something analogous to war-weariness might well set in, especially if the outside world remained demonstrably resolute. Since exports represent 19.1 percent of South Africa's gross domestic product and imports 18.7 per cent (1966 figures), the loss of even half of her foreign trade would more than wipe out South Africa's economic boom and quite possibly plunge her into a severe depression. South Africa has not had such a depression since the twenties and early thirties, though there was a recession in 1945–47. The psychological impact might be formidable, just as it was in the United States from 1929 to 1932.

Some of the effects could no doubt be shunted onto the nonwhite population; unemployment would certainly hit that group first and hardest. But nothing could prevent injury to the whites as well. And as month after month of stringency went by, the government would more and more be called upon to answer the question *Why?* Its answer would be "survival." But if the outside world were in a position to reach a South African audience—as, for example, through a powerful radio transmitter—this explanation could be challenged.

Apartheid and survival are not synonymous, however persistently the government may argue that they are. Sooner or later this fact could be brought home to many South Africans. Then, if it is true that support for the nationalists is like sand driven against a piling, the drift away from them would begin. That portion of the electorate which has supported the government because its policies have produced gracious living, a booming economy, and a docile labor force would be disillusioned. Forced to choose between their ideology and their pocketbooks, a considerable number might choose the latter. The many moderates and liberals who have previously hesitated to speak out in public would be emboldened. Provided the democratic process had not meanwhile been suspended beyond retrieving (which, of course, could all too easily have happened), the extreme right wing might be unseated.

Who would replace it, and whether the new government would be a dramatic improvement, is less clear. The Nationalist Party has a huge parliamentary majority, and need not go to the polls until 1971. To buttress its position, however, it might bring to the fore a group of less illiberal people. Ideology is a useful tool to help retain political power, but when it ceases to serve that purpose or actually risks the loss of power, it usually is highly expendable.

Also possible would be an offer to form a coalition "government of national union" of the kind that often emerges when a country is at war. Or, the extreme Nationalists having been discredited, the party might split, taking its left wing into the United Party. In that event, Graaff would have a chance to show whether he is the imaginative leader his friends believe or the polished mediocrity his critics contend.

Just what his policies would be, he has never made entirely clear. It is presumed he would loosen up the police state, open the country to constructive external influences, and try to moderate the cruelty of white rule without changing its essence. This would not satisfy South Africa's black majority. For them, nothing but a dramatic transformation—a major effort at reconciliation and reform—would be adequate, and even that would not satisfy some of Black Africa. It is hard to picture Graaff in this role. But perhaps he would be able to play it.

The Progressive Party, with its farsighted program for a qualified franchise, could conceivably emerge on top because of its greater acceptability to nonwhites. But this presumes a tremendous national change of heart which, while theoretically possible, does not seem likely, even (or perhaps especially) under a state of international siege. It seems more probable that the Progressives would join with the UP in a new coalition of moderates and exert their constructive influence from within. Their voices would now carry greater weight for their having been right so long.

All of this assumes that conditions during sanctions would be such as to permit a peaceful and orderly transition from apartheid to gradual integration—which is quite an assumption. It is at least equally possible that the opposite would be the case. Encouraged by the crisis and aroused by the privations it would produce, including severe unemployment and shortages, the black majority might rise up in rebellion.

Whether or not it did so in the initial stages, there would almost certainly be a wave of sabotage. The whites, angry, desperate, and fearing revolt, might crack down on them with maximum force. This would provoke whatever resistance the blacks were capable of. The Organization of African Unity would undoubtedly seek to smuggle weapons, ammunition, and personnel into the country at such a moment (presumably having anticipated the need). If an oil embargo were eventually effective, there might come a time when the army and security police began to lose mobility and effectiveness, still further encouraging and facilitating revolt.

Sanctions, especially if enforced by a blockade could, in short, touch off a major emergency inside South Africa. Hope and expectation of such upheaval could be one reason why the Soviet Union is all out for sanctions, whipping on Black Africa and discouraging gradualism and moderation. The Kremlin clearly thinks Communists would pick up the pieces, and it could be right. If order did break down, the chances of restoring it before racial conflict had run its course would not be good. A United Nations peace force to protect white South Africans who wished to perpetuate apartheid would be totally out of the question; it could not get 15 votes (out of 124) in the Assembly, or 4 (out of 15) in the Security Council. Only if the purpose were to assist the revolutionaries, to hasten their victory and install by force a government acceptable to the blacks, would a United Nations majority favor police action at this stage—and this would be highly undesirable.

Compromise terms of reference, in which the United Nations force would be instructed to remain neutral and simply restore law and order, would be virtually impossible to carry out in practice, as experience in the Congo proved. Merely identifying the persons who were disturbing law and order would be a political act, necessarily reflecting the views of the majority in New York —which is to say, the views of the Black Africans and their allies. A United Nations force could not be injected into South Africa *after* a breakdown of law and order to do anything but hasten majority rule.

Among many other reasons why this would be undesirable would be its difficulty. Hastening majority rule would be a far more challenging operation than anything the United Nations has ever attempted before. It would be military occupation of a country against formidable resistance. Die-hard Afrikaners would be likely to conduct, at the very least, a resistance operation like that of the OAS (French-settler army) in Algeria, which tried to sabotage Gen. Charles de Gaulle's peace settlement in 1958. They might attempt something more ambitious; they certainly would if they could. As of today, South Africa claims it can muster 250,000 men in three to six weeks, and probably can. If the government lost control, the hard core available for white guerrilla-type resistance might be much smaller; but there would be few in the United Nations who would eagerly volunteer to take on active opposition even one-fifth that strong, unless they came from the Soviet bloc (which the West would certainly not be eager to see) or from Black Africa, whose soldiers might not conduct the operation with restraint, to say the least. Moreover, African or Soviet "blue helmets" would inflame white indignation inside South Africa and ensure maximum resistance. This kind of thing would have to be avoided at all costs.

Thus the imposition of sanctions, if attempted, would require great skill and sensitivity in determining how far to go and how fast. Too much pressure on South Africa could be as injurious as too little. It would be all too easy for the operation to get out of control. The task would be a little like cracking the shell of a walnut—exerting enough pressure to get inside but taking care not to crush the nutmeat.

Moreover, as Haekkerup pointed out, there should be provision for United Nations intervention of the right kind at the right time to "contribute to the maintenance of law and order and the protection of life and civil rights of all individuals." A United Nations force would be completely unacceptable to Pretoria in the early stages of sanctions; and to dispatch it after bloodshed began would simply be to involve the United Nations as a belligerent in race warfare. The problem would be to select a moment in between. Perhaps there would be a few fleeting days or weeks between the realization by white South Africans that change was inevitable and the onset of chaos—a period when the balance, in Pretoria and in New York, would permit of cooperation.

If so, a United Nations force comprised largely of white Commonwealth troops could be sent in at this point to prevent a breakdown of order. Ideally, it should be made ready in advance and kept on a standby basis, to minimize delay when the moment came. Cyprus is a kind of precedent, where the United Nations helped a national government restore and maintain law and order in the face of intense communal tension and under the threat of armed invasion. There would be no need to view such precautions as a reflection on the ability of either whites or nonwhites to govern the country. United Nations help was not regarded as an intolerable humiliation in Cyprus. The precautions would be designed for a period of interregnum before a new political order, under adequate safeguards, had been fully established.

The availability of such a stabilizing force could serve both to reassure the whites and to restrain the blacks. It would be an answer to Paton's conundrum: "how to offer a man a chance to do what is right, and security at the same time." It could make the decisive difference between evolution and a hideous explosion. The overall objective, after all, would be to persuade a majority of the whites to cooperate in a planned transition, not to exterminate them or to reduce to chaos the society they have done so much to build.

CHAPTER SEVEN

Running with the Hounds

In the last analysis, the question as to whether a modern Commodore Perry is to set sail for Pretoria rests with Washington and London. Balancing the hard-nosed national interests of the United States and Britain in southern Africa, and coming up with the answer—that is, with a clear, consistent policy line toward apartheid—is by no means a simple task. It is, indeed, one of the most difficult assignments a policy-maker can undertake.

Much less difficult is a description of what has been done in the past. The answer: very little. Somehow, the American tradition of government by consent of the governed, of equality before the law, of men "created equal, . . . endowed by their Creator with certain inalienable rights" has run afoul of "practical" considerations in southern Africa.

Anglo-American denunciations of apartheid have been as eloquent as any that have been voiced; it was a British delegate who came up with the oft-quoted description: ". . . morally abominable, intellectually grotesque, and spiritually indefensible." President Johnson told a group of African diplomats in May 1966 that "waste and injustice . . . result from the domination of one race by another." He went on: "Just as we are determined to remove the remnants of inequality from our own midst, we are also with you—heart and soul—as you try to do the same. We believe, as you do, that denial of a whole people's right to share their national future is morally wrong. We also know it is politically and socially costly. . . . As a basic part of our national tradition, we have supported self-determination and an orderly transition to majority rule in every quarter of the globe."

Just how effective and consistent this "support" has been in southern Africa is open to serious question. Both the United States and Britain have given way slowly, with great reluctance, to pressure for action which might significantly influence South Africa's conduct. There has been a significant gap between desire for change and action to achieve it. Aware that they hold the key to meaningful economic pressure—that, as Verwoerd once said, they are "the only countries whose attitudes or actions could be of importance to South Africa"—they have nonetheless resisted the application of such pressure, running interference for South Africa in United Nations lobbies when the chips were down. Their policy could be described as running with the hounds, but making sure not to catch the fox.

This policy is based in part on concern for the legality of sanctions as a remedy for a human rights problem. Washington and London concede that the situation in South Africa "seriously disturbs" international peace and security, but deny that it is as yet a "threat to the peace" in the Chapter VII sense of the phrase. They have argued that however abhorrent the policies of South Africa might be, commercial pressures should not be employed to influence those policies. The attitude might be summarized in nonlegal language as, "It's a rough deal, but it's their problem, not ours." To what extent this view springs from genuine conviction, and to what extent it is a device to fend off steps which for other reasons Washington and London want to avoid, has never been wholly clear. Probably the legal and practical motives converge.

"It is a basic principle," British delegate Lord Caradon said in December 1965, "that trade is not a weapon to be used to express political detestation of a regime in a particular foreign country. [Rhodesia apparently was a special case.] We trade with many countries in which the policies pursued by the governments for the time being in power are in our opinion misguided or worse. There is nothing dishonorable in this. If trade had to be dependent on satisfying a prior political test of the government temporarily in office in the country concerned, world trade would soon wither away." In accord with this "principle" of trading with anyone, anywhere, at any time, British merchants happily sold all they could to Sukarno's Indonesia in the midst of the "confrontation" with Malaysia, which pitted British soldiers against Indonesians in an undeclared war. Much to the distress of the United States, Britons have traded with Castro's Cuba and even with North Vietnam.

The United States, on the contrary, does have a history of using trade as a weapon—not merely against Cuba, but against the Soviet Union, Red China, and Eastern Europe. Still, Washington has pulled back from its use against South Africa.

"My government continues to believe," Adlai Stevenson said in June 1964, "that the situation in South Africa, though charged with somber and dangerous implications, does not today provide a basis under the Charter for the application by the Security Council of coercive measures. Nor can we support the concept of an ultimatum to the South African Government [such as had been proposed by the Myrdal Committee] which could be interpreted as threatening the application of coercive measures in the situation now prevailing, since in our view the Charter clearly does not empower the Security Council to apply coercive measures in such a situation." This remains the American view today, four years later.

More important than legal misgivings—which were, after all, submerged in the Rhodesian case—are a number of practical considerations. One is concern over the possibility that sanctions might be ineffective, even counterproductive, and drive South Africa deeper into extremism and/or touch off the bloody revolution which Washington and London fervently hope to avoid. There is no eagerness to test the willingness of the Afrikaner Nationalists to go down in flames in a Wagnerian immolation rather than "mix with kaffirs." The ability of South African moderates to step in and take control is doubted.

Some strategists also are impressed with the argument that sanctions would injure first and most severely the people they are designed to help—the nonwhites, who comprise the most vulnerable part of the population. This argument infuriates nonwhites. They consider it either shortsighted or hypocritical (or both). They are willing, they say—indeed, eager—to undergo this ordeal for the sake of the larger purpose. They beg the world not to hold off out of real or pretended concern for them.

Miriam Makeba appeared before the United Nations Apartheid Committee at one of its sessions in 1964 and read the lyrics

of a song which made this point. They were by Vanessa Red-
grave, and went in part:

> *You say that you want to make me free,*
> *Then don't trade with the men who are killing me,*
> *Or don't say you pity me.*
>
> *And don't you say, "It's a risky thing to do,*
> *I'm worried that the boycott might be bad for you,"*
> *I know how to live on nothing much better than you,*
> *So please don't say, oh, don't you say you pity me.*

*   *   *

> *Your leaders say they pity me*
> *But your thousand million pounds*
> *Are the seed of the tree*
> *On which they're hanging, hanging, hanging,*
> *On which they're hanging me.*
>
> *Oh, my loving friends,*
> *I can't get from my mind*
> *Those white bones in the sun*
> *That whispered in the wind:*
> *"If there's no help soon,*
> *Then hanging from this tree*
> *Will be thousands and thousands like you and like me."*
> *No money-making then and no ships upon the sea,*
> *Just white bones in the sun*
> *A-hanging, hanging, hanging on my tree.*

Most important of all, among the reasons for resisting sanctions, there is hesitancy in Washington and London to imperil
the solid advantages they derive from association with South
Africa. No policy-maker need apologize for weighing the national
interest, provided he has weighed it realistically. Indeed, he
would be derelict if he did not.

Thus the possibility of a $300,000,000-a-year injury to the
American balance of payments, and an $840,000,000 injury to
that of Great Britain, cannot lightly be brushed aside. Nor is a
total—counting both Britons and Americans—of $3,330,000,000
in investment a stake to be ignored. Moreover, South Africa
is a potential base for antisubmarine warfare in the South Atlantic. It is a way station en route to the East, an alternative to

Suez, which the West will find useful until nuclear power makes frequent refueling unnecessary. The availability of Suez under emergency conditions, including conditions of limited war, is at least doubtful, as the Mideast war of June 5–10, 1967, and the consequent closure of the canal so graphically proved. By the end of 1967, 1,000 diverted ships had passed through Cape Town.

There is a complex of American missile-tracking stations in the vicinity of Pretoria which is valuable both to NASA and to the Air Force. (The first picture of Mars relayed by Mariner IV in mid-1965 was picked up by the NASA station in South Africa.) Switching these operations to alternative tracking facilities in the Malagasy Republic would be costly. Using ships at sea more extensively would render instrument readings less accurate.

Unusually deep South African mines, 10,500 feet down, are well suited to certain experiments with nuclear particles produced by neutrinos. The Case Institute of Technology in Cleveland, in cooperation with Witwatersrand University, Johannesburg, has conducted such experiments. (Although uninformed critics have charged that they were atomic-bomb tests, they have nothing to do with weaponry.)

American astronomers and space scientists make use of a remarkable "hole in the sky" over South Africa—an area through which, because of special conditions, it is possible for telescopes to conduct exceptionally long distance observation. There are only a few other such "holes in the sky," and none of them is as good (the next best is in Spain), though satellite observatories and deep-space probes can now serve some of the same purposes.

Finally, there is the fact that South Africa is firmly (if not effectively) anticommunist and speaks of herself as a military ally. She fought at the side of Britain and America in World Wars I and II, and again in Korea. It should be pointed out, however, that there was much sympathy for Germany in South Africa in both world wars, and her contribution to Korea was small. No South African troops are in Vietnam, or would be asked to go; nor did they join the British in Malaysia, the predictable damage to the American and British posture in Afro-Asian eyes from fighting beside South Africans being prohibitive in each case. Moreover, the utility of South Africa's asserted anticommunism is in serious doubt, since Communists gain much advantage by assisting Africans against her. Yet the alliance argument is widely used.

There is no question that South Africa, were it a stable society and widely accepted by world opinion, would be well worth American cultivation. Even with the future in serious doubt, the advantages of cooperation with her are a formidable temptation to policy-makers. The really decisive question, however, is whether the advantages which will be available from such collaboration over the short and medium run add up to justification for a policy of "running with the hounds," of evasion and inaction in defiance of African pressure and of American traditions.

The answer turns in part on whether, by remaining aloof from meaningful pressure on South Africa, the United States will antagonize the rest of Africa to the point where other national interests are done incommensurate injury. No useful purpose would be served if interests in South Africa were to be preserved at the cost of losing even more substantial values north of the Zambezi. Nor would it be expedient, in the long run, to bet on the wrong horse in South Africa, alienating the people who, one day, will constitute the government of the country. Interests both north and south of the Zambezi would then have been placed in jeopardy.

There are highly important stakes to be lost in Africa north of the "white redoubt." They are not merely ephemeral and sentimental, as is sometimes suggested: the goodwill of 200,000,000 people and respect for America as a champion of human liberty (though this, too, is important). They are hard-nosed and realistic.

One example is trade and investment. In 1966, American investment in Africa exclusive of South Africa (direct investment only) amounted to $1,477,000,000 (by comparison with $508,200,-000 in South Africa). In Nigeria alone, Americans had invested more than $300,000,000. Diamonds, iron ore, crude oil, copper are only a few of the riches of this largely untapped continent.

Some parts of North Africa and Black Africa are not readily available for investment, and others have yet to provide a congenial political climate, but some warmly welcome American capital. And South Africa, for its part, could become a high-risk area on relatively short notice.

Exports from the United States to independent countries of Africa, other than South Africa and Rhodesia, totaled $442,400,-

000 in the first six months of 1967; imports $371,300,000 (by comparison with $272,500,000 and $131,700,000, respectively, for United States trade with South Africa in the same period). And the potential market, as Black Africa develops purchasing power, will one day be tremendous.

The United States has a massive, semisecret communications facility near Asmara, Ethiopia (the Kagnew station), which is one of the largest, if not the largest of its kind in the world. It is a highly important military and intelligence asset. There are American satellite tracking stations at Kano, Nigeria, and Tananarive, Malagasy Republic. Furthermore, the Voice of America has a 1,500,000 kilowatt transmitter in Liberia which blankets all of Africa.

The United States' position in the United Nations is profoundly affected by the attitudes of the 39 African-bloc countries. In a General Assembly of 124 members, operating by two-thirds majority, a bloc representing some 31 percent of the votes is obviously a significant force. And Africa seeks to maximize its influence by voting as often as possible as a monolithic entity. On such issues as seating Red China, African countries can hold the balance of power. On others, such as Vietnam and the Middle East, they have added to United States' embarrassment and difficulty. Increasingly, of late, the West has found them aloof to hostile.

Finally, there is, for any administration in Washington, the important practical consideration that 20,000,000 American Negroes, of whom some 10,000,000 are eligible to vote, have a latent and growing interest in Africa, related as it is to Negro prestige and racial equality. In some big cities such as New York, the Negro vote is of great political importance; and as a result of the Voting Rights Act of 1965, it is becoming a significant factor even in the South.

For an administration to side with South Africa would be for it to risk considerable political backlash—a backlash that is likely to grow in importance and severity. In June 1966, for example, a group from the Congress of Racial Equality (CORE) staged a demonstration at the United States Mission to the United Nations, protesting American "hypocrisy" in dealing with South Africa. Two protesters refused to leave the building and had to be wrestled out. Such pressure on Washington tends to counterbalance the weight cast in the opposite direction by business interests, or could if it were as well organized. The American stand in the United Nations for the creation of Israel is an example of how a politically potent minority in the United States can significantly affect government policy, and through it, the course of history (though in this case, there was no strong domestic counterforce at work).

Thus it is by no means a simple matter to balance the practical advantages of supporting South Africa against the advantages of joining in pressures on her. It is not a question of weighing interests against emotions, or practical considerations against ethics. To be sure, the moral case is almost wholly on the side of pressures, but the tangible considerations are much more evenly divided.

The United States has tried to solve the problem by an obvious device: it has tried to work both sides of the street. This is the real explanation of the policy of "running with the hounds" —that is, of opposition to apartheid in words (the declaratory policy) and resistance to meaningful pressures in practice (the action policy). Washington has cushioned Black African irritation by economic aid, by verbal sympathy, and by holding out the hope that one day, under the right circumstances, it might help crack down on Pretoria. United States support for United Nations sanctions on Rhodesia has helped nourish the latter hope. Africans cannot afford to disregard or lightly forfeit any of this American help. They have, therefore, with some exceptions, contained their dissatisfaction with Washington and continued to try to draw the United States to their side.

Washington's handling of South Africa has similarly contained the deterioration of relationships with that country. Criticism of apartheid has introduced tension and acerbity into these relations, Pretoria showing its displeasure by such things as public criticism of interracial receptions at the American Embassy. The American Consulate in Cape Town used to be able to free tipsy American sailors from South African jails with a simple phone call; now it is a process that takes twenty-four hours.*

---

* There have been extraordinary lapses in communication. South Africa once seriously asked the United States for help in training its army and police in counterinsurgency. The United States asked South Africa (along with other countries) to issue an Eleanor Roosevelt commemorative postage stamp. Both requests produced raised eyebrows.

Still, relations between Embassy and government remain reasonably satisfactory, the United States continuing to try—with less and less success—to influence Pretoria's policies, while South Africa, for her part, has not wished or dared to take any decisive measure of reprisal against Washington, lest the vital commodity, American resistance to sanctions, be lost.

The American policy of straddle is, therefore, achieving its minimum objective. It is preventing or delaying serious damage to the national interest. However, there is little future in such a stance. It offends both sides. The talk antagonizes Pretoria; the inaction, Africa.

It is, moreover, awkward and ineffectual from the point of view of positive accomplishment. It lives from hand to mouth, accumulating irritations. While temporarily it may fend off spectacular setbacks of the kind that sway electorates, it does not lead to the cure of fundamental ills. Nor does it prevent slower and less dramatic erosion of the national interest.

There can be little question that American and British interests are eroding in some parts of Africa. Mali, Tanzania, Congo (Brazzaville), and Guinea are major targets of communist subversion. In one nine-month period (September 1964 to May 1965) the Soviet Union delivered 1,142 tons of arms, ammunition, and military vehicles at Dar es Salaam, the Tanzanian capital. In the same period, Communist China delivered 1,025 tons there. Total deliveries as of March 1966 were estimated at 22,000 tons—roughly half from Moscow and half from Peking.

There are both Russian and Chinese military training camps on Zanzibar (at Chukwani and Mtoni, respectively), and both Chinese and Russian technicians work closely with refugee revolutionaries from the "white redoubt." Some 250 to 300 Chinese are in Tanzania. Elsewhere in Africa, governments sometimes seem to shuttle between Western and communist influence like badminton cocks, the West (at this writing) doing well in Central and much of Western Africa, but less so in North Africa. The ex-Belgian Congo, with its rich minerals, was for some time held together with CIA safety pins.

No one can say for sure that this would have been drastically different if the United States and Britain had urged, and joined in, pressures on South Africa. But there is every reason to believe that such a policy, combined with other intelligent and sympathetic attitudes toward Black Africa's problems, would have enhanced Western influence and made communist penetration much more difficult. This, surely, is the least it would have done.

By every objective criterion, American influence should be mountainous in Africa. The United States contributed considerably to Africa's emancipation. It is extraordinary that Washington should be not much more than holding its own in a contest with Russia and China—countries which have little or nothing to offer except new, unwanted upheaval. Clearly we must be doing something wrong.

One need not look very far to see what it is. What is lacking in the first instance is a wholly realistic scale of priorities. The principal Anglo-American objectives in Africa, in order of importance, should be these:

1. To keep Africa out of Chinese and Soviet sphere of influence.

2. To avert the catastrophe of race war in South Africa.

3. To preserve and enhance legitimate military, economic, and political interests north of the Congo and Zambezi.

4. To preserve and enhance similar interests south of that line.

5. To end cruelties and injustices which offend the conscience of mankind and can inflame nonwhites against whites in many parts of the world, including the United States.

6. To win and retain political power at home.

7. To strengthen the United Nations and advance the rule of law in the world.

These objectives, of course, are closely interwoven. They cannot be artificially compartmentalized. To list them in order of importance, however, is useful because it provides a practical test for any proposed line of action. Does this action achieve a minor objective and defeat a major one? Does it, for example, cling to facilities such as the Simonstown naval base, which could be useful in fighting World War III, a war which may never occur, while smoothing the way toward World War IV—a war between the races—which is much less unlikely? Does it preserve an existing economic stake (such as an investment in South Africa) at the cost of risking a much larger one (in the rest of Africa)? Does it buy time at the prohibitive cost of facilitating Sino-Soviet incursions—that is, does it buy time which only the Russians and Chinese are using to good advantage?

A policy which achieves these end results is not a contribution to the national interest, however advantageous it may appear in a limited context. Yet much or all of the above is a valid criticism of the present policy of talking but not acting on South Africa, of running with the hounds but not catching the fox.

One reason for the continuing tragedy of lost opportunities is that it is hard to get the State Department and the White House to focus on Africa for very long. Other things, notably Vietnam, take precedence—as, of course, some of them should. It is often said, however, that the only continents with lower priority than Africa in the United States Government are Australia and Antarctica. While this certainly has not been true during periods like the Congo crisis, there is a considerable element of truth in it—too much for comfort. Like much of the rest of the country, the government is only gradually making room for Africa at the top of its consciousness.

The Red Chinese have not made this mistake. A Chinese army document on foreign policy dated April 1961, which fell into Western intelligence hands, said: "The center of anti-colonial struggle is Africa; the center of struggle between East and West is Africa. At present, Africa is the central question in the world." This is an exaggerated view, and in the light of what has happened since 1961 in Southeast Asia, it may not now represent Peking's thinking; but it is indicative, and it may be closer to the objective truth than the American tendency to underestimate the miscalled "dark continent."

Washington and London are going to have to assign Africa a much larger share of their attention. Obviously it is not more important than preventing atomic world war, containing Red China, encouraging an East-West détente, and getting the North Atlantic community back on the rails. But short of supreme objectives of national policy such as these, preventing race war in Africa and eliminating opportunities for communist infiltration there should be among the first concerns of the government.

If they are not given such a position, they may demand it. At almost any time, Africa may thrust itself violently and unexpectedly onto front center of the stage. The theory that South Africa is a distant problem, the rightful concern only of those immediately involved, does not stand up under careful analysis. A storm is brewing there which can no more be confined to a given locality than a spring tornado in the Texas panhandle.

The United States cannot control, and may not be able to influence, the day and hour when this storm breaks. Black Africa, with help from the Soviet Union, can precipitate a showdown with the "white redoubt," forcing Washington and London to choose sides—quite possibly under the most disadvantageous conditions imaginable.

Suppose, for example, that a two-thirds majority of the United Nations General Assembly, fed up with American and British temporizing, voted to appeal for a blockade of South Africa. (The Assembly would have the legal right under the Uniting for Peace resolution to issue such an appeal if an American, British, or French veto had blocked action in the Security Council.) Suppose further that the Soviet bloc, reversing present policies, decided to cooperate with the scheme, volunteering naval vessels to patrol the South African coast. Such a reversal is not likely, given Moscow's attitude toward United Nations peacekeeping; but it is possible. (In 1967, Russia swallowed profound legal objections to the Uniting for Peace resolution and invoked its provisions herself, summoning the General Assembly to act in the Middle East crisis.) Russian warships enforcing a blockade of South Africa on behalf of the United Nations would be a nightmare in the full daylight. Prime Minister Wilson's phrase "Red soldiers in blue berets" would come to life (substituting "sailors" for "soldiers").

The cost to Moscow in rubles would be formidable, but the gain in political influence would be beyond measure. In one stroke, the Soviet Union would make of itself the idol and hero of Black Africa. Men who shot down Hungarian freedom fighters in the streets of Budapest would become, in Africa's eyes, champions of human freedom. A nation which persecutes Jews and discriminates against African students (to the point of provoking student strikes and demonstrations) would become a "torch bearer of racial justice." If the blockade were prolonged, as it might well be, the propaganda bonanza for Moscow would continue month after month, perhaps year after year. Nor would the gain be measured solely in propaganda mileage. The Soviet Union would obtain very extensive power to influence African government policies, since it would have life-or-death power over a project the Africans would want continued. Communist influence would be implanted in Africa for generations.

The United States and Britain would be in an impossible position. If they permitted their ships to run the blockade, those ships could be sunk by Soviet men-of-war on behalf of the United Nations, with all of Black Africa cheering. If Washington and London sought physically to protect their ships, thus combating the United Nations on behalf of continued trade with South Africa, Western interests in Africa (and much of Asia) would be incinerated in popular fury as by a hydrogen bomb. As a practical matter, such a course would be inconceivable, not least because it could lead to World War III by pitting Western and Soviet naval power against each other (with Russia on what much of the world would regard as the right side).

Yet to pull back Anglo-American shipping and stand aloof from a showdown would also be costly. The money value of the trade would be lost, and there would be no compensating gain in African goodwill. On the contrary, Africa would credit the Soviet Union with having forced the United States and Britain to break with South Africa, and again the Russians would be heroes. No Black African leader would dare or wish to remain a friend of the West if Moscow, but not Washington and London, acted to stamp out racism in South Africa.

It is easy to see why this possibility—by no means wholly hypothetical—has long been referred to by State Department planners as a "Horrible" (with a capital H). There would be no attractive option available. For Washington and London to allow themselves to be carried along in a climactic showdown against South Africa would be less damaging than to be neutral or an opponent; but it would not produce any positive benefit, and would minimize Anglo-American chances of influencing the pace and character of the showdown. The man who climbs aboard a bandwagon after it is well under way has little chance of getting his hands on the steering wheel. Having refused, until it was too late, to help bring about peaceful change in South Africa, the United States and Britain would have lost control of the instrument of forced change; while communism, which did cooperate with Black Africa—indeed, which undoubtedly would have helped to incite the Africans—would emerge the victor, whatever happened, both in South Africa and much of the rest of the continent as well.

This is precisely what can happen if things are allowed to drift. Time clearly is not on the side of the man who stands still. He may be able to delay the showdown for a while, playing it by ear and hoping something will turn up. But sooner or later the tornado will strike. A much better course would be to seek by every available means to prevent the crisis from arising, and failing this, to cooperate willingly with the African juggernaut soon enough to get a hand on the steering wheel and a foot on the brake.

It is by no means too soon to attempt such control. Indeed, the best time to get aboard and help guide the bandwagon has already passed.

What Washington and London need to do is to *apply as much pressure as necessary to force a process of peaceful change in South Africa.* They must, moreover, adopt this course well before events require it. Otherwise, they will not be able to derive maximum benefit from the action.

They must make unmistakably clear, both publicly and privately:

• That there must and will be change in South Africa, and that they want it to come without chaos and bloodshed.

• That their disapproval of apartheid is not a lightly held or passing phenomenon, subject to alteration if and when they become disenchanted with Black Africa.

• That these objections are directed toward policies, not people; that no one has "written off" the white South Africans or decided they are expendable; that least of all do Washington and London want them sacrificed in a bloodbath to satisfy someone's lust for revenge.

• That Washington and London are not asking white South Africans to "get on a slippery slope" or "commit suicide"; that, on the contrary, what they want is to save both their lives and their standards.

• That little can be saved unless everything is shared, and shared equitably.

• That what South Africa should do, in the first instance, is to open up its society to full, free discussion with all segments of the population taking part and the rule of law restored so as to protect the freedom of that discussion—all this to be a constructive outlet for revolutionary fervor, not a preliminary to violence.

• That thereafter there must be steady progress toward a shared society.

• That if this does not happen, the international crunch on South Africa will come—progressively, step by step, with as much severity (and only as much severity) as is necessary to achieve the end.

If this policy were adopted merely to save what is good in South Africa—to open up hope in a situation where hope is in desperately short supply—it might be open to the rejoinder, "Thanks just the same, but we South Africans know better than you do what is good for us"; or, "Mind your own business: you have plenty of skeletons in your own closet." But it would not be adopted primarily for South Africa, though South Africa would be its principal beneficiary. It would be adopted for the reason that it well serves the national interests of America and Britain; that no other available course would serve them as effectively, if at all; and that world stability, perhaps even world peace, may depend upon it. Even South Africa might eventually come to recognize the wisdom of what had been done. Robert Kennedy, as Attorney General, was burned in effigy on the campus of the University of Mississippi for sending troops to integrate its student body. In 1966, he went to Ole Miss and got a rousing ovation.

The kind of pressures that should be applied in an effort to bring about constructive change have been outlined in detail earlier. They should begin with things Washington and London can do on their own, quite independently of the United Nations: intensified persuasion and enlightened propaganda; clear moral disapproval, in both words and deeds; and pocketbook pressures. Thereafter, if these first steps did not produce the desired results, further graduated pressures should be applied, stage by stage, in cooperation with other countries and primarily through the United Nations.

Washington and London would have to be prepared to see this process through to the end. Specifically, they would have to be willing, as a last resort, to go all the way to total economic sanctions and a blockade if, unhappily, such extreme measures proved necessary. If limited pressure were employed vigorously enough and soon enough, it might never be necessary to use the ultimate weapon. That would be the purpose—to bring about an awakening in South Africa without extreme measures. Sanctions should be regarded as something to avoid at virtually all costs—because of their difficulty, the expense they would entail, and their uncertain effect. But if all else failed, they would have to be envisaged. Bad as they would be, the alternatives would be worse.

To minimize the prospect of using sanctions, the threat to invoke them should be made completely credible. To this end, it could not be a bluff. There would have to be a genuine willingness to follow through, made wholly clear in advance to South Africa—perhaps by actual contributions to a "blockade fund." (The money could always be used for education and economic development.) South Africans, for all their bold defiance, might well ease their policies before absorbing a blow this serious if they really were persuaded it was coming. At any rate, the alternative—a racial bloodbath—is so grim that to fail to try would be an utter abdication of responsibility.

Much attention should be given to the psychological aspect of the crackdown. The United Nations Security Council should set up a committee to plan in advance, and make public, a comprehensive program of graduated pressures which, when endorsed by the Council, would be applied in stages, from the milder to the more severe, until there was a positive response from South Africa. The United Nations thus should try to create a kind of inevitability about the prospective progression from one stage to another, with the result that relatively mild measures would not be sloughed off as insignificant but rather regarded as evidence of an intent to go on to still more damaging ones, the exact nature of which would be on the public record to confront South African scoffers. Under these conditions, steps taken to absorb and adjust to initial measures would lose much of their morale value; they would merely be temporary expedients, with worse sacrifices to come (which South Africa could anticipate and psychologically "feel" in advance). To be sure, a detailed program of future action would also assist the government in planning counteraction; but Pretoria has long been doing this in any event. The principal effect would be to encourage early capitulation.

One major difficulty with a course such as this is that govern-

ments are extremely reluctant to commit themselves in advance
to a course of action when all the relevant circumstances may
not be predictable. Neither the United States nor Britain, for
example, would wish to be irrevocably committed to follow
through with sanctions regardless of what happened. Nor should
they. But neither should they inch their way into the crunch,
minute step by minute step—so slowly that, as the pressure was
applied, South Africa would become economically and psychologically adjusted to it. The principal result of such a course
would be tension between the Africans on the one hand and the
United States and Britain on the other, since Africa would constantly wish to step up the pace.

The two policy extremes—total commitment and total freedom
of action—could to some extent be reconciled. It should be possible to provide both a commitment to a complete program,
demonstrating to South Africa the futility of resistance, and control over its progressive application, maximizing American and
British influence over the pace of events. One device to this end
might be to incorporate the program of graduated pressures into
a document similar to the stage-by-stage disarmament plans presented from time to time over the past fifteen years. Progression
from one stage to another could be made automatic in the event
of a finding by the Security Council that specified conditions
had not been met or specified acts undertaken. Such Council
findings would be subject to the great-power veto. The Soviet
Union, France, and China would then share power to halt the
juggernaut and to influence its direction. But except for France,
they would be more likely to use the throttle than the brake.

A useful by-product of Anglo-American control would be an
ability to slow the pace in case sanctions seemed likely to touch
off revolution. Similarly, it would provide a reasonable amount
of protection for South Africa from irrational continuance of
punitive measures after she had modified her policies. This, in
turn, would remove an argument which would otherwise be used
in Pretoria against capitulation. South Africans frequently argue
that "there is no concession we could make which would satisfy
world opinion." Still a further benefit for Washington and London would be the fact that South Africa would remain dependent
on their goodwill. She could not look to anyone else, except
France, to control the Security Council buzz saw as it approached,

and with Anglo-American cooperation, a French veto could be by-passed in the General Assembly. There would therefore be a powerful incentive for Pretoria to abstain from some of the retribution she might otherwise take on British and American interests in South Africa.

From a Machiavellian point of view, the United States and Britain probably could "sell" their diplomatic support to the Black Africans for a considerable diplomatic price in terms of African support for (or abstention from opposition to) American objectives elsewhere in the world. (Logrolling and vote-swapping are common practices in the United Nations.) There would be a limit to the available "price" in the area of the cold war, since Africans would also have to keep the Soviet Union in line; but for practical purposes, Africans need the United States and Britain, which are heavy traders with South Africa, much more than they need Russia, which has relatively little economic leverage on Pretoria. The "sale" of Anglo-American cooperation would have to be conducted with some subtlety, or it would antagonize a lot of people; but it could be done. To be brutally frank about it, the commodity could probably be sold periodically, over and over again. The only limitation would be the possibility of an African appeal to the veto-free General Assembly in embarrassing circumstances—this, and the fact that once committed to a course of action of this nature it would be embarrassing for the United States and Britain to pull back for less than persuasive reasons. There would be immense pressure from Black Africa and the Soviet bloc to follow through.

The real problem would be to resist pressure for a continuing crackdown in circumstances where partial South African compliance satisfied, or encouraged, Britain and the United States, but did not satisfy or encourage Black Africa. An important part of the program, therefore, would be to define as clearly and simply as possible, from the beginning, what compliance with the standards of the world community would mean. This definition of the United Nations' goals could not consist of a detailed solution for South Africa's domestic problems. Outsiders who do not fully understand those problems would be unqualified for the task, even if they could agree on a solution—which they would be most unlikely to do. Much of Black Africa would want immediate majority rule—one man, one vote. This the

South Africans would not accept short of revolution, whatever the outside pressure, and the West would not try to force it on them. Others at the United Nations, including some of the more moderate diplomats from Africa, would settle for extension of the franchise to all persons, of whatever race, who met certain standards. And there would be many variants of these solutions—partition and federation, for example.

All of this is ground over which intellectuals of many countries, including South Africa, have gone for years. To debate it in the United Nations would be pointless. It would bog the United Nations down in an eternal wrangle from which nothing useful would emerge. Nor would it be proper for foreigners to attempt to draft and impose upon South Africa what would amount to a national constitution. Any country in the world, even the Africans in South Africa, would resent, and quite properly resent, such an undertaking. It would certainly cross the border between legitimate international concern and "matters which are essentially within the domestic jurisdiction of any state." The United Nations would have to define the criteria for "compliance" in broad terms, leaving the specifics to South Africa.

One practical approach would be the one suggested by the Myrdal Committee in 1964: that the United Nations call upon South Africa to summon a constitutional convention fully representative of all the people of the country. This would be an entirely proper first step for the world community to request, since it would be a means of relieving serious international tension.

As of today, no word spoken or written by any person "banned," let alone in prison, may be published or broadcast in South Africa. A call for a national convention, therefore, would be a very radical demand in the government's eyes. Since the broadest possible airing of views, from all segments of the population, would be the point of the exercise, it would be necessary to free political prisoners, lift bans, and give opponents of apartheid a national platform from which to set forth their views. It would be necessary to recognize that these views are of value and that they should be given weight in determining the country's course —a revolutionary proposition for many South Africans. The Nationalist Party might well regard such action as political suicide, since its grip on power depends heavily on limiting the free access of South Africans to facts.

To summon a national convention would not be to guarantee that it would reach agreement. If a convention were to be called and were to break down in deadlock, a difficult judgment would have to be made. Was the convention held in good faith? Were all segments of the political spectrum adequately represented? Did the government take a responsible and active part? Was there free expression of views? Were there any improper restrictions on press coverage? Was there evidence of genuine effort to agree? Did each of the extremes offer to compromise? And so on.

If not, United Nations pressure could usefully be applied. If so, and if agreement had nevertheless proved impossible, United Nations influence could perhaps best be employed to keep the dialogue in motion and assure continued full participation in it.

This would not satisfy radical critics of apartheid, but it could have tremendous impact within South Africa. It would give the nonwhites a voice they do not now have, and would be a substantial increment to their political power. It would involve— the United Nations could properly insist that it involve—due process of law, a permanent end to banning (and hence muzzling) of nonwhite leaders, opportunity for peaceful demonstrations, and in general full freedom of participation in the political process, short of the immediate right to vote in national elections.

Explosive pressures which now have no peaceful outlet would thus obtain one. Having opened the door safely to limited political rights, South Africans might come to regard economic freedoms for nonwhites, such as the right to organize, collectively bargain, and strike, as less radical and drastic. Indeed, such freedoms might emerge irresistibly; and what would be even better, whites might discover that the results, so far from being catastrophic to their way of life, were actually beneficial to everyone, resulting in greater productivity, a more stable and efficient work force, a wider market for goods, and other benefits which responsible trade unionism has produced elsewhere.

If nonwhites did not exercise their new political and economic freedoms responsibly, or if they interpreted greater freedom as a license for (or even an encouragement to) violent revolution, it might be possible for the West to readjust the power balance by easing some of the pressures on Pretoria, or at least blocking the application of further pressure. If the process of reform were begun soon enough, before too much desperation and bitterness had set in, the opposite would be more likely: many nonwhites would join in good faith, and with much enthusiasm, in the effort for peaceful evolution. They would themselves have been given an enhanced stake in stability.

To the extent that nonwhites did react responsibly, the more open-minded of the whites would awaken to the fact that they had underestimated their fellow beings. Many a well-meaning South African today will point to an African and say, "He no more wants to vote than he wants to climb into a rocket and go to the moon." In fact, that African may be a cell leader in Poqo. With greater recognition of the real aspirations and capabilities of Africans would come a gradual erosion of prejudice. Just the discovery that "our blacks" are not "content" and are not being "blessed" would be a great eye-opener for many.

Discussion is not a cure-all, and it could not be relied upon indefinitely if there were no tangible results. But the free exchange of ideas in a free society is an immensely potent force, and it would be likely to have many constructive results. It would be educational for all segments of the population. It would be the fastest way to bring about the fundamental change of heart that is required. "Men are never so likely to make the right decision," Macaulay once wrote, "as when there is open discussion." Should the whites refuse to permit such a process, the world community could crack down progressively, with a clear conscience and a good legal and political foundation.

CHAPTER EIGHT

Storm over South Africa

An Indian, apparently the victim of a hit-and-run driver, was allowed to bleed to death on a sidewalk in Durban in 1964, while hundreds of people passed by, each assuming that someone else had called an ambulance (a nonwhite ambulance, of course). In point of fact, no one had. Something comparable happened in New York that year when the rape-murder of Kitty Genovese was observed by at least thirty-eight people and not reported. But the reaction in New York was one of horror at the indifference shown. In Durban, the incident caused little more than a ripple of indignation. It was considered rather unusual when a white man wrote a letter to the editor complaining about it.

The shoe can also be on the other foot. In August 1967, a white man was critically injured in an automobile accident near Mtunzini, eighty miles north of Durban. He lay on the road for an hour and a half awaiting help. The first ambulance that arrived on the scene was for nonwhites only. It had to, and did, leave him where he was.

A friend of mine gave her part-time maid six eggs—at a total cost of about 20 cents (U.S.)—at Easter. They were for the maid's six children to paint and eat. A white neighbor, learning of the gift, berated my friend sharply and at length for "spoiling the Africans." The maid's salary, for half-time work, was 5 rand ($7) a month, or about 25 cents (U.S.) a day.

The Johannesburg city Department of Non-European Affairs, in an official manual, "Your Bantu Servant and You," describes $22 a month as a good wage for full-time, live-in servants, if they are efficient. (The cost of living in South Africa is on roughly the same order of magnitude as that in the United States.) The pamphlet further counsels employers that, since servants "are human, with social, recreational and other interests," they should not be worked more than 10 hours a day for this salary and should get every Thursday afternoon off, plus every other Sunday afternoon. A 65-hour work week should be the maximum, the manual suggests. It counsels employers about servants' "feeding habits" and says a male servant should be called by his name rather than "boy," since "in his own mind he identifies himself with his name."

Such attitudes point to a kind of sickness. What is the cure? Is there, as the Prophet Jeremiah asked, "no balm in Gilead? Is there no physician there?" The fury of the outside world is not a cure. It will only make the disease worse, provoking in those afflicted a great wave of self-pity and self-justification, overlain with fear.

Violent protest by those subjected to cruelties and injustices can perhaps, by a crude kind of surgical operation, cut out some of the worst manifestations of the disease, but it can only intensify the attitudes from which they spring. Pressure from outside of the kind I have recommended can do little more than create conditions in which a cure may be possible.

What is needed is first a recognition by those who are the initial victims of racism—those who practice it—that it is an affliction which needs to be healed. This is by far the hardest step. Many South Africans seem wholly unaware of any wrongdoing, and many more consider discrimination perfectly proper, but feel it should be carried on in subtler and less inhumane ways. There is an almost universal assumption among whites that of course white men are superior to nonwhites—not just in education but in capacity to absorb it.

This attitude is not unique in South Africa. Millions of people in the United States will say they are color-blind, but will favor restrictive housing covenants "to protect real estate values"; will insist that all men are equals, but regard a Negro chauffeur as a status symbol, marking the employer as a kind of latter-day slave-owner; will say they are completely free of prejudice, but be shocked at an interracial dance. There is scarcely a major city in the United States, South or North, where Negro housing is not *de facto* segregated, and efforts to bring about genuine desegragation of schools, as distinct from token desegregation, meet with strong resistance, both in North and South.

Immigration laws in the United States have for decades had

heavy racial overtones. In Britain, some years ago, the large-scale arrival of Jamaicans was followed by what South Africans would call "influx control." When the Labor Party sought to ease the restrictions, signs were scrawled on walls in Smethwick (a Labor stronghold) reading, "If you want a nigger neighbor, vote Labor." And the Labor candidate, Patrick Gordon-Walker, was defeated. In 1968, when a community of Indians in Kenya holding British passports were crushed under "Africanization" laws and sought to migrate en masse to Britain, the Labor Government clamped strict restrictions on the flow. Both Kenya and Britain had obviously been motivated in part by racial prejudice.

Racism is by no means solely a white-man's disease. Caste distinctions in India are not essentially different; and though they have been outlawed on paper, they have by no means been eliminated in practice. People of Malay stock in Indonesia and Malaysia actively resent the Chinese, and riot against them (and did so before there was an ideological motive in the equation). Chinese, for their part, seek advantage in the struggle with Soviet rivals by pointing out to Africans and Asians that the Russians are white. South Vietnamese clash for racial reasons with Montagnards (mountain tribesmen) who are dark-skinned aborigines. They have been known to object (strenuously) on grounds of color to serving under American Negro advisers. Puerto Ricans and Negroes stage "rumbles" with switch-blades in Harlem. Indians and Blacks killed each other in Cheddi Jagan's Guiana (now independent Guyana). Scarcely a country is completely free of the disease.

Even in Africa, racism can be detected. Kenya's treatment of Indians is a case in point. There also have been violent outbursts against Indians in Uganda. Light-skinned Sudanese from the north of the country, Moslems, fight bloody riots against black-skinned southerners, whom they regard as an inferior race, as pagans—indeed, as *abeed* (slaves). The short, coarse-featured, and more dark-skinned Hutu in Rwanda slaughter the tall, patrician, lighter-pigmented Tutsi, wreaking vengeance for generations of treatment as inferiors by the Tutsi. Arab and Berber clash in Algeria. Mulattoes look down on Africans in South Africa, and Indians and Africans knife each other, producing some of the bloodiest riots the country has known.

So why single out South Africa for special condemnation and

punitive action? the superficial observer may ask. Let him who is
without prejudice cast the first stone. Is not South Africa a white,
Anglo-Saxon, Protestant ally, resolute against communism? Why
pull Afro-Asian chestnuts out of the fire? Are the Afro-Asians
concerned about the plight of Jews and dissident intellectuals in
the Soviet Union, or of Protestants in Spain? Have they gone to
bat to get self-determination for the Germans? Was there a hulla-
baloo about arbitrary arrests in Ghana, or communes in Red
China, or slavery in Yemen? Are there not scores of places where
human rights are scandalously violated, including parts of the
United States? Is the United Nations to be asked to intervene in
them all?

The answer is in two parts. First, South Africa is the only place
in the world where racial discrimination is proclaimed as a deliberate government policy, enforced with the ruthless power of
the state, and practiced for the purpose of keeping one race on
top of all others. South African leaders are not ashamed of race
prejudice and seeking ways to eradicate it. They are proud of it
and are seeking ways to perpetuate it. Indeed, through Bantustans,
they are inviting the establishment and perpetuation of a localized
form of black racism. Denials of civil rights in the Soviet Union,
Red China, Ghana (under Nkrumah), and elsewhere have
stemmed from political, not racial, motives. Cruel and intolerable
as such denials are, it at least is possible for a man to change his
politics. He cannot change his race.

Second, South Africa is a potential cause of what I have called
World War IV, a race war. Africans will not tolerate an island
on their continent where the white man, simply because he is
white, dominates the black man, simply because he is black.

Domestically, South African nonwhites have exhausted all forms
of protest short of large-scale bloodshed. From 1912 to 1944, Africans did their protesting, via the African National Congress,
through strictly constitutional channels: resolutions, petitions,
delegations to Parliament, airing of grievances. The net result
was one further constraint after another.

From 1944 to 1961, African nationalism in South Africa still
used peaceful, though more militant, and after 1949 illegal, methods of protest. These included demonstrations, strikes, and defiance campaigns. The culmination of all this was Sharpeville.

Only in 1961 did the nationalist movement, by then split into two parts, choose a course of violence. But still it was not primarily violence against people, it was violence against property—against the infrastructure of the economy and against symbols of apartheid. Now, today, having been frustrated in all these alternative courses, Africa is groping for the final weapons: guerrilla warfare, terrorism, and open revolution.

"Who will deny," Chief Luthuli has asked, "that thirty years of my life have been spent knocking in vain, patiently, moderately and modestly at a closed and barred door? What have been the fruits of moderation? The past thirty years have seen the greatest number of laws restricting our rights and progress, until today we have reached a stage where we have almost no rights at all." Nor are Africans permitted to have what would be, in such circumstances, the most precious commodity of all—hope. The government deliberately and ruthlessly crushes it.

On November 6, 1964, when three ANC leaders were hanged for sabotage which involved fatalities, Duma Nokwe, Secretary-General of the ANC—an organization which for almost fifty years resisted demands for violence of any kind—wrote the United Nations: "The African people will no longer tolerate a situation in which the loss of life is on our side only. The systematic murder of our people will be replied to on the basis of a life for a life." It was not true that until then no whites had lost their lives. But it was true that few had been killed intentionally, as a form of protest against apartheid. Now, it appeared this policy had been or would soon be scrapped. How soon, Nokwe did not say.

If it is, and if nothing is done to prevent it, a storm will break over Africa which will rock the world to the core, stirring emotions rarely seen since the days of the religious wars, if then. "The confrontation based on color," President Kaunda of Zambia has said, "will be the major factor in international unsettlement in the rest of the twentieth century as ideology and the cold war have been in its first half." Independent nations of Black Africa will be involved from the beginning. The communist states undoubtedly will soon follow. To think that the West will be able to stand on the sidelines is dangerous self-delusion. When this problem hits the fan, no one will be able to remain neutral.

Just what form the conflict will take remains to be seen. The presumption is that it will consist of a feedback of saboteurs and guerrillas from training camps in Africa, the Soviet bloc, and

China. There would also be volunteers from such countries as Algeria, penetrating South Africa via Zambia and Botswana, or, if feasible, from Rhodesia or from along the shorelines. The Soviet Union and Red China have already begun to finance preparations. So has the Organization of African Unity, through its Liberation Committee. There will be sabotage, terrorism, and thousands of individual acts of violence and revenge.

The army and police power will be, as in the case of Hungary, on the side of the government. Much of world opinion, mobilized actively by Africans at the United Nations, will be with the rebels. This world sympathy will provide a kind of moral umbrella under which the Sino-Soviet bloc will be able to step in, to its immense profit. The United States and Britain will not be free, even if they should wish, to aid the white South Africans without massive, catastrophic damage to their other interests in Africa and without delivering Africa to communism. They will be under immense pressure to intervene on behalf of the Africans. If they hold aloof, they will also suffer reprisals. Their normal action, to plead for a cease-fire and belated reforms, will not be very persuasive at this stage. Whatever they do, communism will stand to make sweeping gains.

The only rational plan is to fend off such a catastrophe before it starts, if possible. This is the answer to those who say South Africa is simply another case of human rights violation, perhaps a bit more cruel than most, but still, one which can be safely allowed to take care of itself.

Timely intervention in South Africa will not be pulling Afro-Asian chestnuts out of the fire. It will be saving our own. It will not be treachery to a white, Anglo-Saxon, Protestant ally, if that is what South Africa is (the description is imperfect at best). It will rather be an effort to awaken those who, while professing the Christian religion, sometimes to the point of fanaticism, are departing very far indeed from the ideals expressed by the Master. Such intervention will not be undercutting resistance to communism; it will be acting to eliminate a formidable breeding-ground for communism. It will not be unwarranted interference in the domestic affairs of a sovereign state comparable to United Nations intervention in Alabama or Mississippi. It will be preventive diplomacy of the highest order. To say that if South Africa can be an object of world pressure, Alabama must also be, is to equate two things which are not at all equal. The only precedent being established will be a healthy precedent of concern by the world community in the cure of an illness which threatens to injure everyone.

The effort to awaken South Africa should not be undertaken with vindictive intent. Those who rebuke South Africa for insufficient Christianity cannot consistently ignore its teachings themselves. "Have I any pleasure at all that the wicked should die? saith the Lord God: and not that he should return from his ways, and live?" (Ezekiel 18:23). The purpose must not be imposition of black supremacy, or any other predetermined solution. It must be to unite moderates within South Africa, to begin healing the disease of racism with the balm of intelligent, free discussion, and thus to set in motion a process leading toward an equitably shared society. The precise outlines of that society the South Africans themselves, of all races, alone have the right to decide.

Everyone will be called upon to make some sacrifices in the interest of the greater good. Black Africans will have to moderate their all-or-nothing demands. Majority rule simply is not obtainable by peaceful means in the immediate future, and the attempt to obtain it is counterproductive. The United States and Britain will have to make very tangible material sacrifices. South Africans will have to let go of *baasskap* and some of the comforts and prerogatives that go with it.

I asked Chief Tutor, son of Chief Poto, Paramount Chief of Western Pondoland, what he meant by multiracialism—the policy he and his father favor for their homeland, the Transkei. Chief Tutor, a striking man with an arc of beard across each cheek, extending to a neat mustache, replied, "Multiracialism means the world is there for everyone; and if everyone would work together, everyone would be happy."

Is this too simple an ideal for our complicated globe? Is it too naïve? The consequences of race domination are so severe that the world will have to learn, either by precept or by suffering, that it has no alternative. In South Africa, an awakening by suffering is too grim to contemplate. The relevant question is not whether to put pressure on South Africa for peaceful change, but when, to what extent, and how. John Donne's immortal warning is again in order: The bell tolls for us all. Alan Paton's beloved country no longer weeps alone.

SOUTH AFRICA CHRONOLOGY: 1652–1968

1652

A Dutch expedition led by Jan van Riebeeck lands near what is now Cape Town, South Africa, and establishes the first permanent white settlement in sub-Saharan Africa.

Nonwhites have already inhabited parts of South Africa: Hottentots and Bushmen are in the Cape and hinterland areas, and Bantu tribes, migrating southward, probably have crossed the Limpopo River—the northern boundary of South Africa—at least several centuries earlier.

1688

French Huguenots arrive in South Africa. (Germans and others follow later.)

1779

White settlers, migrating from the Cape, clash with Bantu tribes in the first of nine "Kaffir Wars" (1779 to 1877).

1795

The rule of the Dutch East India Company ends as the British, fearing that France will seize the Cape Colony during the Napoleonic wars, carry out a "preventive occupation."

1803

The Treaty of Amiens ends hostilities between France and Great Britain, and Britain withdraws from the Cape.

1806

War erupts again between France and Great Britain, and the British reoccupy the Cape—this time to stay until 1910.

1814

Holland cedes the Cape Colony to Britain.

1820

Five thousand British colonists arrive at Port Elizabeth.

1828

English is declared the official language of the colony, and all free men, regardless of color, are given equality of status—two British policies, among many, that convince the Dutch inhabitants their own traditions and separate identity are being jeopardized by colonial "intruders."

1836

Partly to escape the political and cultural influence of the British and partly to free themselves from British-imposed policies that would undermine master-servant relationships established by the Dutch, the Boers (Dutch farmers) undertake the Great Trek, a profoundly important and symbolic event. Some 12,000 Voortrekkers (pioneers) venture from the Cape in thousands of ox wagons to claim the resources and virgin lands of the interior.

1838

In the "Battle of Blood River" (still commemorated annually), migrant Boers defeat the Zulu tribe and establish the Boer Republic of Natal.

1843

Anxious to deny the Boers permanent control over a vital port area, the British annex Natal.

1852

Boers establish an independent Transvaal Republic. Its constitution (1858) prohibits "equality between colored people and the white inhabitants, either *in Church or in State*" (italics in original).

1854

Boers establish an independent Orange Free State.
Creation of the first Cape Parliament marks the beginning of representative government there.

1860

Needing labor for Natal sugar plantations, British planters import indentured Indian workers. By the end of the decade, there are 5,000 Indians in Natal.

1867

Diamonds are discovered near Hopetown.

1868

Britain annexes Basutoland (which, in 1966, is to become independent Lesotho).

1870

Britain annexes the Kimberley diamond fields.

1877

Britain annexes the Transvaal. But after defeat in the first Anglo-Boer War (1880–81), London grants it internal self-government.

1884

Germany proclaims a protectorate over South-West Africa.

1885

Bechuanaland (now independent Botswana) is made a British protectorate.

1886

Gold is discovered in the Transvaal.

1899–1902

The Boer War is fought, culminating a century of mistrust and hostility between Briton and Boer. Britain wins.

1903

Swaziland is made a British protectorate.

1910

The Union of South Africa is created, the former British Cape and Natal Colonies joining with the Boer republics of the Transvaal and the Orange Free State to form one country, a member of the British Commonwealth.

1913

The Union Government prohibits acquisition of land by Bantu except in the "Reserves."

1919

The League of Nations entrusts the Union with a mandate over South-West Africa.

1930–31

To bolster "European" (white) electoral power, the Union enfranchises white females and, in the Cape and Natal, removes property and educational vote-qualifications for white males.

1936

African voters are removed from the common roll in Cape Province.

1948

March

A Nationalist Party pamphlet explaining and defending apartheid is published, foreshadowing twenty years of legislation which is to transform white supremacy from a customary practice to a legal system. "Either we must follow the course of equality, which must eventually mean national suicide for the white race," it reads, "or we must take the course of separation (*apartheid*). . . ."

May

The Nationalist Party of Dr. Daniel F. Malan and its electoral ally, the Afrikaner Party, wrest a parliamentary majority from Field Marshal Jan Christiaan Smuts's United Party, though the latter obtains an electoral plurality.

	Seats	Votes
Nationalist Party	70	401,834
United Party	65	524,230
Afrikaner Party	9	41,885
Labor Party	6	27,360
Others	0	71,940

1949

January

Race rioting in Durban between Africans and Indians leaves at least 145 Africans and 122 Indians dead, 1,800 injured, and

2,000 buildings destroyed or damaged. Indians blame the disturbances in part on the government's apartheid policies.

1950

South Africa enacts a spate of racial and suppressive legislation implementing apartheid. Most significant are:

(1) *The Group Areas Act,* which empowers the Government to demarcate territorial sectors throughout the Union exclusively for residence by one or another racial group (White, Colored, African, Asiatic).

(2) *Suppression of Communism Act,* which grants broad and severe repressive powers to the Minister of Justice. This measure defines communism as, *inter alia,* "any doctrine or scheme which aims at bringing about any political, industrial, social, or economic change by the promotion of disturbances or by unlawful acts or omissions; and which aims at the encouragement of hostility between European and non-European races."

July

The World Court delivers an advisory opinion on South-West Africa, which South Africa has refused to transfer from League of Nations mandatory status to United Nations trusteeship. The Court holds that the League Mandate remains in force and that South Africa is obliged to submit to United Nations supervision over the administration of the Territory.

June 1950 to December 1952

The ANC (African National Congress) and the South African Indian Congress launch a nonviolent "defiance against unjust laws" campaign. "Defiance" takes the form of "technical offenses" against apartheid legislation. By the time the campaign is called off, shortly before Christmas, 1952, some 8,000 people have been imprisoned.

1953

April

In the first test at the polls of the government's apartheid policy, the Nationalist Party obtains an increased parliamentary majority. The results:

	Seats	Votes
Nationalist Party	94	598,297
United Party	57	576,074
Labor Party	5	34,730
Independents	0	1,290

August

A three-member United Nations Commission, established by the General Assembly in December 1950 to "study the racial situation in the Union of South Africa," reports that "the doctrine of racial differentiation and superiority on which the apartheid policy is based is scientifically false, extremely dangerous to internal peace and international relations. . . ."

November

Eighty-year-old Prime Minister Malan is replaced by Dr. J. G. Strijdom.

1955

April

South Africa withdraws from UNESCO because of that organization's criticism of apartheid.

1956

March

A Tomlinson Commission, appointed by the Government in 1950 to investigate the "socio-economic development of the Bantu areas," suggests that the Reserves should be consolidated into separate, partially self-governing ethnic areas to be known as Bantustans.

May

Cape Coloreds are deprived of their place on common electoral roll after a five-year constitutional struggle.

November

South Africa decides to maintain only token representation at the United Nations until the Assembly discontinues "interference" in the Union's domestic affairs. (This near-boycott lasts until 1958.)

1958

April

In the first "all-white" general election, the Nationalist Party increases its parliamentary majority by 10 seats:

	Seats	Votes
Nationalist Party	103	647,468
United Party	53	503,635
Labor Party	0	3,552
Independent Party	0	2,934
Natives' Representatives	3	2,607
Cape Coloreds' Representatives	4	1,205

September

H. F. Verwoerd succeeds Strijdom as Prime Minister.

1959

June

Acting on the Tomlinson report, the government authorizes gradual consolidation, over a period of years, of some 264 scattered native Reserves into eight partially self-governing Bantustans.

1960

February

British Prime Minister Harold Macmillan delivers his widely quoted "wind of change" speech to the South African Parliament, seeking—unsuccessfully—to awaken South Africans to fundamental changes in the world about them.

March

South African police at Sharpeville kill 69 Africans and wound 178 others engaged in a nonviolent protest against the pass laws. Reaction is swift and worldwide. The United Nations Security Council, involved for the first time, declares that the situation in the Union of South Africa "if continued might endanger international security."

April

The Government outlaws the ANC and the PAC (Pan Africanist Congress), two principal protest organizations.

June

The Addis Ababa Conference of African States invites African members of the Commonwealth to press for South Africa's exclusion from the Commonwealth, and calls on all African States to sever diplomatic relations, close their ports to vessels flying the South African flag, boycott South African goods, and refuse landing and passage rights to South African aircraft.

October

In an all-white referendum, South African voters approve the establishment of a South African Republic, thus breaking with the British Crown (though not yet with the Commonwealth). The vote is 850,458 to 775,878. The decision comes into effect May 31, 1961.

November

Ethiopia and Liberia initiate contentious proceedings against South Africa in the International Court of Justice (World Court), charging maladministration of South-West Africa.

1961

March

Confronted with continuing Commonwealth pressure, South Africa decides to withdraw from the Commonwealth. This, too, is effective May 31. It is regarded as reversing the effects of the Boer War. The Boers now have won in the political realm what they had lost on the battlefield.

October

Foreign Minister E. H. Louw defends apartheid in the United Nations General Assembly. Several angry African states move to have the speech deleted from the official records. Failing this, they ask for a censure motion, the first of its kind in United Nations history, which is then adopted in a vote of 67–1–20.

At home, the Nationalist Party retains a clear parliamentary majority, though polling fewer than 50 percent of votes cast.

	Seats	Votes
Nationalist Party	105	370,431
United Party	49	338,547
Progressive Party	1	69,042
Liberal Party	0	2,461
Independent Republican	0	2,251

1962

June

The Government intensifies its efforts to silence opposition. A so-called sabotage law imposes prison and death penalties for acts ranging from trespass to murder. The ANC's "Spear of the Nation," an underground terrorist organization, commits more than 200 acts of sabotage (1962–64).

November

The United Nations General Assembly requests member states, separately or collectively, to: (a) terminate or refrain from establishing diplomatic relations with South Africa: (b) close ports to all vessels flying the South African flag; (c) enact legislation prohibiting their ships from entering South African ports; (d) boycott all South African goods and refrain from exporting goods, including all arms and ammunition, to South Africa; (e) refuse landing and passage facilities to all aircraft belonging to South Africa. No major trading partners of South Africa vote for the recommendation, and few countries fully comply.

December

The World Court holds by an 8 to 7 majority that it has jurisdiction to adjudicate the South-West Africa case on its merits.

1963

May

Parliament empowers the Minister of Justice to arrest and detain for repeated periods of 90 days—that is, indefinitely—any person suspected of committing, intending to commit, or having information about specified types of political offenses.

The Transkei Constitution Bill, establishing the first of the projected Bantustans, is promulgated on May 24. The powers of the Transkei governing organs are limited and made subordinate to the South African Government.

July

South Africa ceases participation in the Economic Commission for Africa, a step ahead of a resolution disqualifying her.

August

The Security Council adopts by a vote of 9–0–2 (France, United Kingdom abstaining) a resolution that "solemnly" calls upon all states "to cease forthwith the sale and shipment of arms, ammunition of all types, and military vehicles to South Africa." The United States announces it will comply. (Previously Washington has barred arms useful in enforcing apartheid.) Britain also later complies, as do many countries.

December

The Security Council (1) enlarges the arms embargo to include equipment and materials for the manufacture and maintenance of arms or ammunition; and (2) requests the United Nations Secretary General to establish a small group of recognized experts to examine methods of resolving the "present situation" in South Africa.

The General Assembly asks the Secretary-General to seek ways and means of providing relief and assistance for the families of those persecuted for opposition to apartheid. A United Nations Trust Fund is the result. As of March 1968, 37 countries have contributed $532,102 and pledged $107,234.

South Africa withdraws from the United Nations Food and Agriculture Organization (FAO).

1964

March

South Africa withdraws from the International Labor Organization (ILO). It has previously been excluded from meetings.

June

The Security Council, acting on recommendations by its group of experts (known as the Myrdal Committee after its chairman, Mrs. Alva Myrdal of Sweden) urges: (1) that "all" the people of South Africa be permitted to decide the future of their country in a fully representative national convention; and (2) that a practical and technical study of the logistics of sanctions be set in motion. The latter is done.

The Security Council also urges South Africa to renounce the death penalty for anti-apartheid acts and to grant an amnesty to all political prisoners, particularly to the defendants in the so-called Rivonia trial of Spear of the Nation leaders, including Nelson Mandela and Walter Sisulu. Two days after passage of this resolution, all but one of the Rivonia defendants are sentenced to life imprisonment. The other receives a lesser sentence.

November

The South African Government suspends the widely criticized "90-day detention" law as of January 11, 1965, but soon replaces it with a similar 180-day law.

1965

March

The expert United Nations committee on sanctions set up in June 1964 concludes that measures ranging from severance of political and diplomatic relations to a total trade embargo might be successful in influencing South Africa's policies if they were universally applied, if adequate enforcement machinery were established and if other practical problems of implementation could be solved.

1966

March

The Nationalist Party wins its most firmly entrenched parliamentary majority to date.

	Seats	Votes
Nationalist Party	126	758,345
United Party	39	482,491
Progressive Party	1	32,803
Other	0	12,278

July

In a surprise decision, the World Court refuses to rule on claims brought by Ethiopia and Liberia against South Africa in the South-West Africa case. Even though the Court had affirmed in 1962 that the Applicants had "standing" to invoke the Court's jurisdiction, the Tribunal now finds that Applicants do not have ' a legal right or interest regarding the subject matter of their claims," i.e., that Applicants do not have sufficient "standing" to obtain a judgment. Accordingly, the Court does not rule on the merits of the case.

September 6

Dr. Verwoerd is assassinated in the House of Assembly. The white assassin, Dimitri Tsafendas, is adjudged mentally disordered, and jailed.

September 13

B. J. Vorster becomes Prime Minister.

1968

January 26

A South African court convicts 30 South-West African guerrilla fighters. The law under which they have been tried (the Terrorism Act) is retroactive in effect; the accused are required to prove their innocence, not to state their guilt; and South Africa's right to exercise any authority over South-West Africa has been declared forfeit. On all these grounds, the United Nations General Assembly, Security Council, Human Rights Commission, and other organs demand release of the prisoners. But on February 9, they are sentenced to long jail terms, 19 of them to life imprisonment. A prolonged tug-of-war between South Africa and the United Nations follows.

February 15

The International Olympics Committee, noting that Pretoria is prepared to send an integrated team, readmits South Africa to the 1968 Summer Olympics. (She had been barred in 1964). African and other states object that tryouts for places on the team will not be interracial and that sports apartheid in South Africa is inconsistent with Olympic traditions. They announce they will boycott the games. The Olympics Committee reluctantly reverses its decision.

Index